LINOCUT PRINTMAKING
IN THE CITY

ELLA FLAVELL

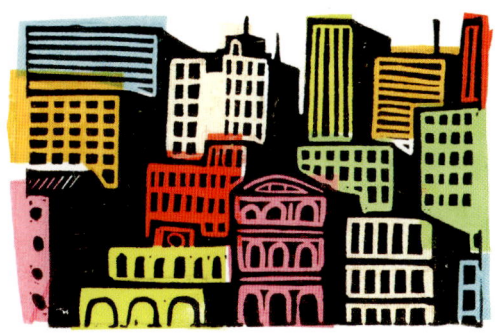

TOOLS AND TECHNIQUES FOR THE URBAN ARTIST

DAVID & CHARLES
—PUBLISHING—

www.davidandcharles.com

CONTENTS

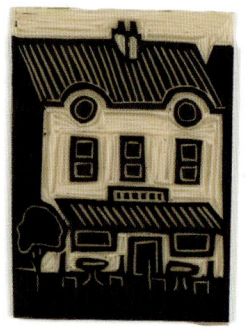

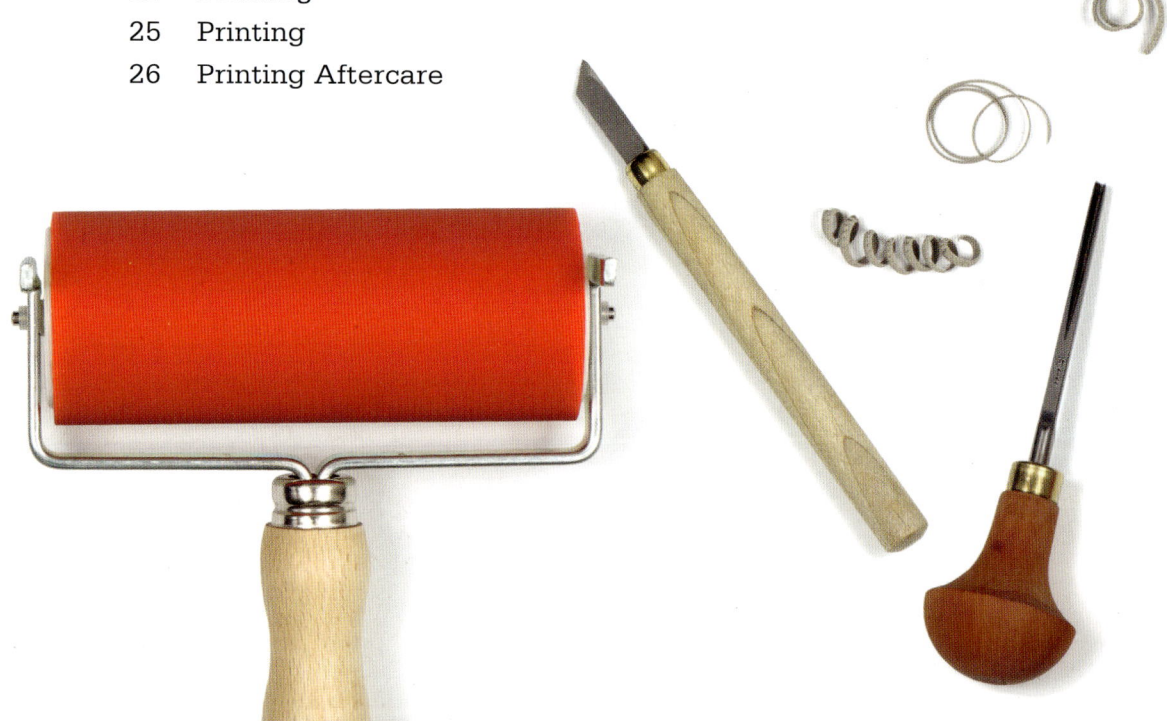

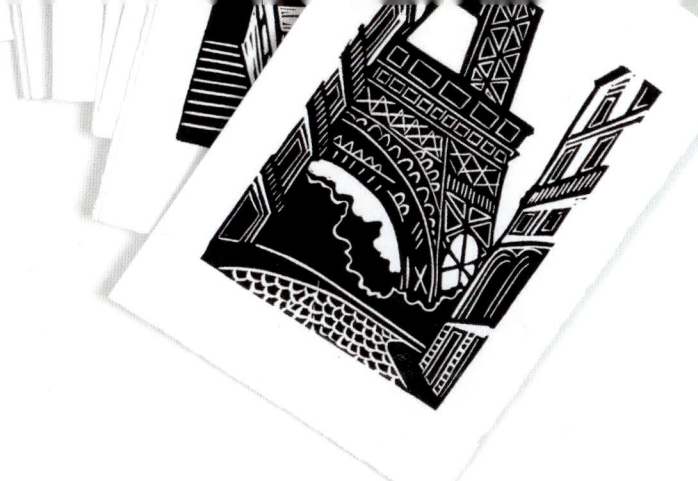
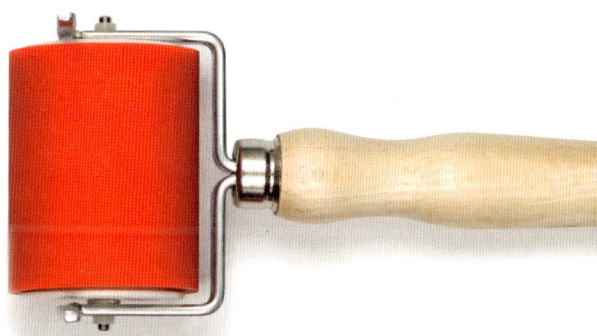

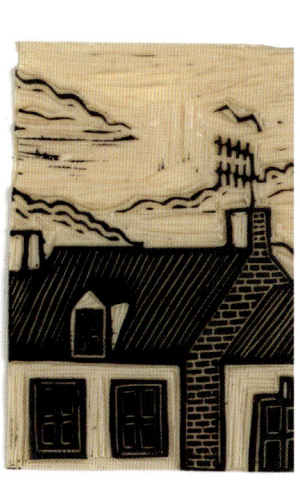
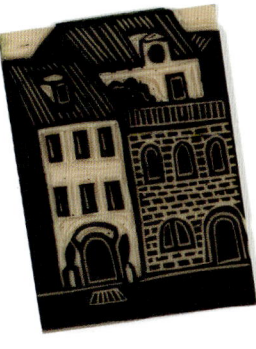
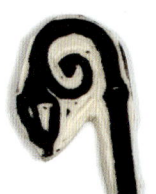

INTRODUCTION

Welcome to *Linocut Printmaking in the City*, a guide to creating linocut prints of the exciting and ever-changing urban environment. This book will introduce you to the key tools and techniques required to make your own prints, as well as providing some inspiration and follow-along projects to help you develop your skills.

Towns and cities are an incredibly rich source of inspiration for artists and printmakers, filled with an endless variety of subjects from the magnificent architecture of old buildings to the utilitarian design of modern conveniences, the peace of inner-city parks to the hustle and bustle of train stations and rush-hour traffic. Cities also offer a range of patterns, textures, and a contrast of light and shade that are ideal for translating into print, and which can be used to create both realistic and abstract interpretations of your subject.

Since 2016, the urban environment – particularly its historic or unusual elements – has been a key source of inspiration for my own linocut prints. I am fascinated by places that have a story to tell, whether it's an important event from history or something more personal, such as a memory from a day spent with friends or family. The search for inspiration for your prints (or printspiration!) can take many forms and can even lead to the discovery of new places, hidden corners brimming with beautiful buildings or secret features in even the most familiar of locations. I love that it encourages you to look at things in a new light, to consider composition, contrast, and storytelling – even the play of light and colour on different surfaces. Printmaking can be a slow process, but because of this it is also incredibly mindful and very rewarding – with the bonus that at the end you have a beautiful work of art.

The first chapter of this book introduces you to some of the key tools, materials, and techniques used in the linocut process, while the second guides you in applying these skills to your first prints. The third suggests some key sources of inspiration for your prints and how you can interpret different subjects. The final two chapters introduce the use of other materials into your prints and offer some further projects to test your printmaking skills and provide the foundation for future prints of your own.

Happy printmaking!

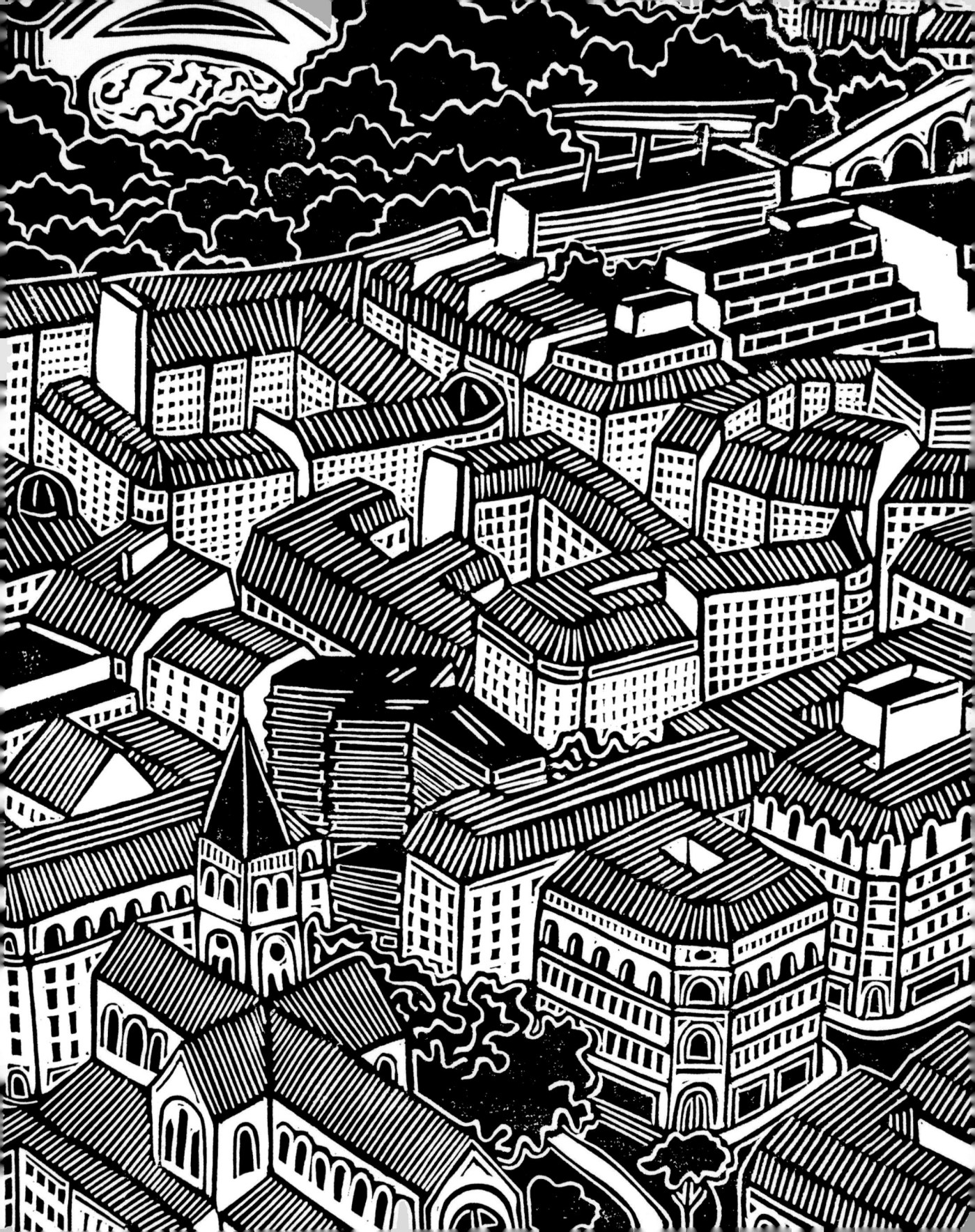

PRINTMAKING AS AN ARTFORM

For thousands of years, printmaking has been a way to produce both practical and aesthetic works, including text, textile designs, posters, tourist souvenirs, book illustrations, and, of course, works of art.

PRINTMAKING

One of the oldest techniques for creating prints is using a woodblock, where a design is carved into a smooth block of wood – a precursor to linocut. However, many other materials have been used as the basis for printmaking, including ceramics, polystyrene, rubber, metal, wax, and stone.

Each of these materials requires their own specific set of tools and methods – some need dipping in acid, others need to be chiselled, some are moulded – but all allow for a single image to be reproduced hundreds, or even thousands, of times. Although each of these prints has been produced from the same block, they are all still unique works of art with their own individual characteristics depending on how ink has been applied or how they have been printed.

As printing blocks are reusable, there is also the potential to try lots of different colour combinations or to try printing the same image onto lots of different surfaces – the possibility for experimentation is endless!

LINOCUT

Ever since linoleum (a solidified form of oil) was invented in the 1860s for durable flooring, artists have been experimenting with it as an alternative to the wooden and metal printmaking blocks that had been around for centuries. This new material was both durable and flexible, did not require complicated processes of printing and carving, and could hold intricate forms without the risk of splintering or breaking.

The technique of linocut became especially popular in the 20th century, as artist-grade lino began to be mass produced, and since then it has become the medium of choice for both professional and amateur printmakers alike. Linocut has been used in everything from advertising to pattern design to high art, with examples of this technique found among the work of artists such as Henri Matisse and Pablo Picasso.

Due to the versatile nature of lino, the technique has been adopted for all manner of subjects, from delicate landscapes to bold, high-contrast abstract compositions. While the linocuts in this book all focus on the urban environment, the techniques that are demonstrated throughout can be adapted for any subject of your choice.

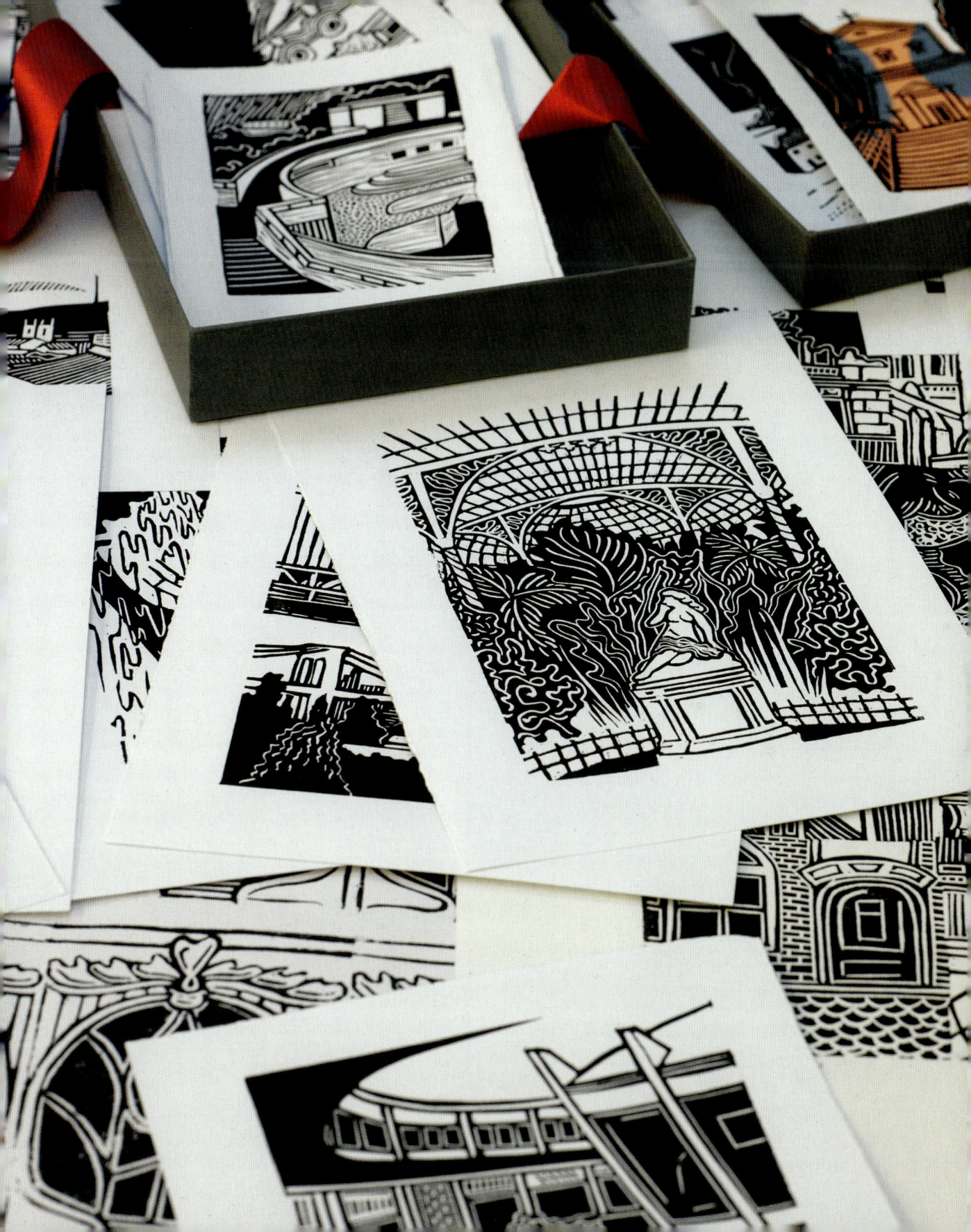

TOOLS AND TECHNIQUES

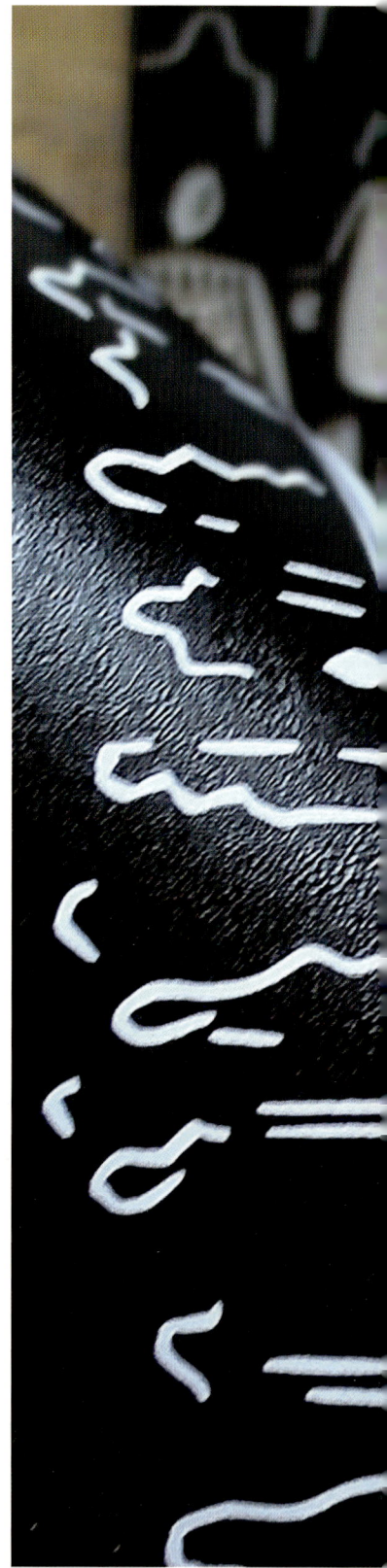

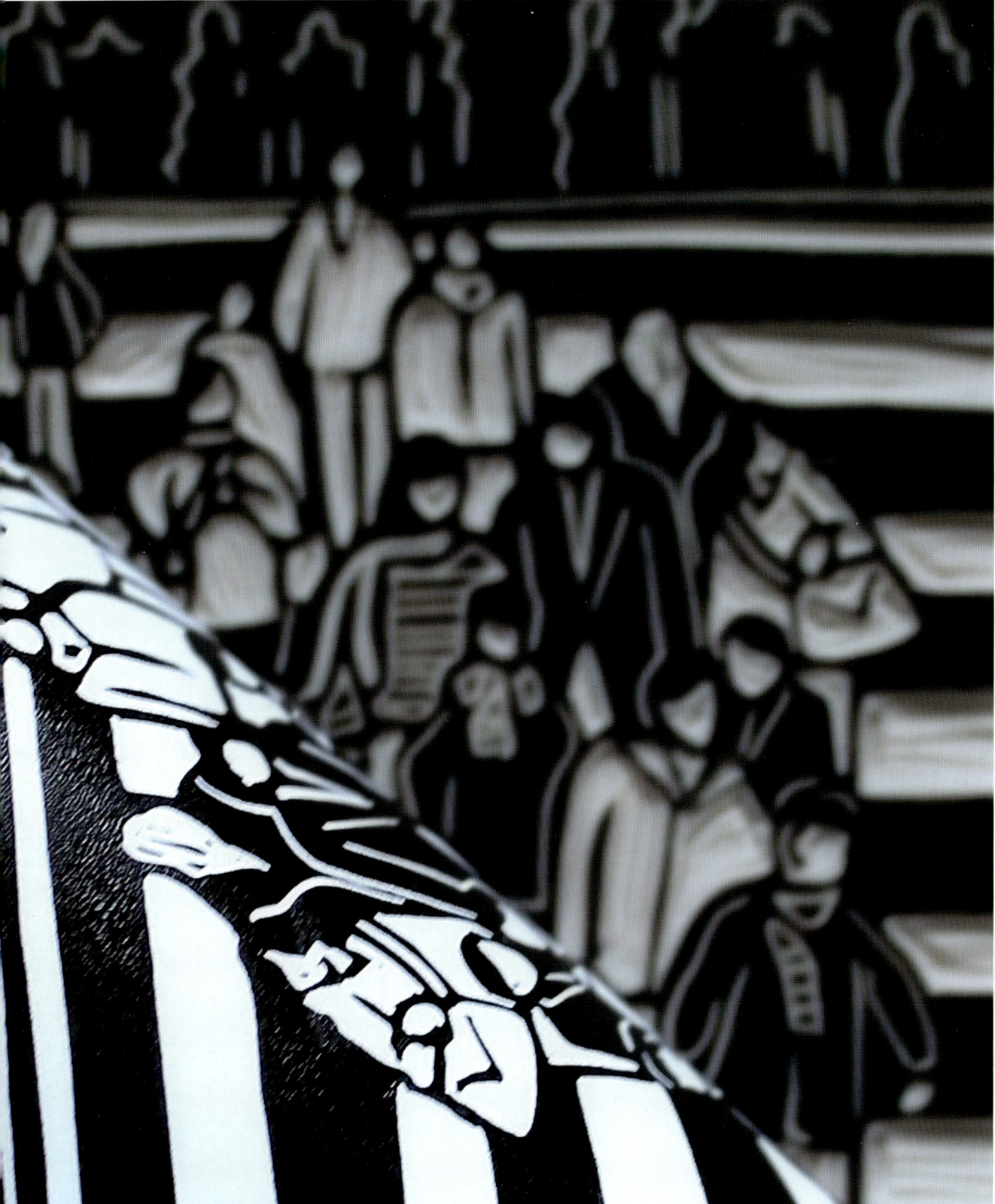

WORKSPACE TIPS

In this chapter, we explore some of the key tools and techniques required for the printmaking process. Before getting started, here are some top tips for setting up a workspace.

SPACE FOR PRINTMAKING

Printmaking can be done in even the smallest spaces, so long as you have a flat, solid area for both carving and printing, and enough room to have both your printing block and ink tray next to each other. As both carving and printing can require exerting a lot of downward pressure, make sure that your surface is stable as this will help prevent the block slipping or tools getting damaged.

TAKE REGULAR BREAKS

Carving can be tough on your hands and back, especially if you are using a harder lino that requires extra pressure to carve. Make sure to take regular breaks during carving and printing to stretch and give your hands a rest – this is particularly important when carving, as it will help prevent accidental slipping.

CLEANING SPACE AND HANDS

Printmaking can get very messy, so it is always good to keep clean paper towels or wet wipes close at hand! Make sure that the areas around your printing surface – and your hands – are free of ink to prevent unwanted smudges on your prints.

CARVING TOOLS

Carving tools – sometimes referred to as cutters, gouges, or burins – are one of the most essential tools for a printmaker and selecting the right one can make a big difference for your prints.

Carving tools usually come with ends of either a 'V' shape or a 'U' shape, or are flat, like a chisel. Both 'V' and 'U' cutters come in a range of widths, from narrower ones for small details to wider ones for clearing away large areas of lino. The projects in this book mainly use a narrow V-shaped cutter, though it is also recommended to have a wider tool to hand.

Cutters come in a variety of sizes and styles, and it's worth experimenting to find which one suits your carving style.

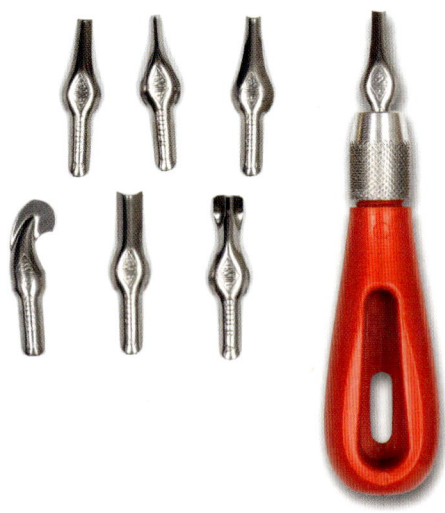

CUTTERS WITH INTERCHANGEABLE HEADS

Tools with interchangeable heads are the best option for getting the hang of using different shaped cutters. These cost-effective handles, often made from hard-wearing plastic, usually come with different sizes of V-shaped heads and are designed to fit snugly in the hand. Replacement heads can be bought separately, for when the cutting edge has become dulled. This type of cutter works excellently on soft lino but will wear down quickly on hard grey lino (see more on this in Carving Surfaces later in the chapter).

BULB-HEADED AND PALM TOOLS

If you are looking for something more hard-wearing that can easily carve both grey and soft lino, professional quality bulb-headed or palm tools are a great option. The cutters on these are usually much more durable than those on the interchangeable tools and as such will wear down much more slowly. These can either be bought individually (depending on what size or shape cutter you want) or as a set. Maintain the sharpness of these tools through stropping (polishing them on leather) or sharpening them by using either a sharpening stone or a professional sharpening service. Tips on how best to care for your tools may vary depending on which brand you use, so always check with the manufacturer before stropping or sharpening.

PEN-SHAPED TOOLS

These straight-handled tools are traditionally used for woodblock printing but work well for lino too. As with the bulb-headed and palm tools, these can be bought either individually or as a set. Wide-angled tools of this variety are particularly useful for clearing large sections of your block.

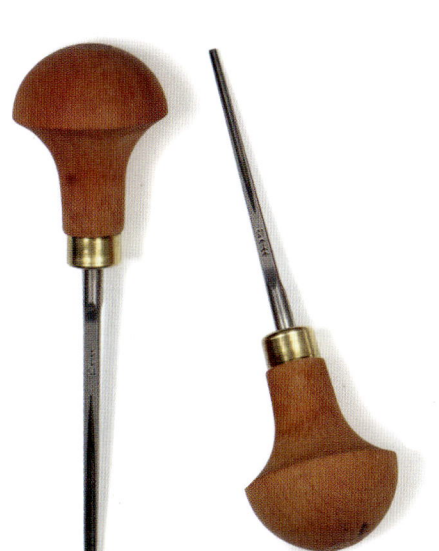

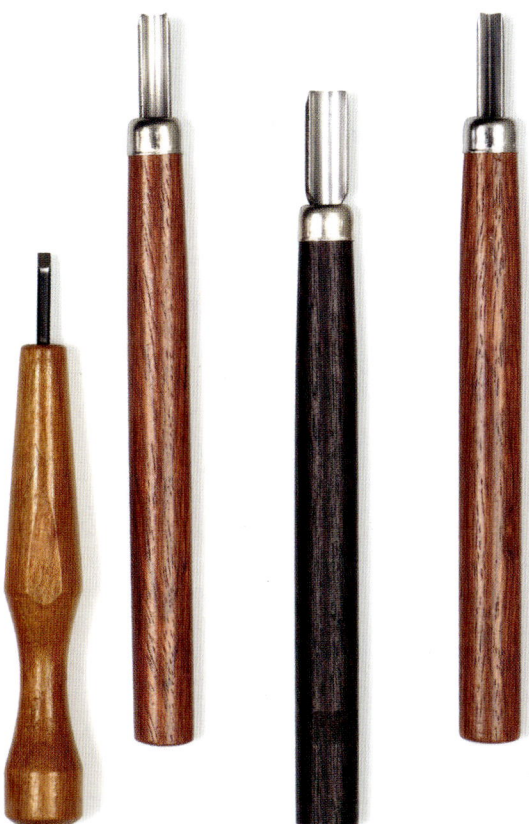

CARVING TIPS

HOLDING THE TOOL

Most lino cutters are designed to be held with the handle resting in the palm of the hand. The blade is held steady and directed by the first finger, which usually points towards the end of the cutter.

There are multiple variations on how you can hold the cutter, depending on your personal preference. Finding a way that helps you carve comfortably is important to reduce strain and to maintain safe carving practices. Experimenting on scrap pieces of lino is a great way to find your own carving style.

THE RIGHT ANGLE

When carving, it is important to find the right angle to get the depth of line you need. A good rule is to keep the cutter around 45 degrees from the surface of your lino, but you can vary the depth of your line by changing the angle. A higher angle, made by raising your wrist, will carve a deeper line. Be careful not to sink the blade of the cutter too deep into the lino, however, as this can cause it to become stuck, potentially damaging both the block and the tool. A smaller angle, made by making the blade almost parallel to the block, will create a shallower line. This can be dangerous as the cutter may slip, resulting in accidental lines across the block or injury. If your lines look too shallow – which can cause them to hold ink and misprint – you can re-carve over the top to make them deeper.

Different tools will require different angles and different levels of pressure, so it is always recommended to test them on a scrap piece of lino first. We will explore how to make different shapes of line throughout the projects in the book, but this scrap piece can also be used to practise different methods of line making (see the Pattern Guide opposite).

SAFETY TIPS

As lino tools are very sharp, mishandling or slipping can cause injuries. The most important thing is to always carve away from your hands and body. This can be tricky as you need to hold the lino with your spare hand, so always make sure it is out of the line of carving. A non-slip mat can help but will prevent the block from moving when creating certain shapes. Bench hooks and hand guards are available that will hold the lino still for you, but, like the non-slip mat, will make carving certain shapes difficult.

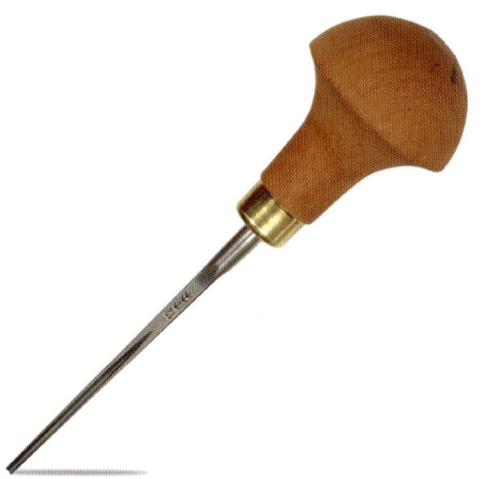

PATTERN GUIDE

As discussed, it is always handy to practise carving on a scrap piece of lino before committing to your block. This image shows some of the main patterns and carving techniques used throughout the projects in this book. Trace this image to transfer it onto scraps of lino or copy the images directly to test out these shapes before carving. In this image, the white space represents the carving line, while the black space indicates areas that should be left solid.

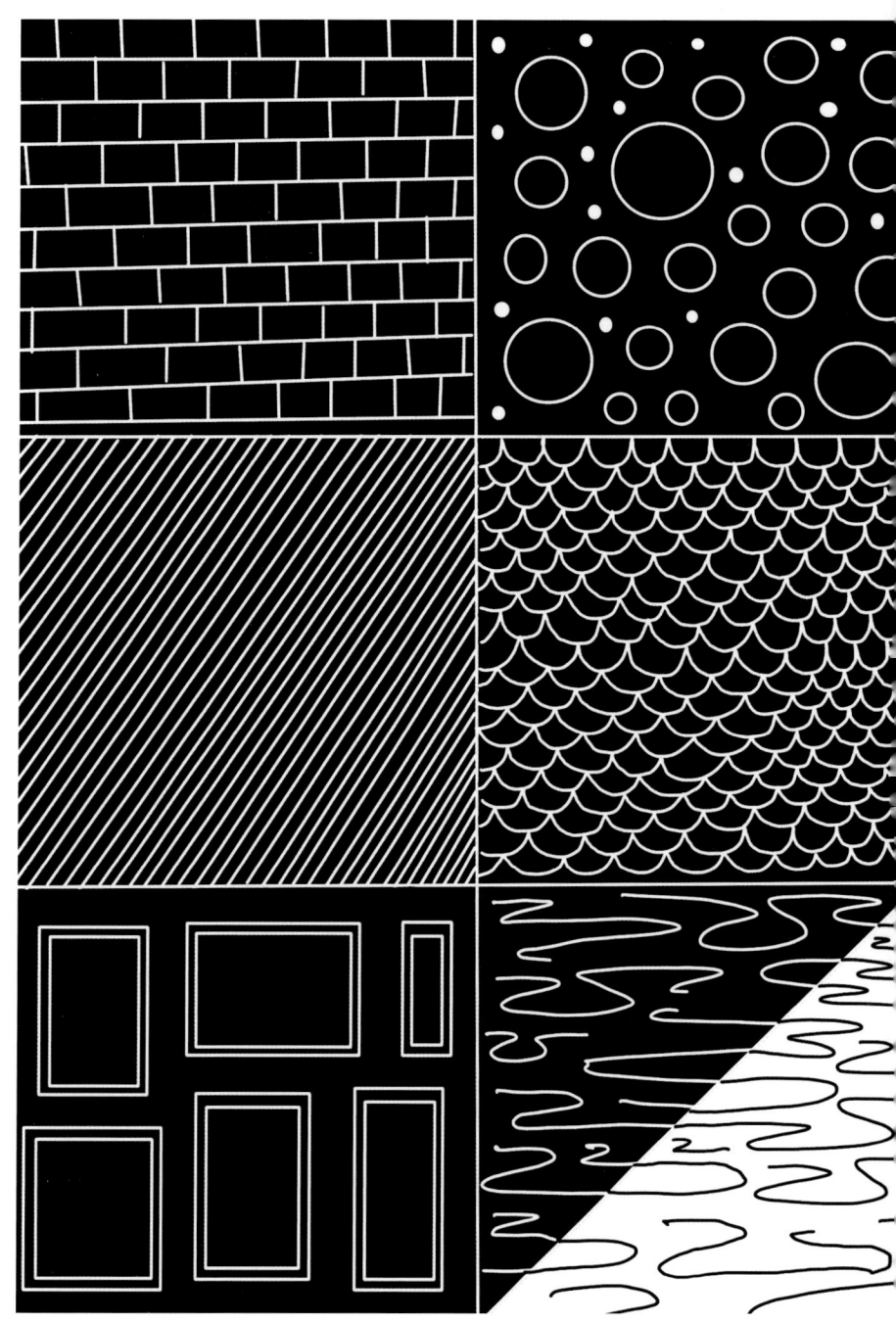

CARVING SURFACES

Lino comes in a variety of shapes and sizes. As with the cutters, it can be useful to experiment with different types to see what suits your printmaking practice.

GREY LINO

Hessian-backed grey lino is the traditional choice for printmaking, as its tough surface can withstand the pressure of a printing press. This is also a great option for hand printing, as it can hold a lot of detail. Grey lino does require a bit of extra care, as after multiple rounds of printing and cleaning it can become brittle. To minimise warping, wash ink off your lino with a soapy cloth and avoid submerging it in water, before storing it flat with some gentle weight on top. In chilly weather grey lino also becomes a bit harder to carve, but warming the block gently on a radiator or with a hairdryer will get it ready for carving in no time!

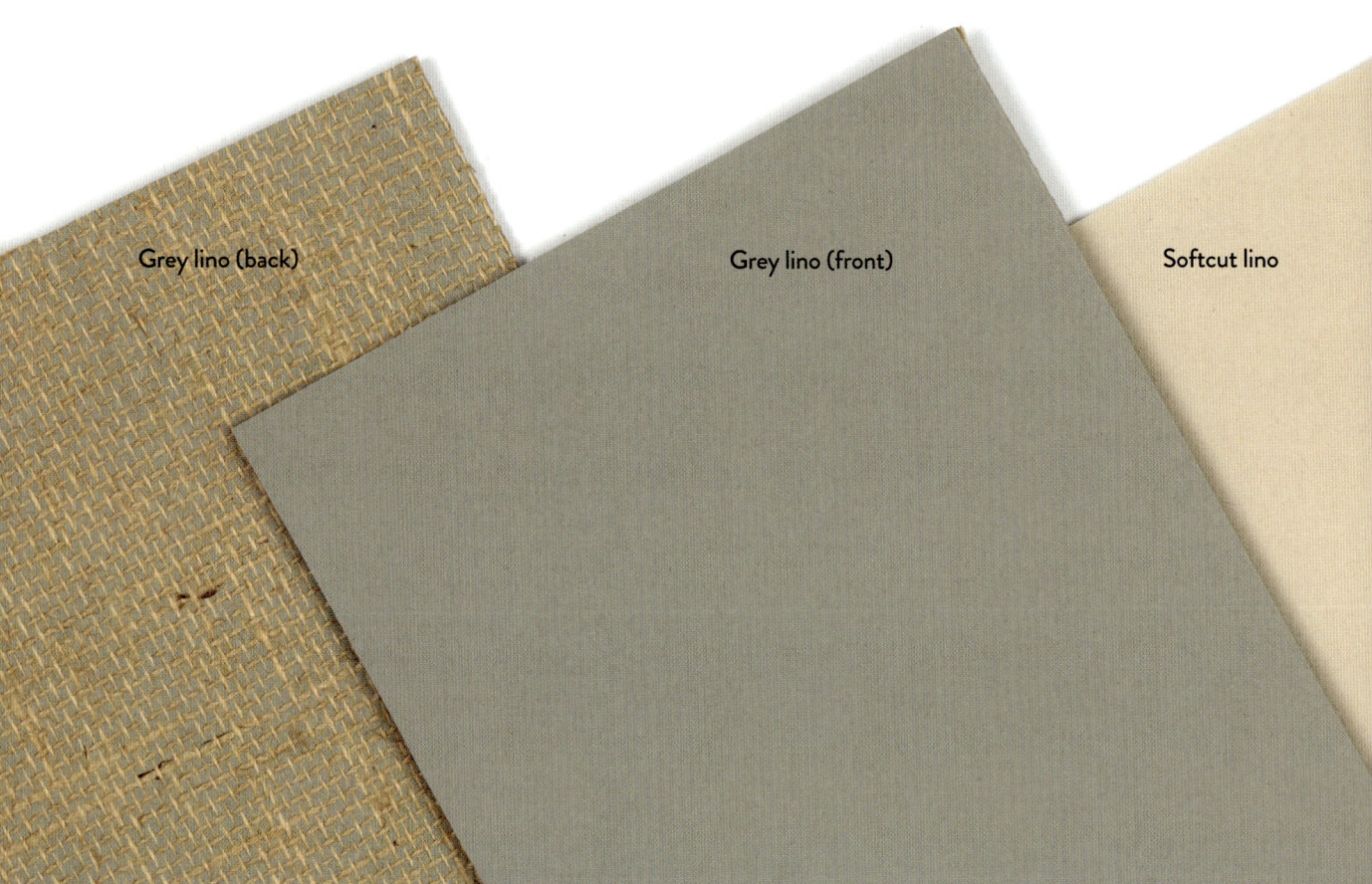

Grey lino (back)

Grey lino (front)

Softcut lino

SOFTCUT LINO

A popular alternative to grey lino is softcut, which comes in a variety of types from very soft, thick lino (perfect for making stamps), to thinner, slightly harder varieties that hold fine detail for more intricate prints. Softcut lino, unlike grey, is usually double-sided, with the two sides sometimes varying in texture for different print effects. This type of lino is also more durable than the grey lino and will withstand multiple washes and printing sessions without warping.

OTHER OPTIONS

Japanese vinyl is a great alternative to softcut lino and behaves very similarly. Vinyl is often coloured, with the top layer being a different colour from the inner layer of the block, which makes it easier to see where you have carved. Stiff foam – like that used in takeaway packaging – can also be used to create prints by embossing the design using a pen or blunt pencil rather than a cutter. Foam is significantly less hard-wearing than lino but is a great option for testing out designs or for smaller projects.

SIZING LINO

If you need to cut a piece of lino down to the size you want, the best method is to cut through the lino with a sharp craft knife, using a ruler as a guide to keep the line straight. For hessian-backed lino, you may need to cut through the backing with scissors to complete the sizing.

Japanese vinyl

OTHER TOOLS

BRAYER

A brayer, or a roller, is used to transfer ink onto the block. Hard rubber rollers are recommended, as foam ones will absorb too much of the ink. Brayers are available in a variety of sizes, from tiny ones for inking small details or mini prints, to large ones for wider blocks. Having a number of different sized brayers on hand is recommended if you are working with different colours of ink in the same printing session.

BAREN

A baren is any item used to add pressure to the back of the paper when transferring a print. Almost anything can be used as a baren – so long as it is hard and smooth, with no sharp edges that could tear the paper. You can buy barens specifically designed for the job in a variety of materials from bamboo to glass. They also come in a variety of sizes, but it is recommended to use one that will be able to get into all the small details of your block (smaller details may require a smaller baren that can focus on specific areas). You can also use household objects such as spoons (both wooden and metal), tin lids, and heavy, flat-bottomed glasses.

BRUSH

A stiff brush, such as a paintbrush, toothbrush, or small household brush, is useful for clearing away any lino shavings that may have got stuck in your block during the carving process.

PALETTE KNIFE

Palette knives are a helpful addition to any printmaking kit. You can use them for getting ink out of tubs, scraping excess off inking plates, or mixing colours.

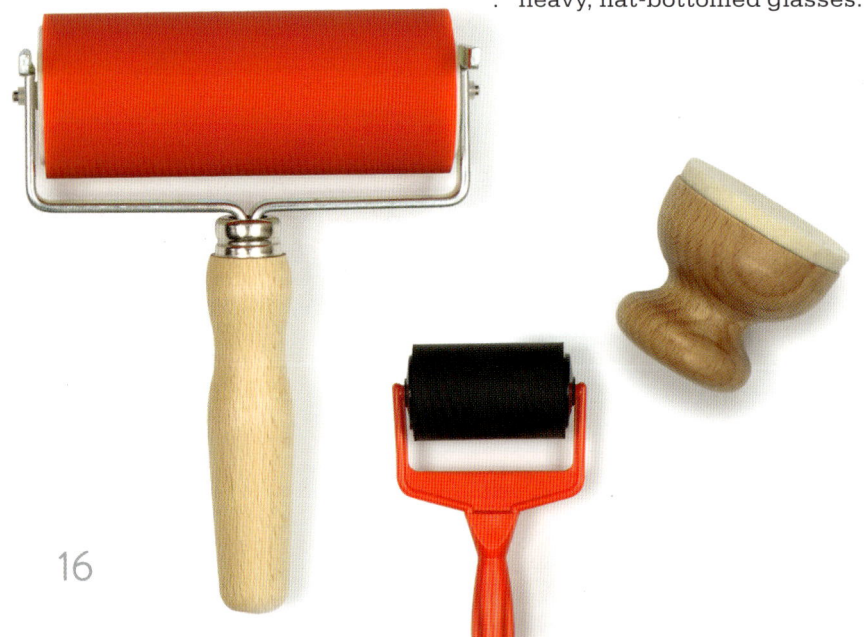
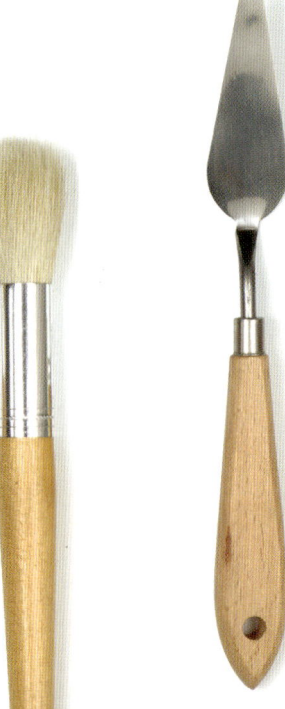

INKING PLATE

The right inking plate can make a big difference – having a smooth surface to roll your ink out on before putting it on the block is key to making sure you are not adding either too much or too little. Inking plates can be bought, or you can make your own using the glass from an old photo frame, a sheet of thick plastic, or a large tile. Your inking plate needs to be completely smooth, so as not to damage your roller or get an uneven roll of ink.

REGISTRATION BLOCKS

A registration block is essential to keep your print still during the printing process. This avoids smudging, and if you are working on a multi-block print it ensures all your layers are aligned. Follow these simple steps to make one of your own.

SUPPLIES

Thick cardboard, larger than your block
....
Ruler
....
Craft knife
....
Glue
....
Pen
....

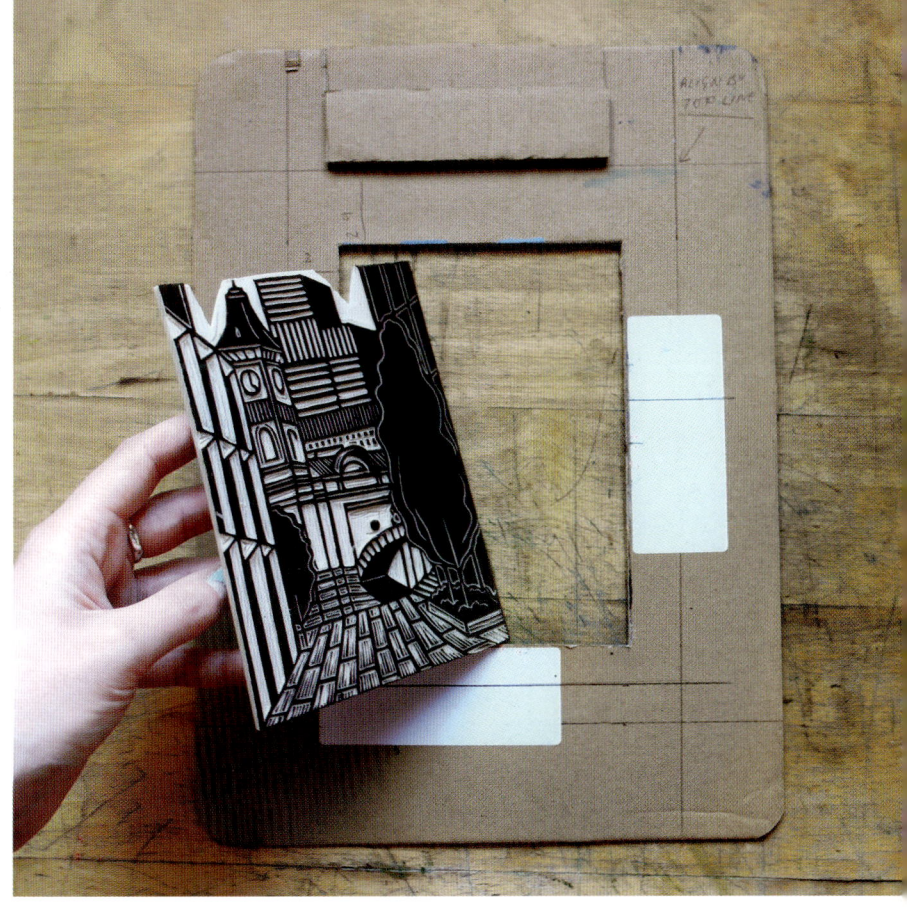

1 Trace around the outside of your lino block in the centre of your cardboard. Using the craft knife, cut out this section to leave a hole into which you can slot the block.

2 Now trace around the paper you want to print onto, using the ruler to make sure the hole you cut for the block is in the centre. This line will give you a guide when it comes to printing.

3 Using the cardboard you removed from the centre, cut some thin strips and glue them at the top edge of the paper line. This will give you somewhere to rest the paper against during printing, to stop it slipping.

4 Ink your lino before putting it into the registration block, to prevent any stains on the edge of the cardboard. The tip of the craft knife can be used to push your block into place, to avoid inky fingers.

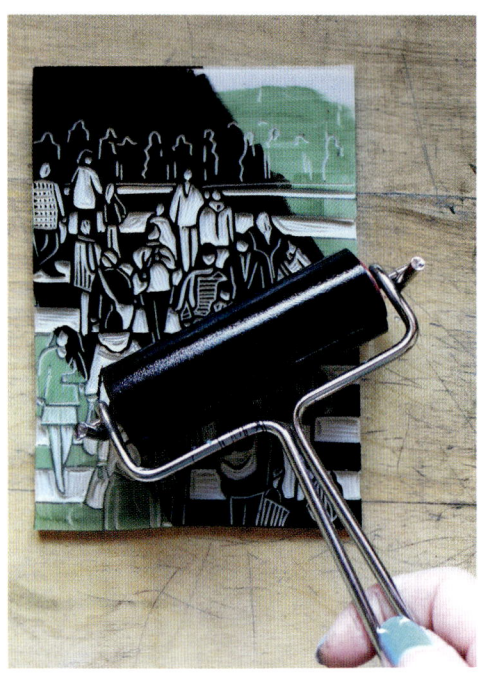

INK

Printmaking ink usually comes in two types: oil-based and water-based. Oil-based ink is generally favoured by linocut printmakers for its depth of colour, even coverage of the block, and the ability to create different tones and effects. Oil-based ink does, however, take a long time to fully dry, and may require specialist supplies to clean both your blocks and tools. Water-based ink has a much shorter drying time and can be washed away with soapy water. Like oil-based inks, good quality water-based inks can give a rich colour and can be mixed to create a variety of shades.

HOW TO INK A BLOCK

1 Start by placing a line of ink at the top of your inking plate. Then, taking your brayer, touch it slightly to this line of ink and pull it down towards you.

2 Repeat this process until you have a thin layer of ink around the whole roller and on the plate. A good way to test if you have enough on your brayer is if there is a shiny, slightly rippled texture to the surface of the ink both on the roller and plate.

3 Applying a light but even pressure, roll your ink over the block. Too little ink is always better than too much – you can add more if necessary, but too much and the ink will get caught in the smaller details of your block, causing them to be lost in the printing process.

4 The amount of ink needed for a block will vary depending on the type of lino and the type of ink you use, so doing some test prints on scrap paper first is always recommended. Now it's time

to print your block, following the techniques in the Printing section further on.

5 Use a palette knife to return any excess ink left on the inking plate to the tub or, if you use ink from a tube, store this excess in an airtight container. Both oil- and water-based inks will generally keep for many months stored in this way.

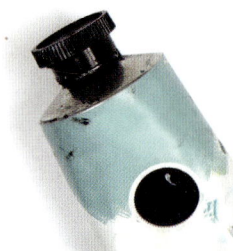

CREATING A COLOUR GRADIENT INK EFFECT

A gradient effect is a great way to add colour to your prints, or to define different areas. Start by selecting your colours, either using pre-mixed inks or mixing your own. High contrast colours work best for gradients, but a subtle effect can be produced by using a darker and lighter shade of the same colour, as with the blue in this example.

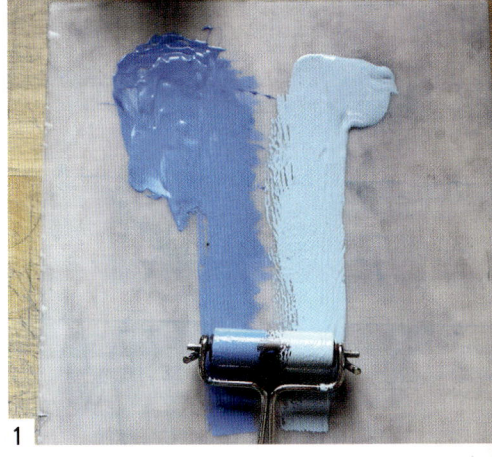

1 Once you have chosen your colours, place them a little less than a roller's width apart at the top of your inking plate. Now pull both the colours down the inking plate towards you to create two separate lines of colour. Either end of the roller should be in a different colour of ink, and it is important not to swap these ends over during the rolling process. It is useful to use a wide roller for this, to maximise surface area.

2 Pull the roller backwards and forwards, and begin to introduce a gentle side-to-side motion so that the two colours meet in the centre of the roller. Continue this motion until you have the desired shade in the centre.

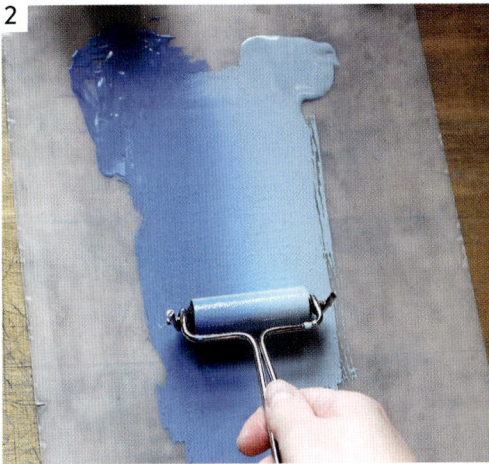

At either end of the roller, you should still have the original colours. This process may need to be repeated with each new inking of the block.

3 When inking the block, it is important not to swap up the two sides of the roller, which will mix up the gradient. Instead, ink in only one direction. If you need to add more colour to the ends, you can either use separate rollers or the edge of the roller with the gradient.

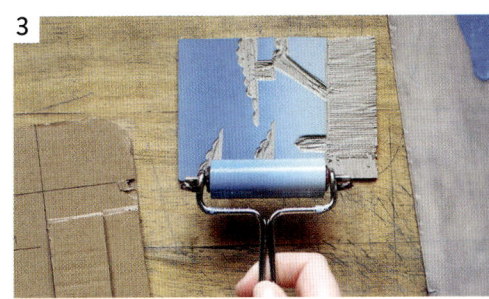

4 Now it's time to print your block. Here, it's ready to be the sky for the Multi-Block Print in the Further Studies chapter.

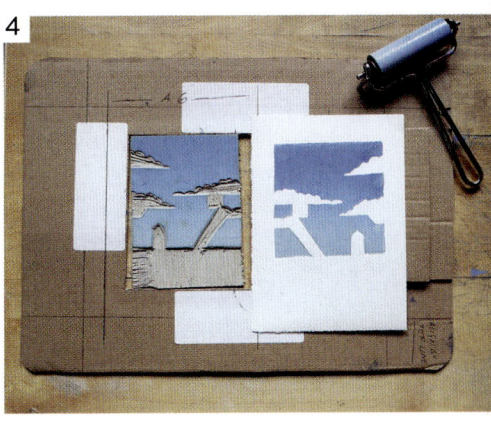

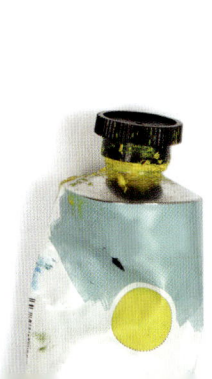

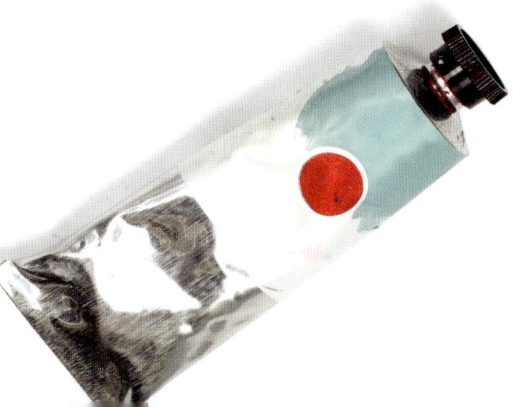

PRINTING SURFACES

PAPER AND CARD

Paper is a favourite topic for printmakers, and everyone will have their own individual preference. Different types and textures of paper will react with ink in different ways, impacting the final look of the print. Smooth papers and card will give a cleaner finish, even with a very thin layer of ink, making it a popular choice, while textured paper may require more pressure and more ink to get a clean print.

Handmade papers, such as Lokta (which is made from hemp fibres) or Washi (traditional Japanese paper made from plant fibres), are often more porous, and as such absorb ink faster than smoother, mass-produced paper. These papers are, however, perfect for printmaking as they are very durable. Their textured surface, irregular (or 'deckled') edge, and handmade quality make them a popular choice for many printmakers. Awagami offers a great range of handmade and traditional papers (see image opposite), but there are lots of alternatives available.

CHOOSING A WEIGHT OF PAPER

The weight of paper is an important factor when choosing a printing surface. The higher the gsm (US lbs) number, the thicker the paper will be. Too thin, and paper can adhere to the block and possibly tear, but too thick and the paper will be hard to print by hand, resulting in a patchy or blurry print.

Extra White Watercolour

Arches Aquarelle Watercolour Cold Pressed Sheet 185gsm

Kitakata Select

A good gsm for first-time printmakers is between 80 and 180gsm (24–50lbs), with the higher number being a good combination of flexibility and durability. Handmade papers such as Lokta and Washi may be lighter than this, but due to their closely woven fibres are very durable and are therefore less likely to tear. Nevertheless, it is worth being gentler when printing with these papers, just in case.

OTHER SURFACES

While the examples in this book focus on printing onto paper, it is also possible to print onto wood, fabric, and some ceramics. To print onto these different materials, you may need specialist inks that can withstand washing (in the case of fabrics) or ones that will bond securely to the surfaces. Printmaking suppliers will usually stock a range of inks and ink additives for printing onto different materials. It is best to check with the manufacturer for information on drying times and durability, as this may vary between inks.

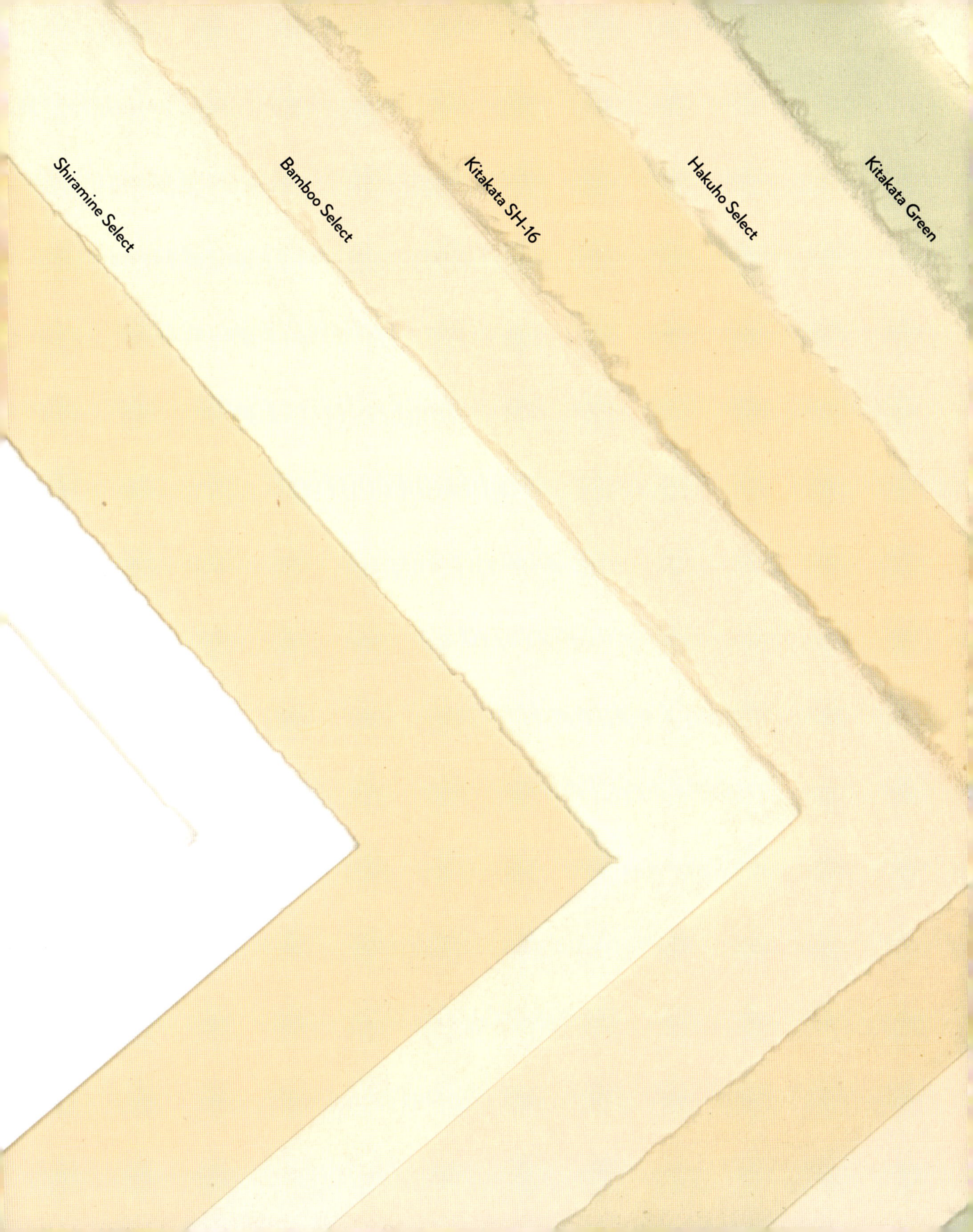

Shiramine Select

Bamboo Select

Kitakata SH-16

Hakuho Select

Kitakata Green

DRAWING

Drawing is one of the key steps in the printmaking process, and keeping a sketchbook handy is a great way to record your ideas. Below are a few tips for creating your preliminary drawings.

COMPOSITION AND SCALE

Whether you are drawing from life or from photos, sketching gives you the opportunity to play with scale and composition to give your prints the biggest impact. Moving buildings or items around, or making them larger or smaller, is a great way to guide your viewer through the image. Think about what story you want to tell and what parts of the image you want to draw attention to. It doesn't have to be accurate – this is your world, arrange it how you want!

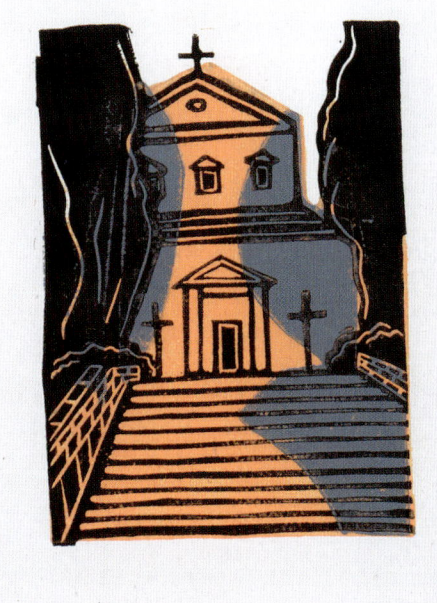

BALANCE

Your drawing can be used to plan out areas of light and shade before committing to carving. Think about where you want to keep some areas lighter (carving away the majority of the block) versus darker (keeping more of the block intact) so that one part of the print doesn't overwhelm the other. This can also be used to change the mood of the print – lighter areas suggest sunny scenes, while darker areas can create a moody, dramatic tone.

TEXTURE

Like the balance between light and shade, balancing areas of texture in your print is also important to prevent it from becoming too overwhelming. Provide places for the eye to rest, contrasting areas of detail with areas of solid colour. Planning this out on your drawing before starting to carve allows you to test how different combinations will work.

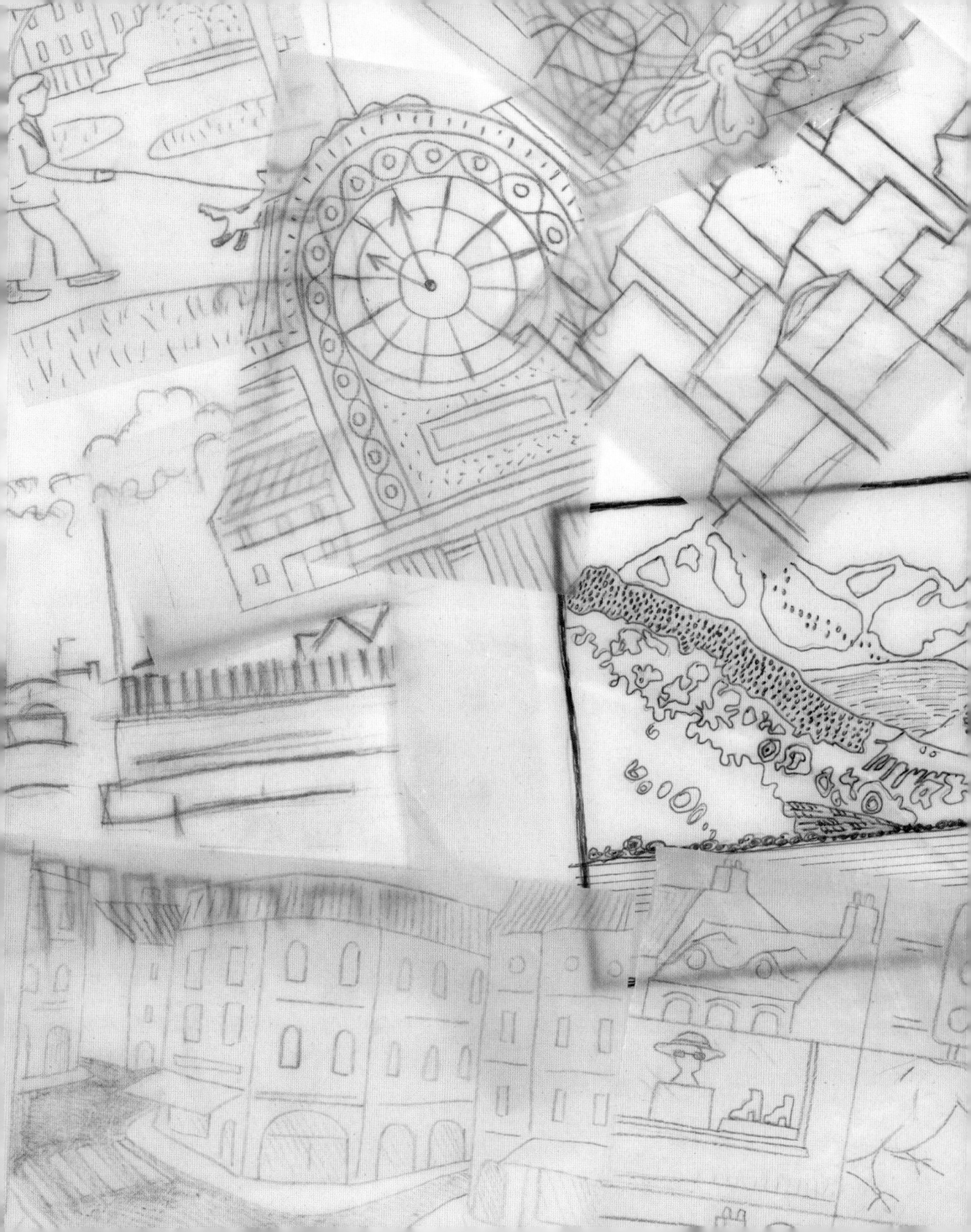

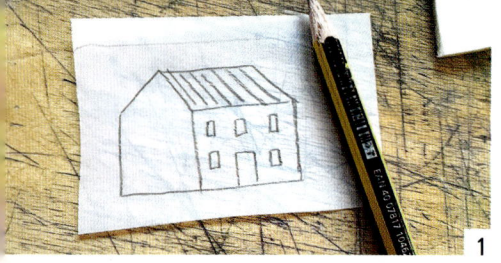

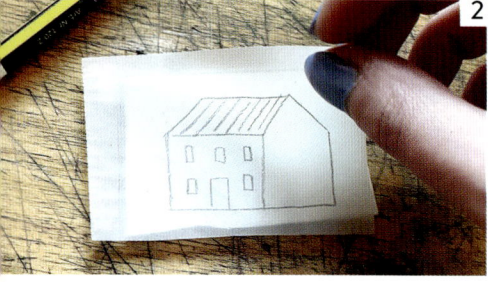

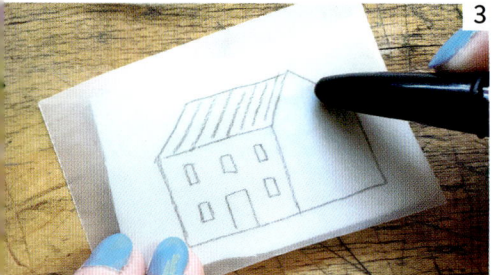

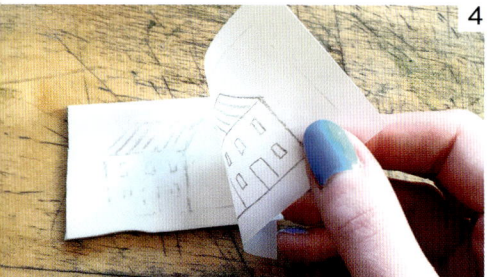

TRANSFERRING A DRAWING ONTO THE LINO BLOCK

Once you are happy with your drawing, there are multiple methods for transferring it onto lino. Some printmakers prefer to use carbon paper, while others draw freehand onto the block. The method described here, however, is the most flexible, and lets you position your drawing exactly where you want it. Nearly every project in this book starts with this process, so it's worth practising. Remember that printmaking works in reverse, so your drawing needs to be backwards on the block to print the right way round!

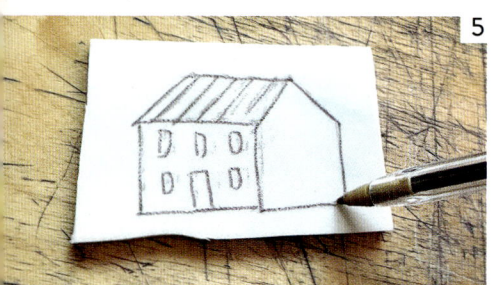

SUPPLIES

Your drawing

Tracing paper

Pencil – HB is recommended

Sticky tape

Ballpoint pen

Thin acrylic paint and brush

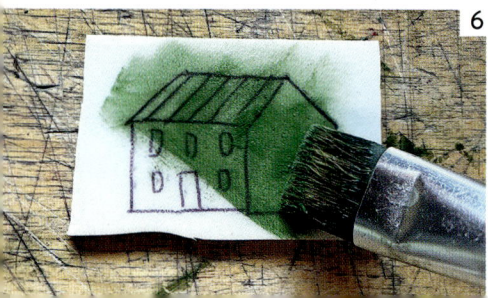

1 Use the tracing paper to trace your drawing – press down firmly with the pencil, as darker lines will make the next steps easier.

2 Flip the tracing paper pencil-side down onto the block. You can secure the drawing with tape for added stability if you wish.

3 Using the end of a ballpoint pen (without removing the lid) scribble over the back of the tracing paper, placing a firm pressure over the pencil lines.

4 You can check to see if the pencil marks have transferred by lifting the tracing paper at a corner, but be careful to put it back in the same place!

5 Once all the pencil marks have been transferred onto the lino, use the pen to re-trace the lines on the block. This will stop them being washed away or smudged during the carving process.

6 Paint a thin layer of acrylic paint over the block – if the paint is too thick, add a bit of water to thin it down. It needs to be transparent enough to see the pen lines below, but dark enough to form a contrasting colour with the block. This will help you to see where you have carved.

PRINTING

Once your block is carved
and your ink is rolled, it's
time to get printing!

1 Place your inked block carefully
into your registration block or
onto a flat surface. If you have
ink on your hands from the inking
process, use a damp cloth to
wipe them clean, to prevent inky
fingerprints on the final print.

2 Gently lay your paper on top
of the inked block – once it
makes contact with the block
it cannot be moved, so make
sure it is lined up carefully.

3 Using your chosen baren,
apply a firm, even pressure
across the block. This pressure
should be enough to transfer
the print, but not too much that
it rips the paper. It may take a
few attempts to get the correct
pressure, as this will vary
between ink and paper types.

4 Holding the bottom edge
of the paper in place with
one hand, carefully peel back
your print. Be extra gentle if the
paper has adhered to the block
in some places, to avoid tearing.

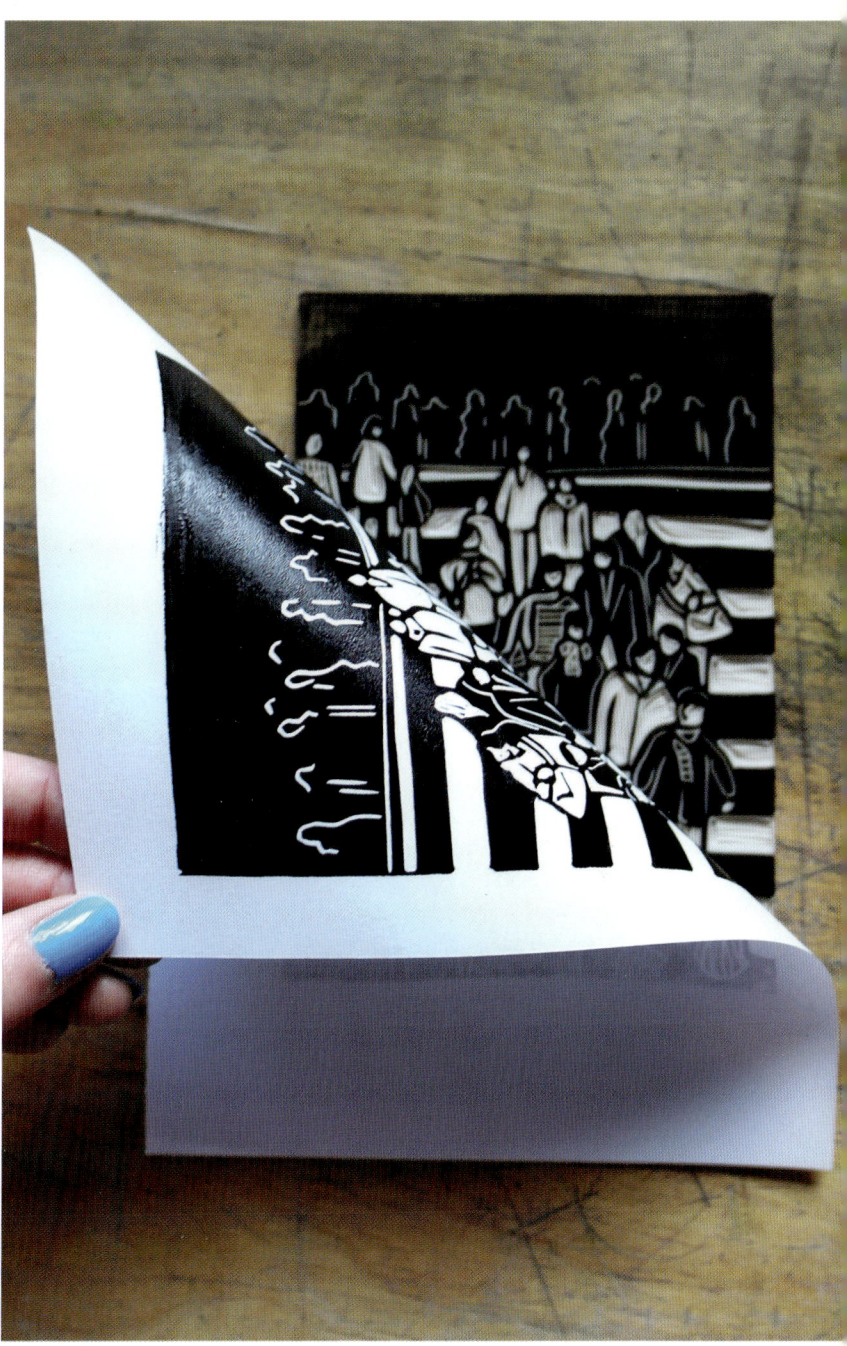

PRINTING AFTERCARE

DRYING PRINTS

Drying times will vary depending on the type of ink you have used. Oil-based inks take much longer than water-based inks (which will dry in a couple of hours). Prints can either be dried by lying them out on a flat surface, such as a table or a clothes airer, or by pegging them on a line. Make sure that your prints are not touching each other while drying, as this can cause them to stick together.

STORING PRINTS

Once your prints are dry, store them in a flat, dry place out of direct sunlight, to avoid the colour fading, until you are ready to frame them. Wrapping them in acid-free tissue paper will add an extra layer of protection and may prevent the ink from rubbing from one print to another.

TOOL CARE

Printmaking tools are very durable and will last a long time but do require some maintenance. Make sure that anything covered in ink is washed thoroughly after every printing session, particularly your brayer, as any build-up of dried ink will prevent it from rolling properly.

Cutters may need sharpening every now and then, which can be done using either a professional sharpening service, or using a sharpening stone or stropping device (a piece of leather used to sharpen blades). Individual tools will have their own care instructions, so check these before sharpening.

STORING BLOCKS

Once you have finished printing with a block, clean the ink away using either warm, soapy water (for water-based ink) or vegetable oil or purpose-made cleaners (for oil-based ink). Softcut lino can be submerged in water, while hessian-backed grey lino needs to remain as dry as possible to prevent warping. To clean grey lino, use a damp cloth to wipe over the carved surface.

Dry your blocks in a tea towel (dish towel) – grey lino may need a gentle weight applied while it is drying to prevent bending. Once your blocks are clean and dry, store flat and in a place where they won't be moved too much, as over time some blocks may become brittle.

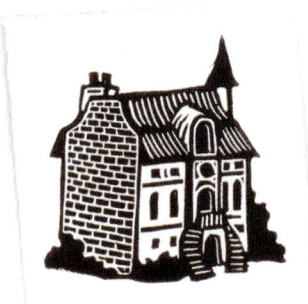
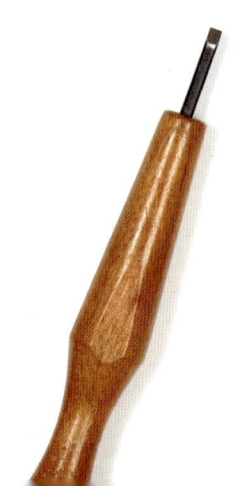
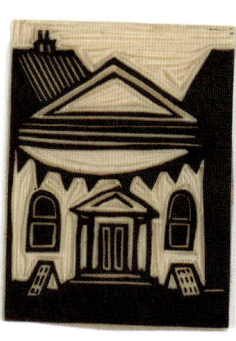
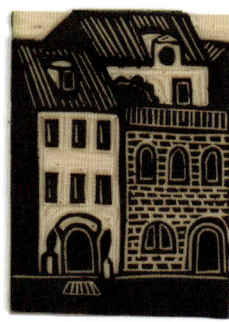

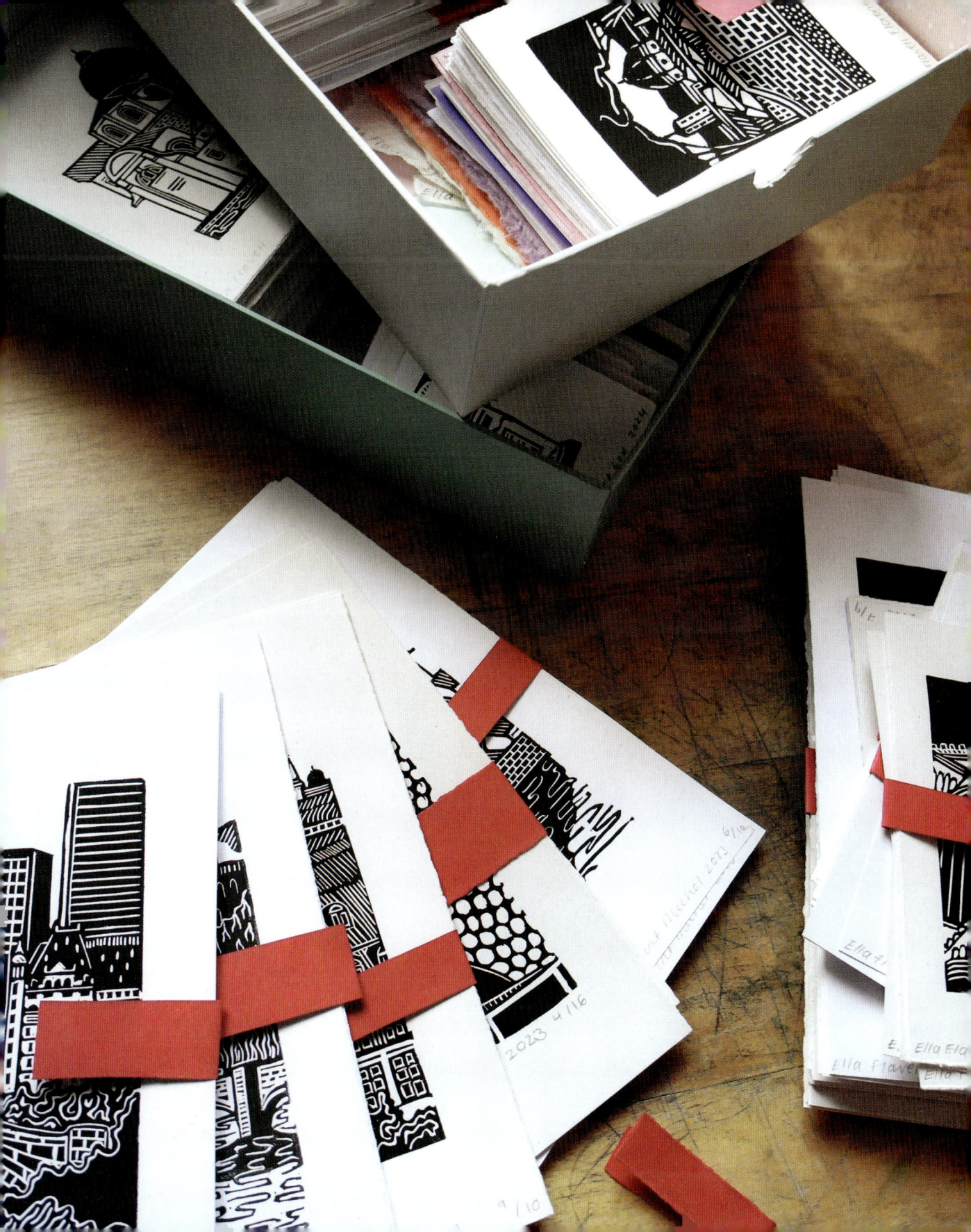

FIRST
PROJECTS

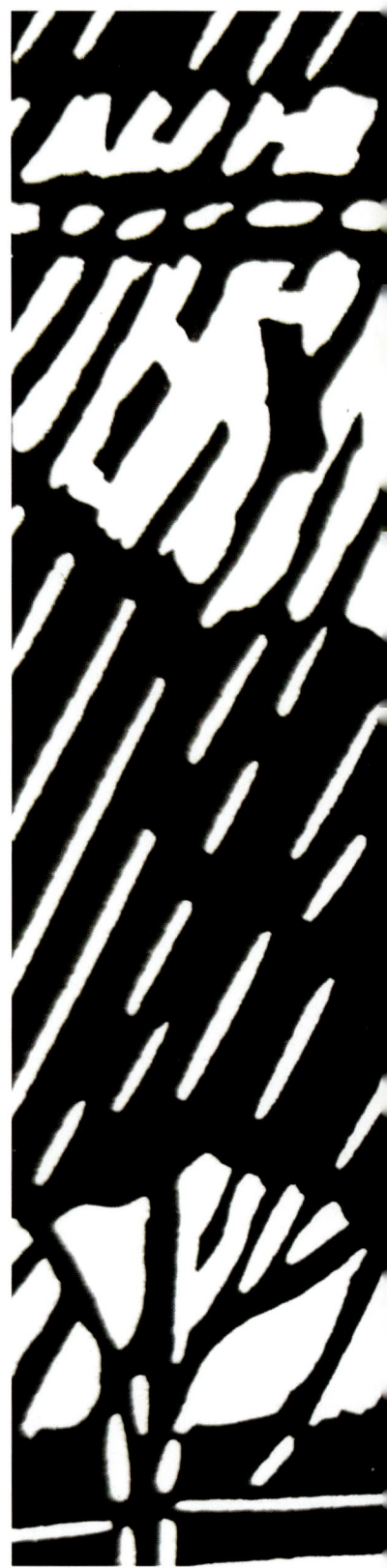

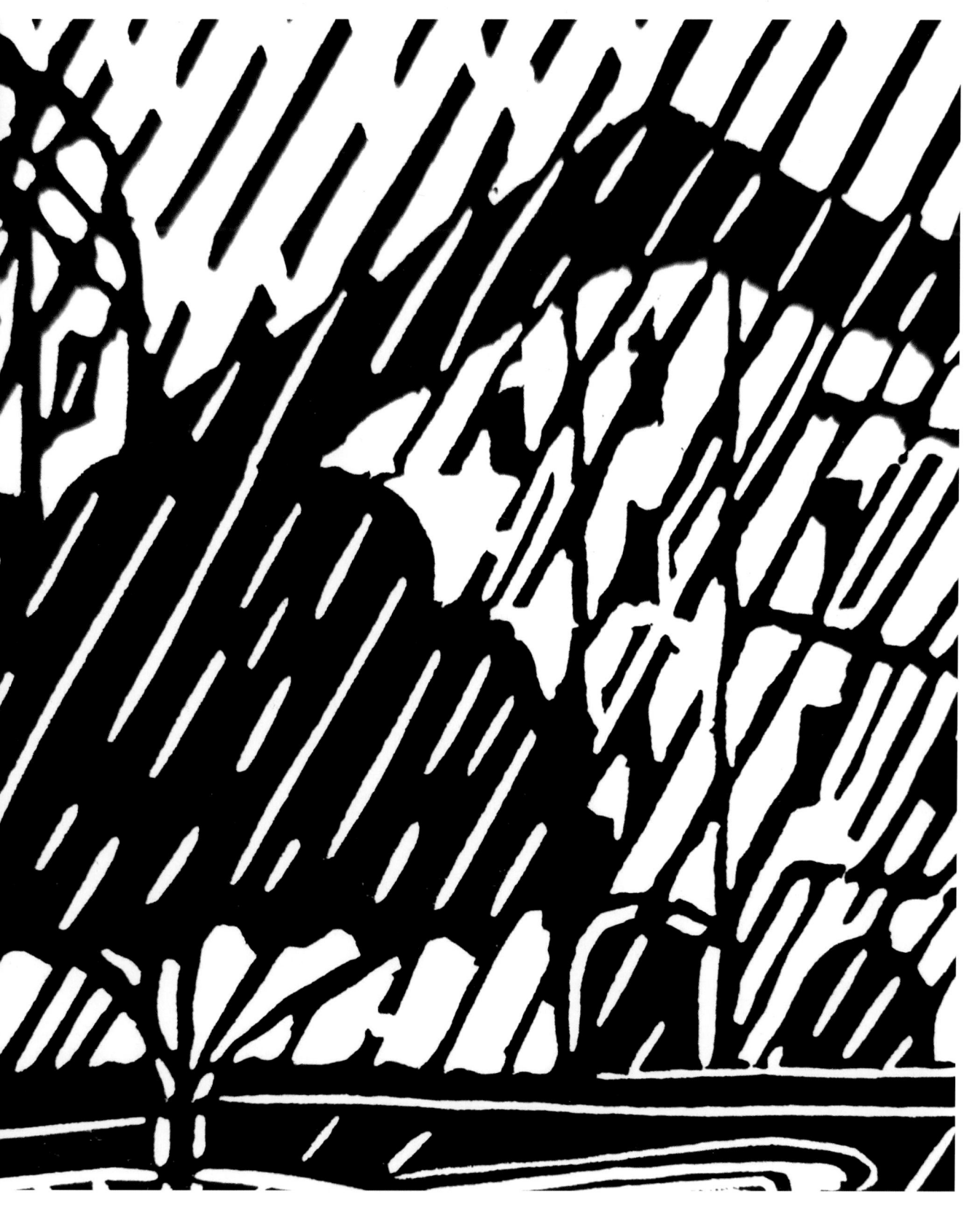

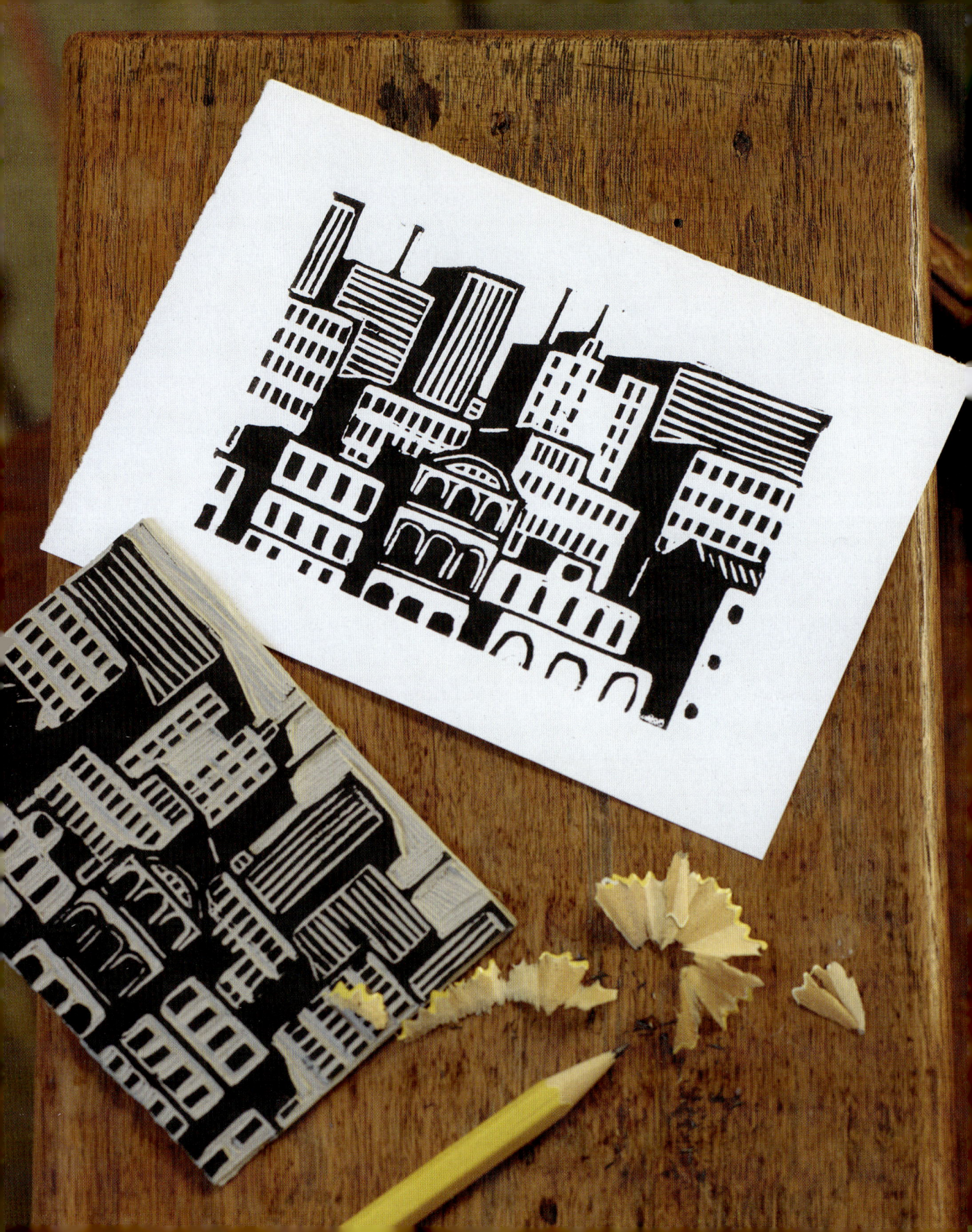

CITY SKYLINE

This city skyline print is a great introduction to the linocut technique, letting you practise carving straight lines and grids. Whether you base your skyline on a real location or an imaginary city, this design is incredibly versatile and can be used as a base for future projects too.

SUPPLIES

Tracing paper

Pencil

Pen

Acrylic paint and brush

Narrow cutter

One sheet of lino
7.5 x 10.5cm (3 x 4in)

Ink of your choice

Brayer

Baren

A6 card

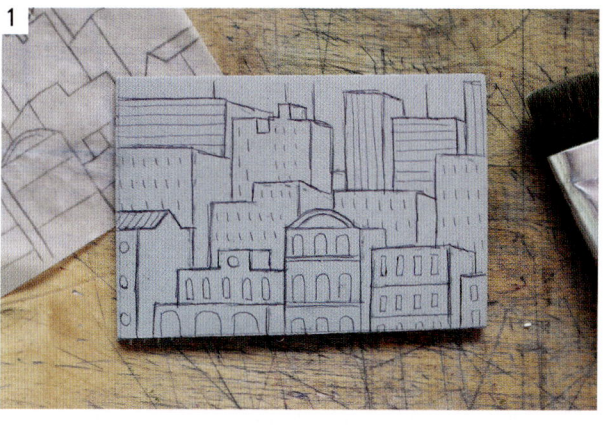

1 Begin by sketching out your design. Create visual interest by varying the size and shape of your buildings. Using the techniques described in the Tools and Techniques chapter, transfer your drawing onto the lino.

2 Add a thin layer of acrylic paint so that you can see where you have carved more easily. This is especially useful when it comes to carving the windows.

3 To add windows to the buildings, begin by carving a series of equally spaced vertical lines.

4 Now carve horizontally across your vertical lines. Carving your lines closer together will produce smaller windows, while carving them further apart will give you larger windows.

5 Use the technique in Steps 3 and 4 for the buildings in the mid-ground of your print. Leaving the sides blank gives a 3D effect, adding to the sense of depth in the image.

6 For the buildings in the background, simplify the windows into either horizontal or vertical lines.

7 Now add extra details to the buildings in the foreground, as these should be the largest in the print. Dividing the floors using lines and adding arches over the windows is a great way to achieve this.

8 Make the most of the extra space in the foreground buildings to vary the shape of the windows. Round and arched windows make a really nice contrast to the angular background.

9 Once you have carved your buildings, you can decide to either leave the sky solid, which will give a night-time effect, or to carve it away for a day-time effect. To finish the carve, add antennas to the tops of some of the buildings.

10 Now that your block is ready to ink and print, use the techniques described in the Tools and Techniques chapter.

11 You might like to use this block as a key block to add colour to, using either the multi-block or chine collé techniques (demonstrated later in this book).

3
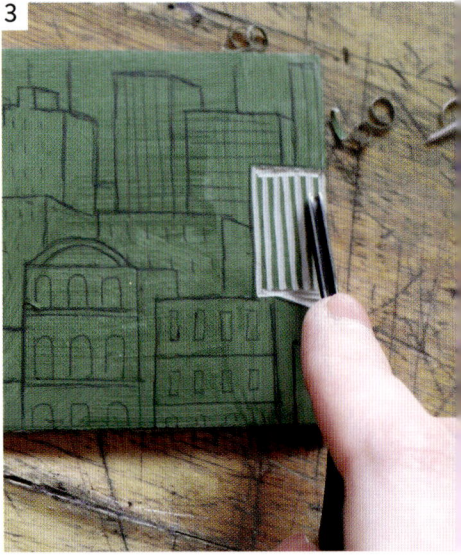

6
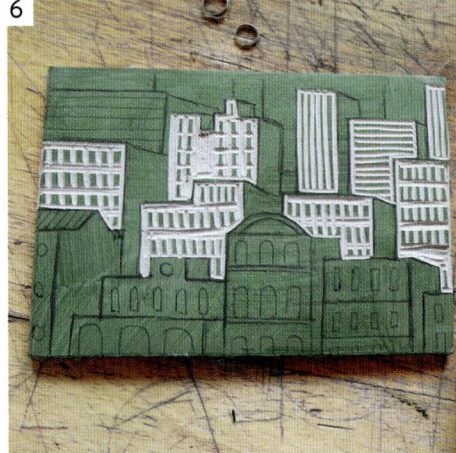

9
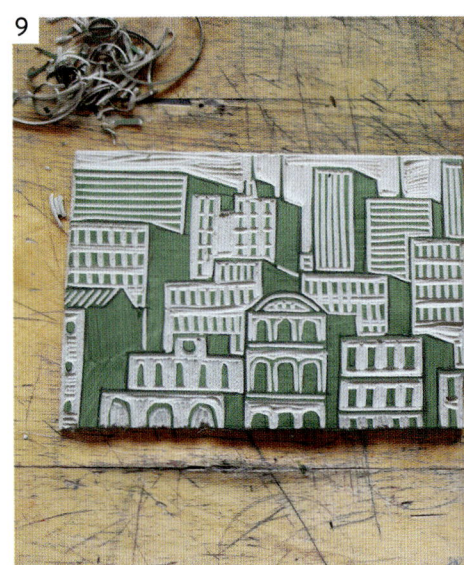

4

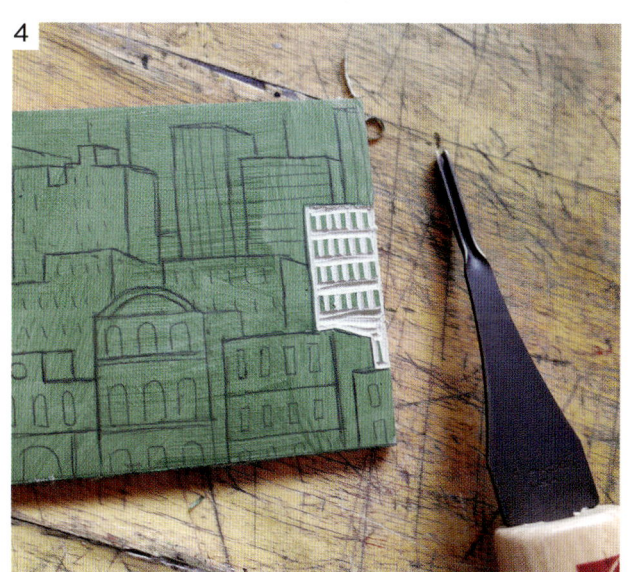

5

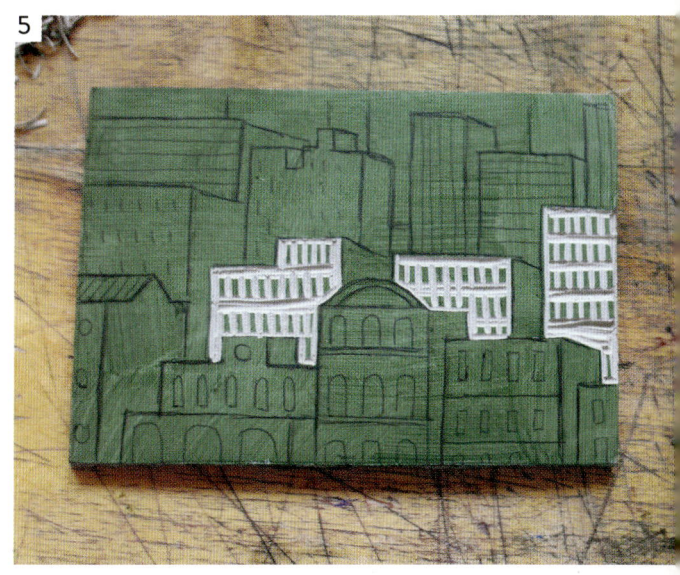

7

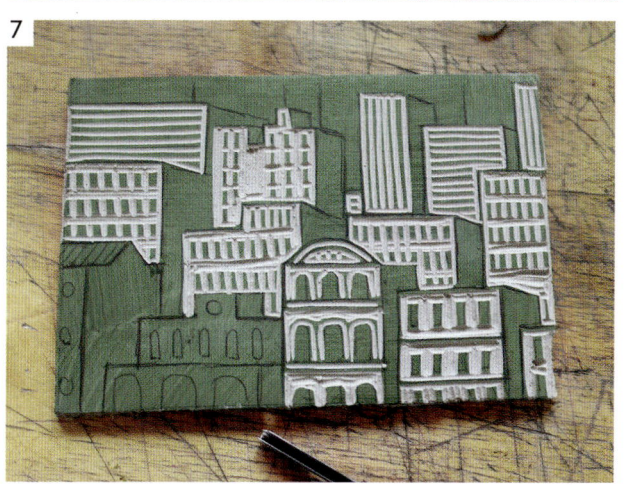

8

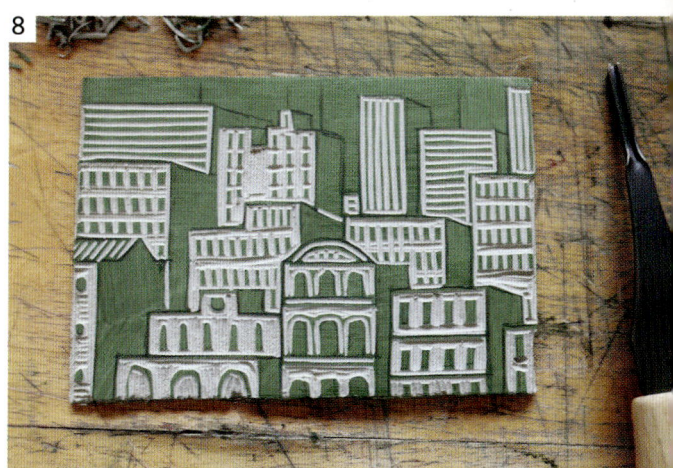

10

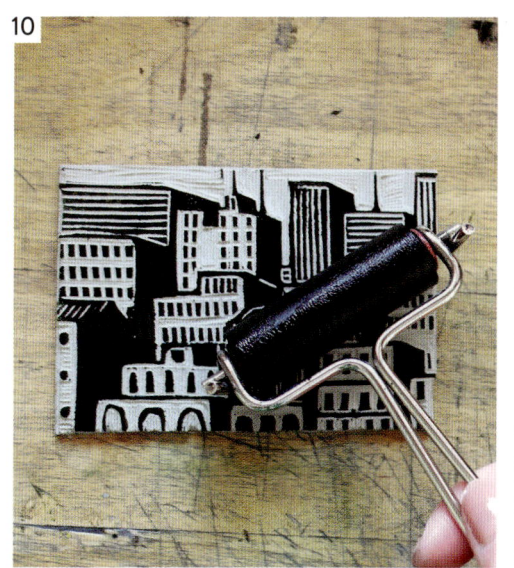

11

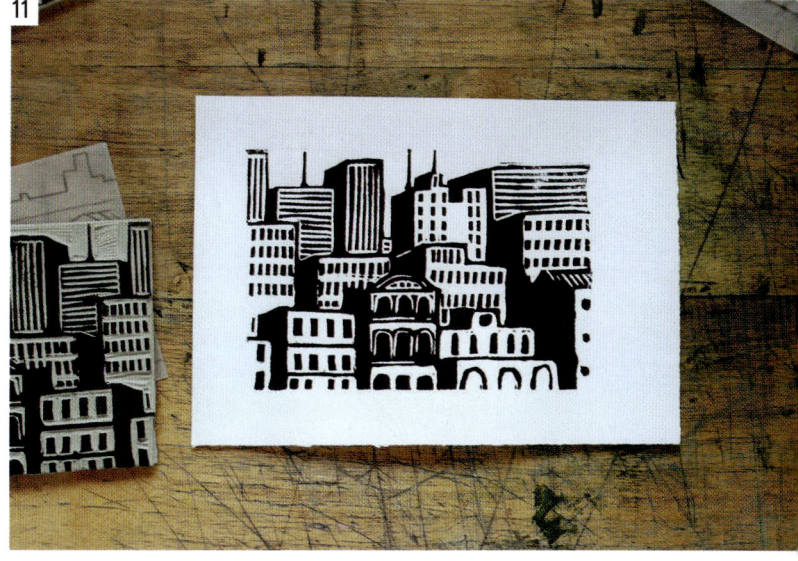

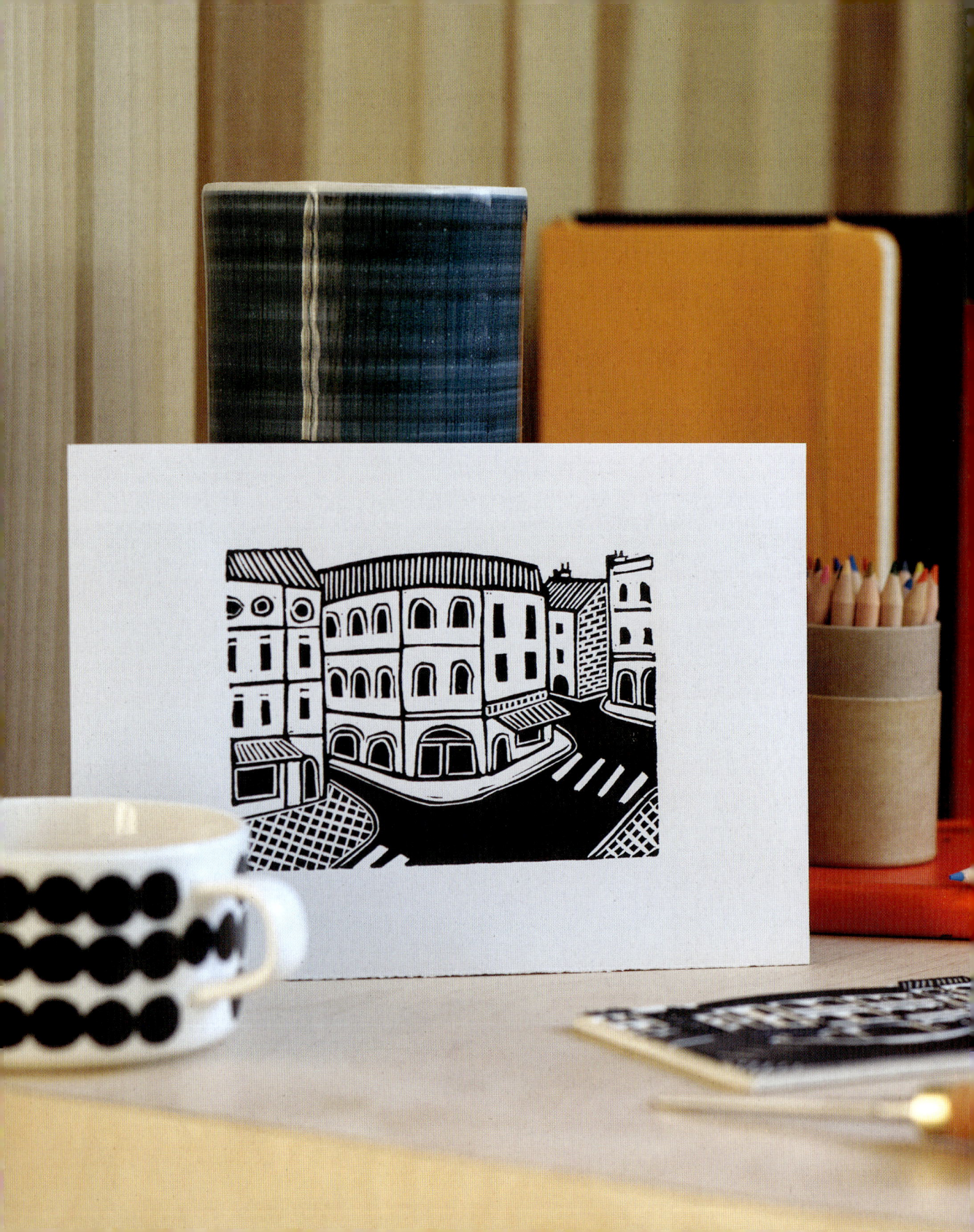

STREET SCENE

Capture a local or an iconic view of your favourite city with this customisable street scene. This block gives you plenty of opportunities to explore new ways of adding texture and detail too.

SUPPLIES

Tracing paper
....
Pencil
....
Pen
....
Acrylic paint and brush
....
Narrow cutter
....
One sheet of lino
9 x 12cm (3½ x 4¾in)
....
Ink of your choice
....
Brayer
....
Baren
....
A5 card
....

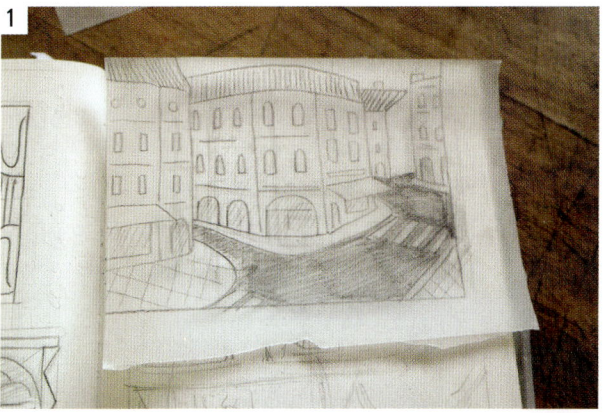

1 Begin with your sketch. The viewpoint here is slightly elevated, as if looking from a high window, which allows for a wider view. Alternatively, you could draw your scene from the view of someone on the street, with the buildings rising up around them.

2 Once happy with your drawing, use the techniques described in the Tools and Techniques chapter to transfer it onto the block. Add a thin layer of acrylic paint to help you see where you need to carve.

3 Carve the details of the buildings. Smaller windows can be solid shapes, but for larger ones add extra detail by carving their outline, which can also be used to distinguish individual panes of glass.

4 Add brickwork to the sides of buildings. To do this, first carve a series of horizontal parallel lines. Then carefully carve vertical lines between each of these horizontal ones, staggering them to look like overlapping bricks. A guide for this technique for carving brickwork can be found in the Pattern Guide in the Carving Tips section of the first chapter.

5 You might like to add other details, such as carving short, parallel lines for roofs and awnings.

6 Add the finishing details to the roads and pavement (sidewalk). Creating a crosshatch effect can suggest paving slabs, while keeping the main road solid will form a good contrast with the pattern and detail of the rest of the block.

7 Once you are happy with your design, it is ready to ink. Because of the smaller details and thin lines, especially around the windows, don't add too much ink to your roller in one go, as it could get stuck in these details. Instead, build up the layers of ink gradually until you have enough to print with.

8 When your block is inked, check the balance of the design, and make sure that no ink has been trapped in the finer details. If any ink has become stuck, use paper towel to remove the excess before re-inking that section.

9 Now you are ready to print your block, using the techniques described in the Tools and Techniques chapter. This is another good opportunity to check the balance of your print and to see if there are any areas where more details can be added or if any areas need fixing or re-carving, and then reprint.

10 You can adapt this street scene to reflect your own local area by changing the architectural style of the buildings, or the types of shops and businesses included. Working on a larger scale would allow you to add even more details, such as people in the street or products in shop windows.

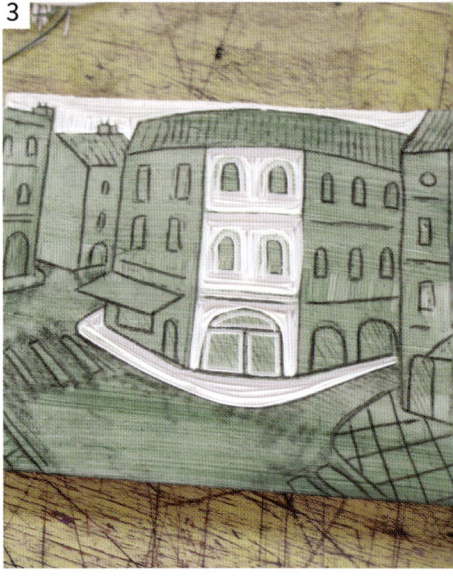

3

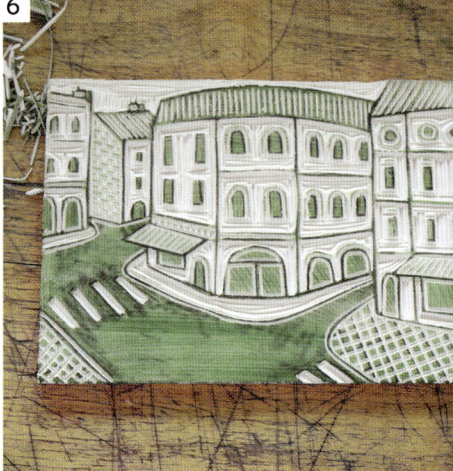

6

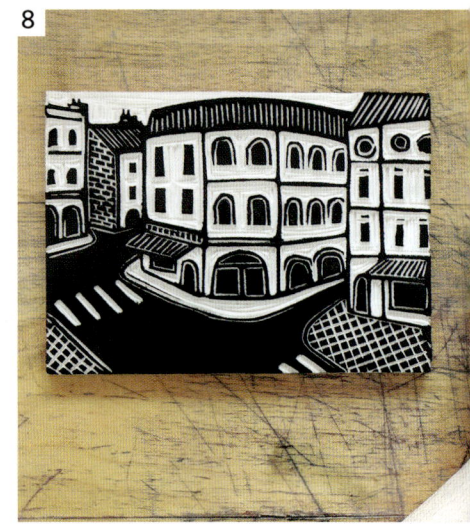

8

4
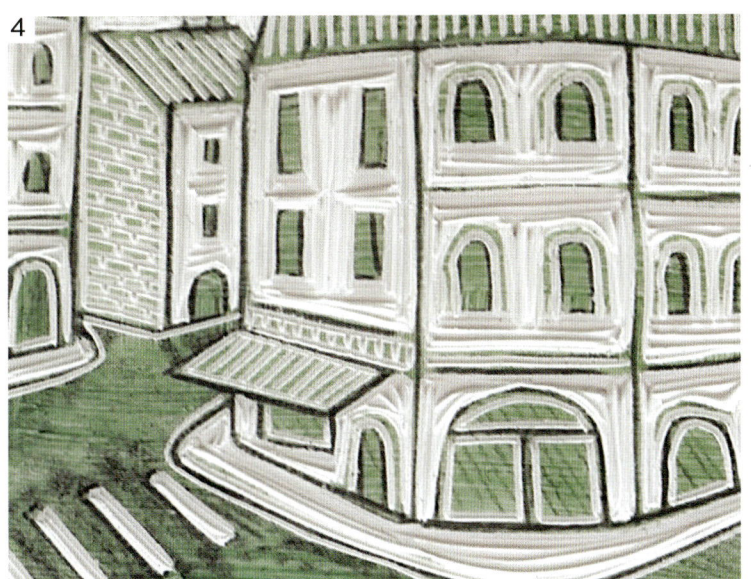

5
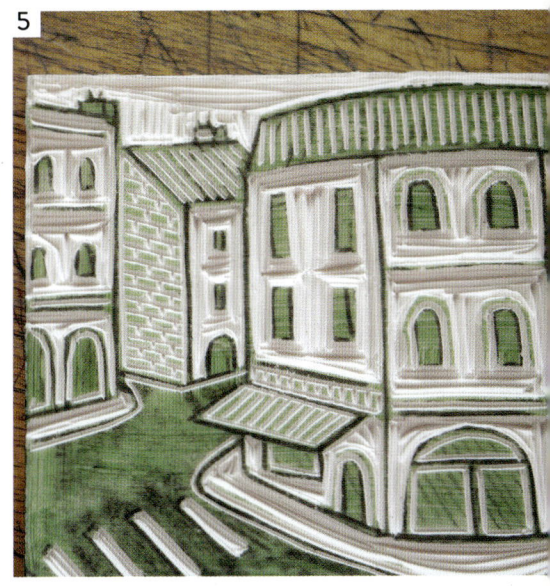

7
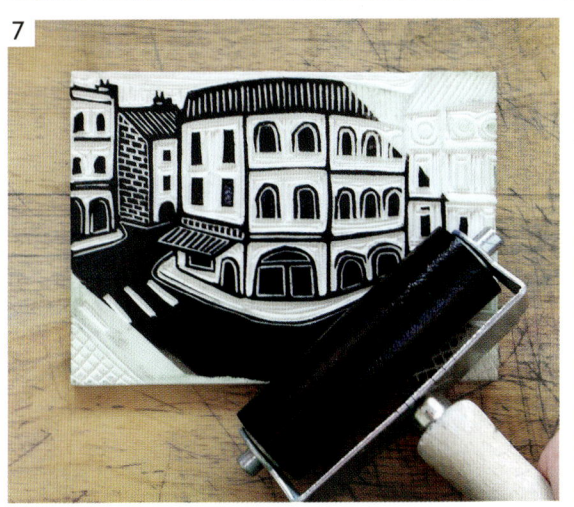

10
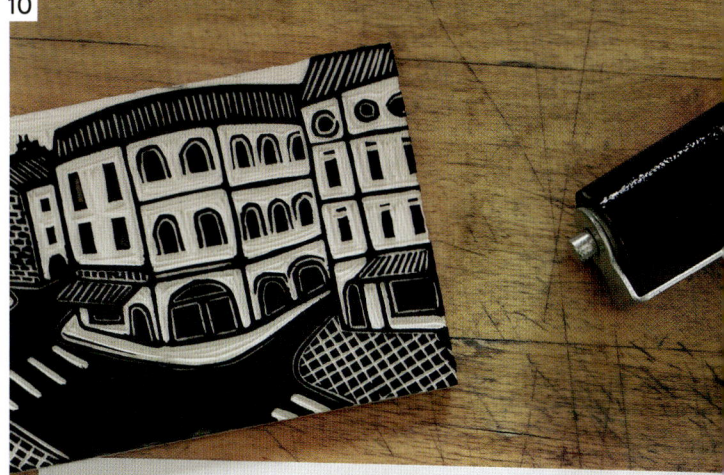

9
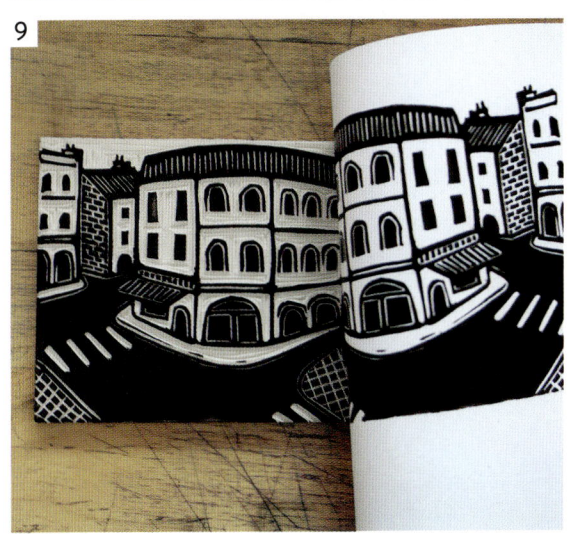

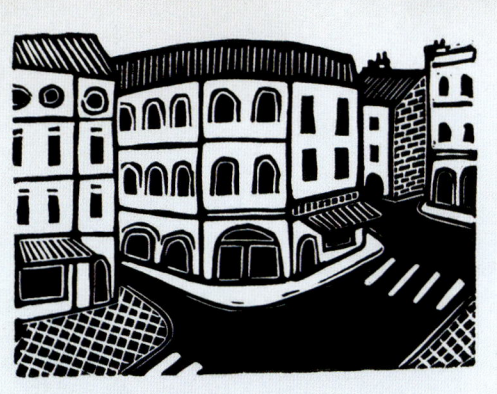

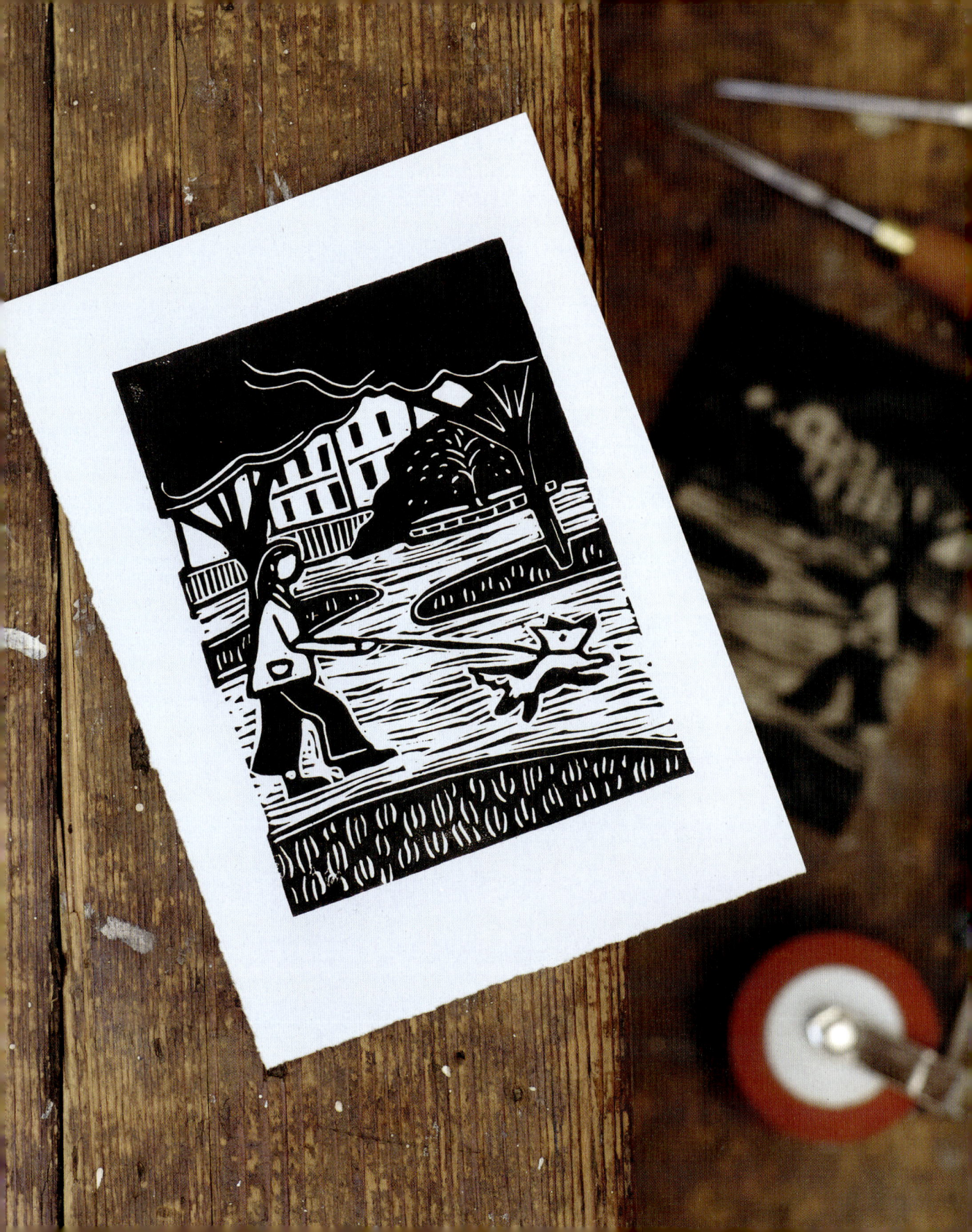

URBAN PARK

Introduce the natural world into your prints with this view of an urban park. It offers the potential to experiment with texture and shape, and is a great way to practise fine mark-making. This print is also really customisable – try swapping out the dog walker for joggers, children, or even a self-portrait.

SUPPLIES

Tracing paper

Pencil

Pen

Acrylic paint and brush

Narrow cutter

One sheet of lino
7.5 x 10.5cm (3 x 4in)

Ink of your choice

Brayer

Baren

A6 card

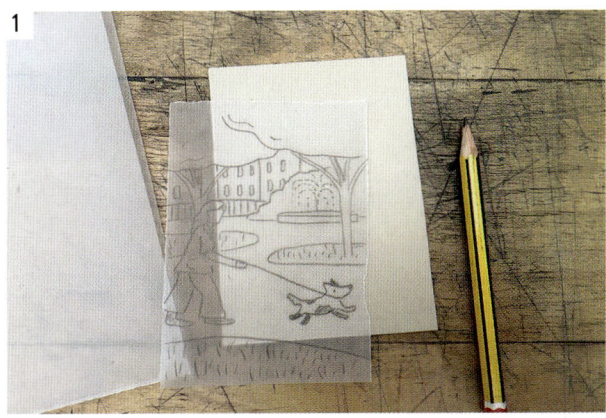

1 Begin by sketching your design, incorporating areas where you can introduce pattern and texture. To make sure these patterns don't overwhelm the final image, test them out first on the drawing – here the short lines used for the grass are balanced by the solid trees.

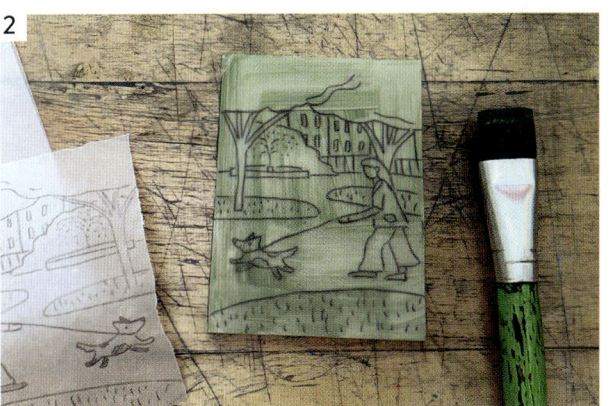

2 Transfer your drawing onto the block and add a thin layer of acrylic paint using the techniques described in the Tools and Techniques chapter. This contrast colour will be especially helpful in this print for working out areas of texture and contrast.

3 Create the texture on the paths by carving away the surface to leave some narrow, raised areas. Leaving raised areas can be used to indicate shadows, while angling them can suggest changes in gradient.

4 Adding figures and animals is a great way to suggest scale in your print. To make them stand out from the surrounding area, keep parts or all of them as areas of solid colour.

5 More texture can be created in the grassy areas. Carve short, slightly curved lines in groups of two or three to indicate blades of grass to avoid overwhelming the block with pattern.

6 Now add in the background details. Using the same technique as the grass, add some water flowing in the fountain by carving some short, curved lines. To create very short lines, place the cutter into the block so the point is submerged, and then flick it up to abruptly end the line.

7 To balance out the texture in the foreground, create an area for the eye to rest by keeping the tree canopy solid. A few organic, curvy lines can be used to divide up the trees. Alternatively, carving away this area would give a lighter feel, or provide a space that could be filled with colour using the watercolour technique discussed later in this book.

8 Add in the final details of the background, including a fence and some buildings, again using short straight lines. Demarcate the tree trunks from the background by outlining them, or alternatively repeat the technique used for the paths to create the texture of bark.

9 Your block is now ready to ink. Before printing, use the inked block to gauge the balance of light and dark and areas of texture.

10 Once you are happy with the block, you can begin printing. Although printed here in black ink on white card, why not experiment with the colour of the paper or ink to change the mood of your print?

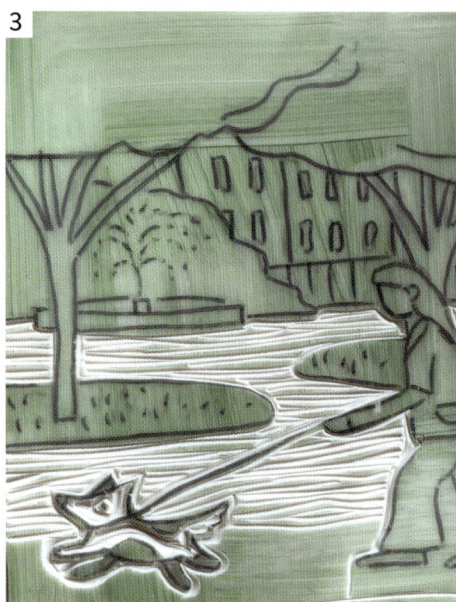

3

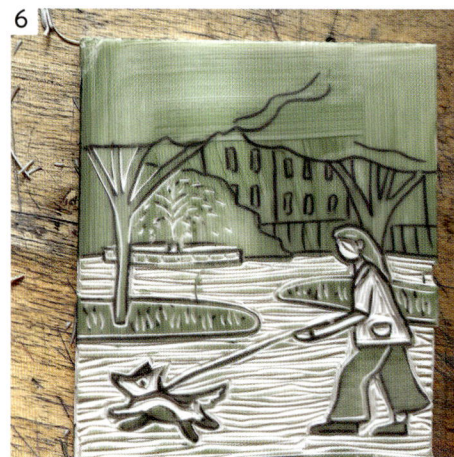

6

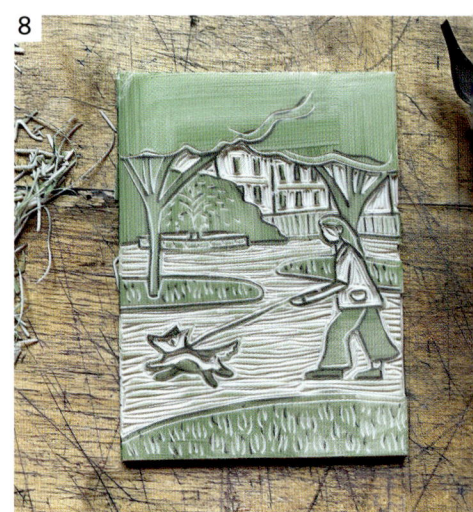

8

4

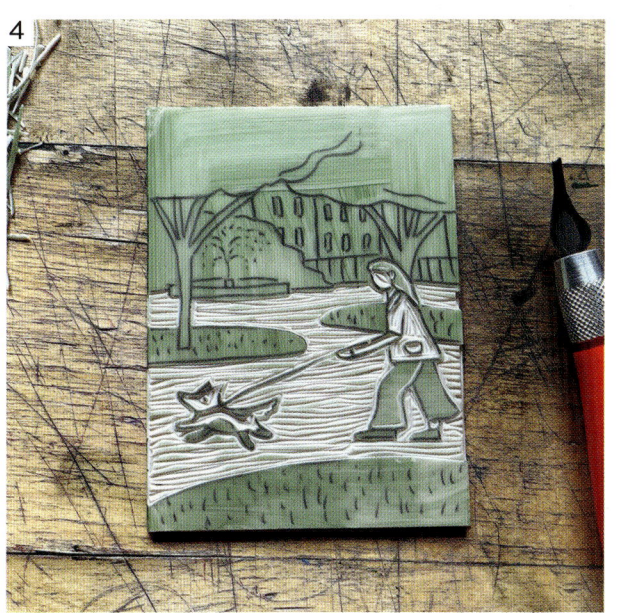

5

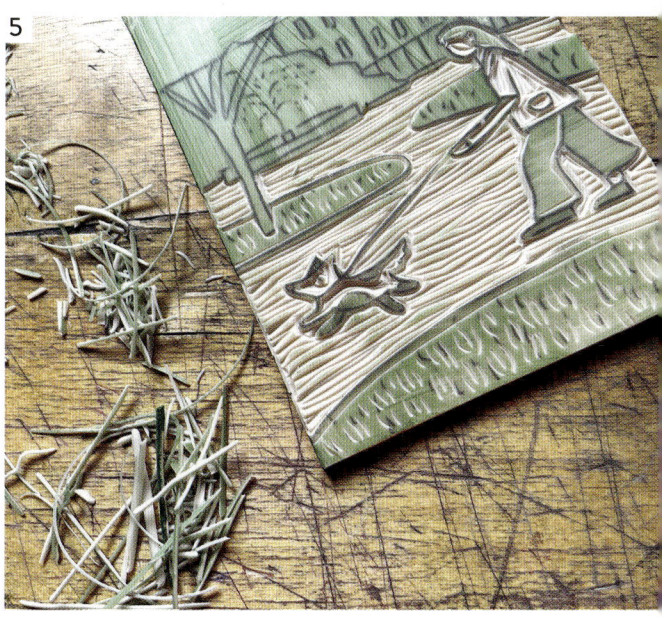

7

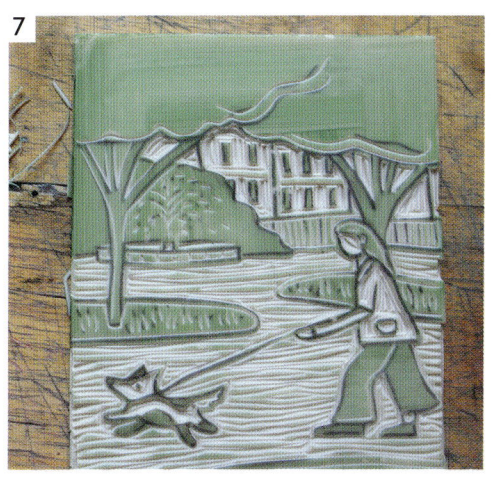

9

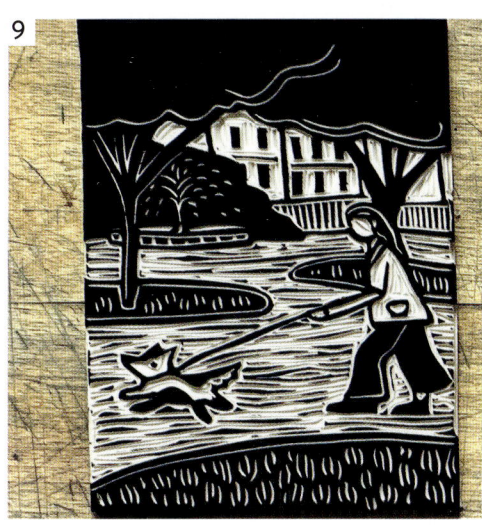

10

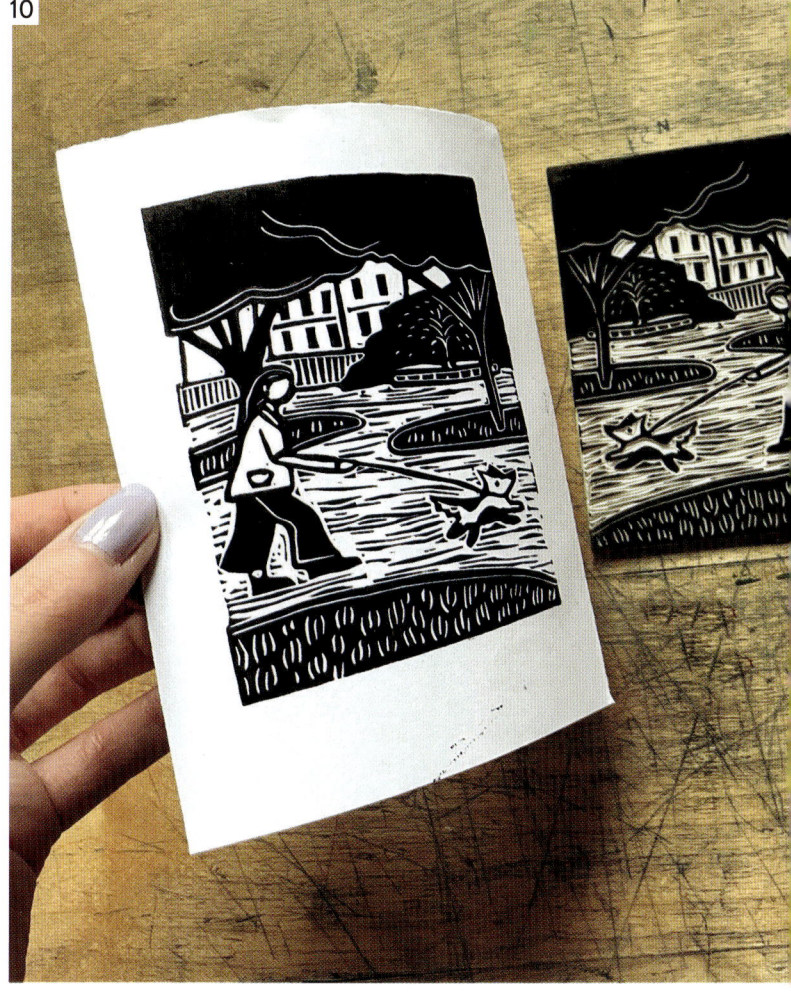

MARKET SCENE

Markets are a great subject for a printmaker, filled with interesting colours, textures, and shapes. There's always something new to discover. This print of an outdoor fruit and vegetable market is a great way to practise different surface effects and carving styles.

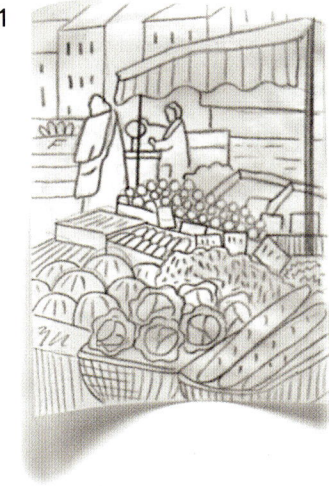

1 Begin by sketching out your design and transferring it onto tracing paper. To draw the viewer into the scene, create different layers. Here, there is a large pile of produce in the foreground (perfect for creating lots of texture), while the background is simpler, using the two figures as a focal point.

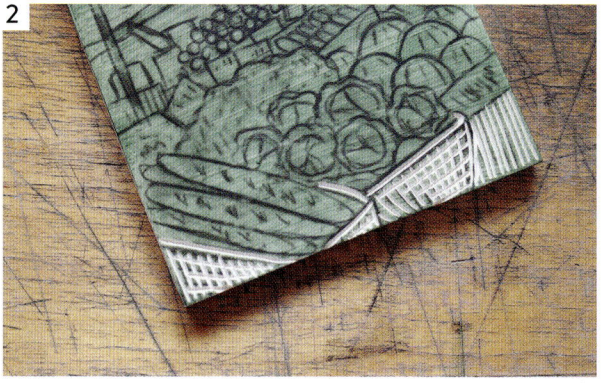

2 Once you have transferred your drawing onto the block, you can begin carving (using the techniques in the Tools and Techniques chapter). Starting in the immediate foreground, create baskets by carving a grid pattern. You can suggest shadows by varying the length of the horizontal line, which can also be curved to suggest the shape of the baskets.

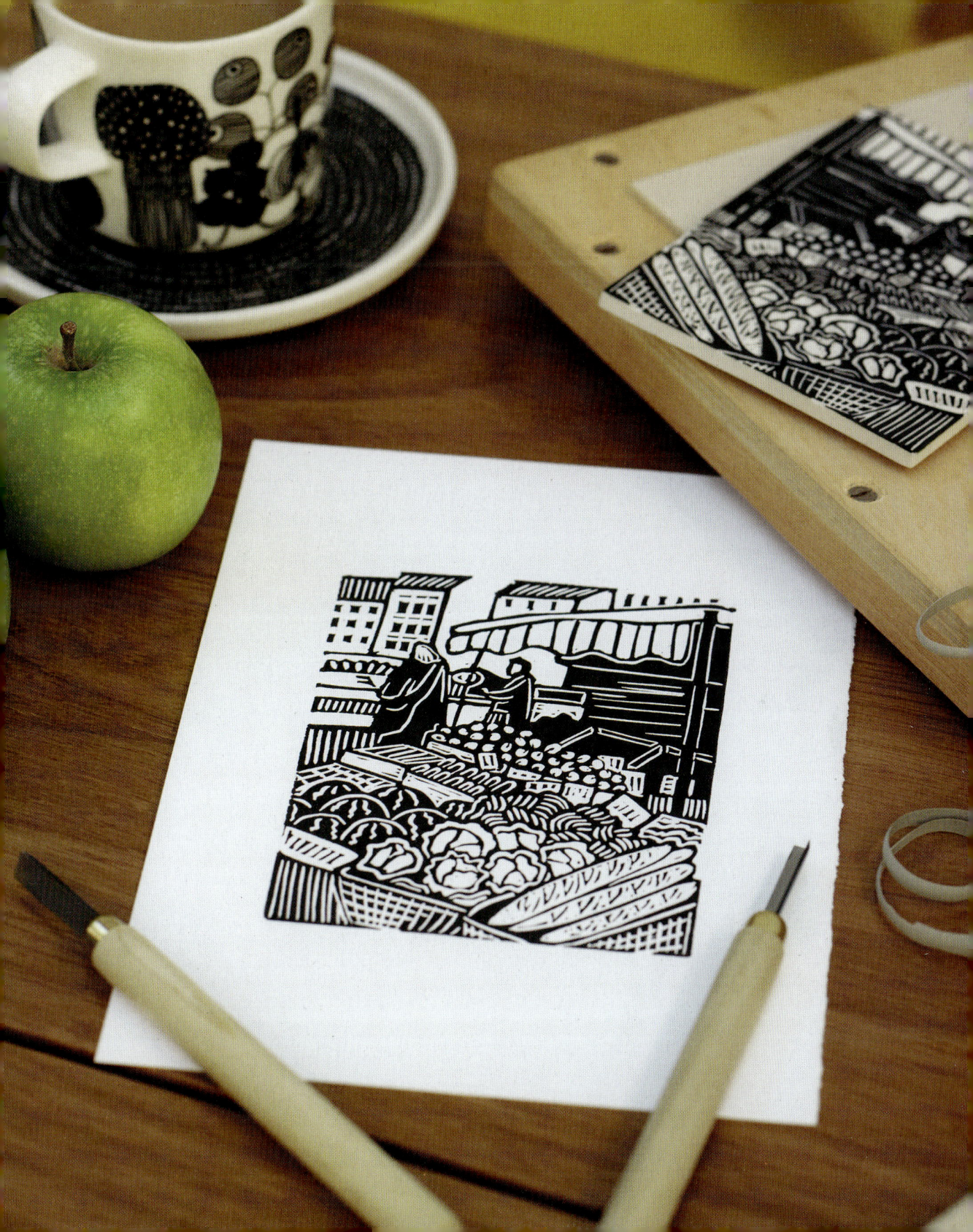

3 The market's produce is a great place to play with texture and explore different ways of moving the cutter. Carve some slightly curved 'V' shapes for the crust of the bread. For the lettuce leaves, create a wiggly circle by rotating the block with your non-cutter hand while slowly moving the cutter in a 'S' shape.

4 Try out different methods of mark-making for each box of produce. Piles of items in the distance can be suggested by short dashes or 'U' shapes. These more abstract shapes will help create perspective.

5 To create small circles for tomatoes, apples, or oranges, press the point of a 'V' gauge into the block and, without moving the cutter, spin the block all the way around.

6 For the figures, a striking effect can be created by keeping details to a minimum. Carve only the outline of the figures to distinguish them from the details of the foreground, helping them stand out in the finished print and creating a place for the eye to rest.

7 Finish by carving the background, which will help situate your market scene. Here, buildings suggest a street market, but you could swap this for the roof of an indoor market hall.

8 The block is now ready for inking. A solid colour has been used here, but colour could also be used to define different areas or different produce, using either smaller rollers to ink individual sections, or using the gradient technique as shown in the Ink section of the Tools and Techniques chapter.

9 Before printing, check that the block is clear of any small shavings of lino – sometimes when carving small details, lino shavings can remain attached or trapped. Once you are happy, your block is ready to print.

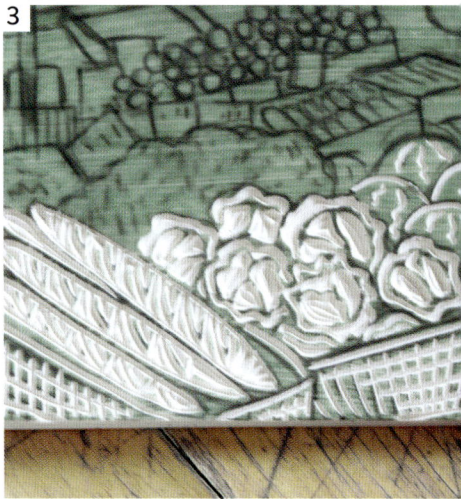

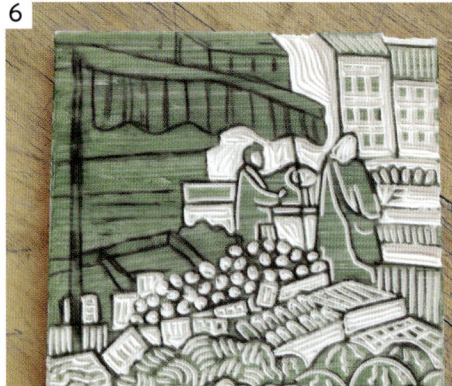

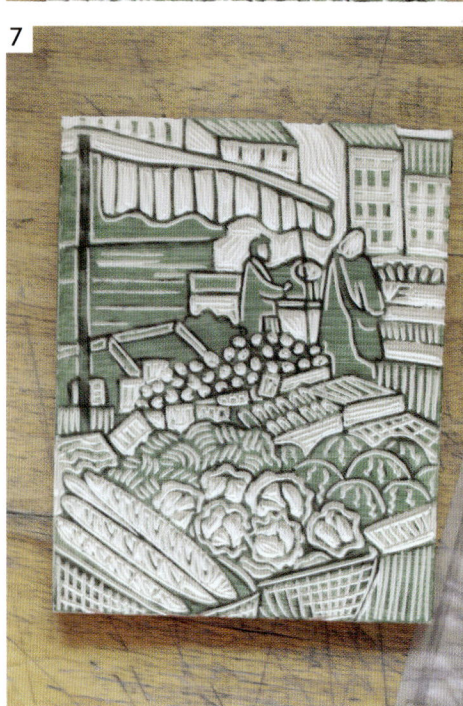

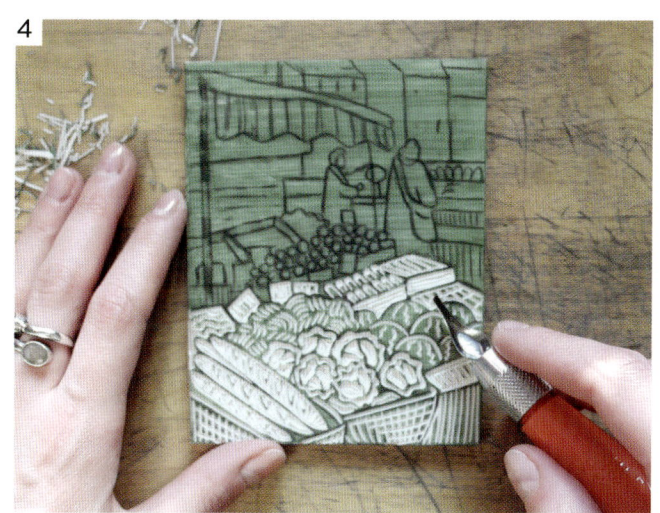

4

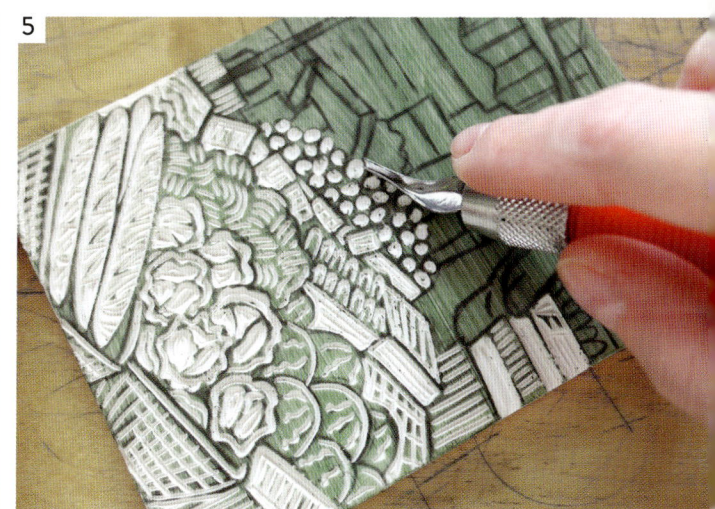

5

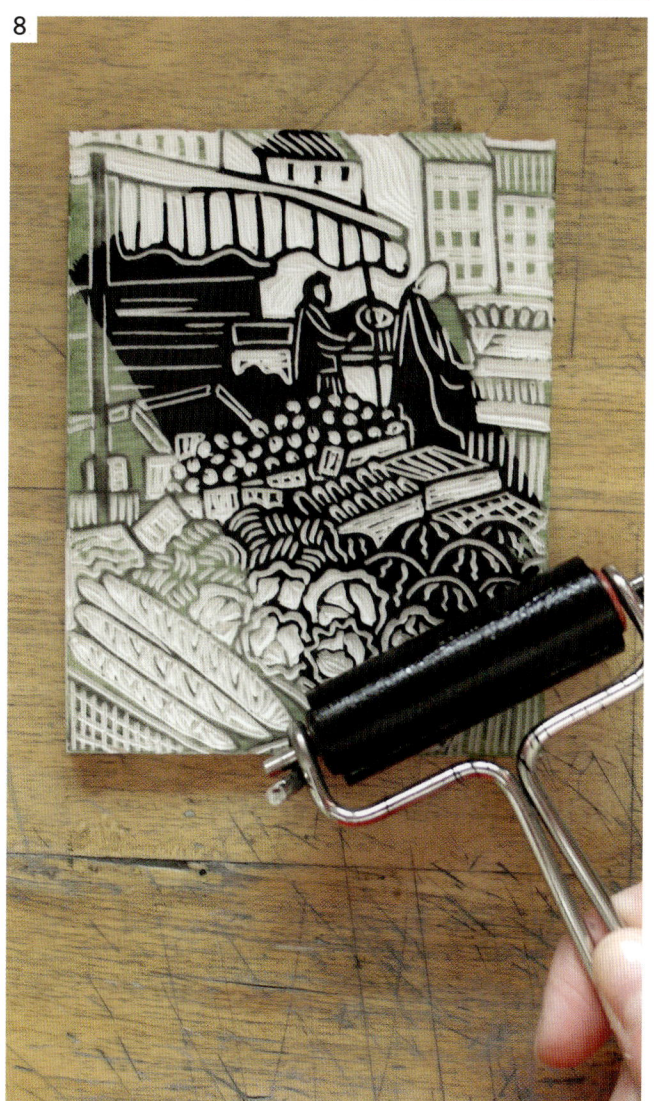

8

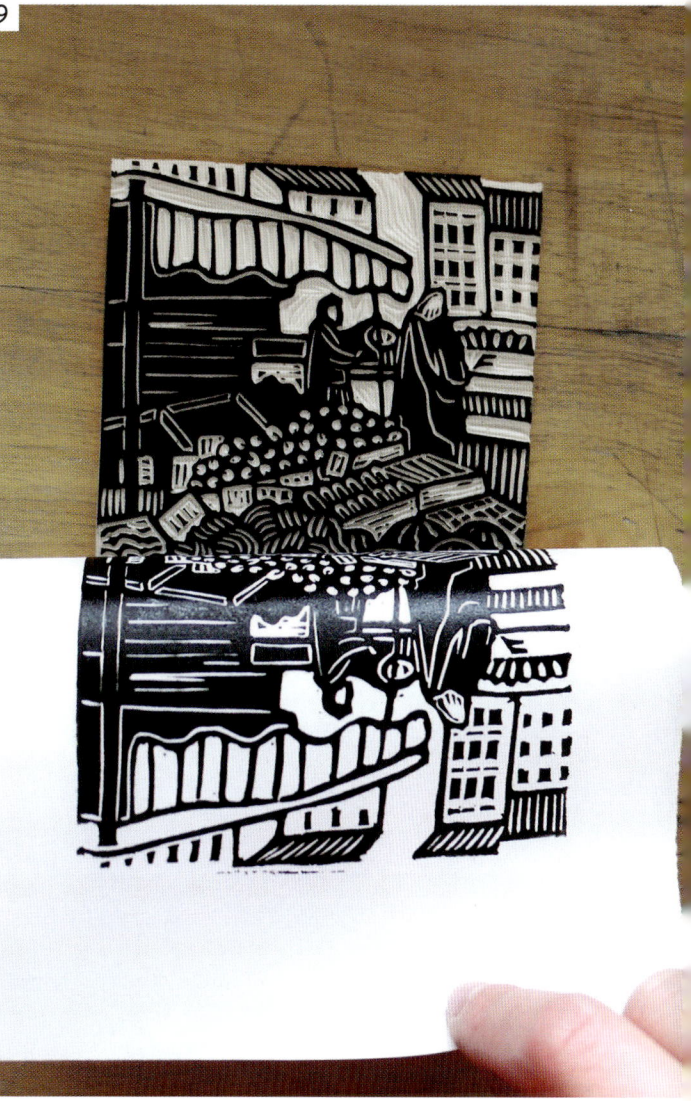

9

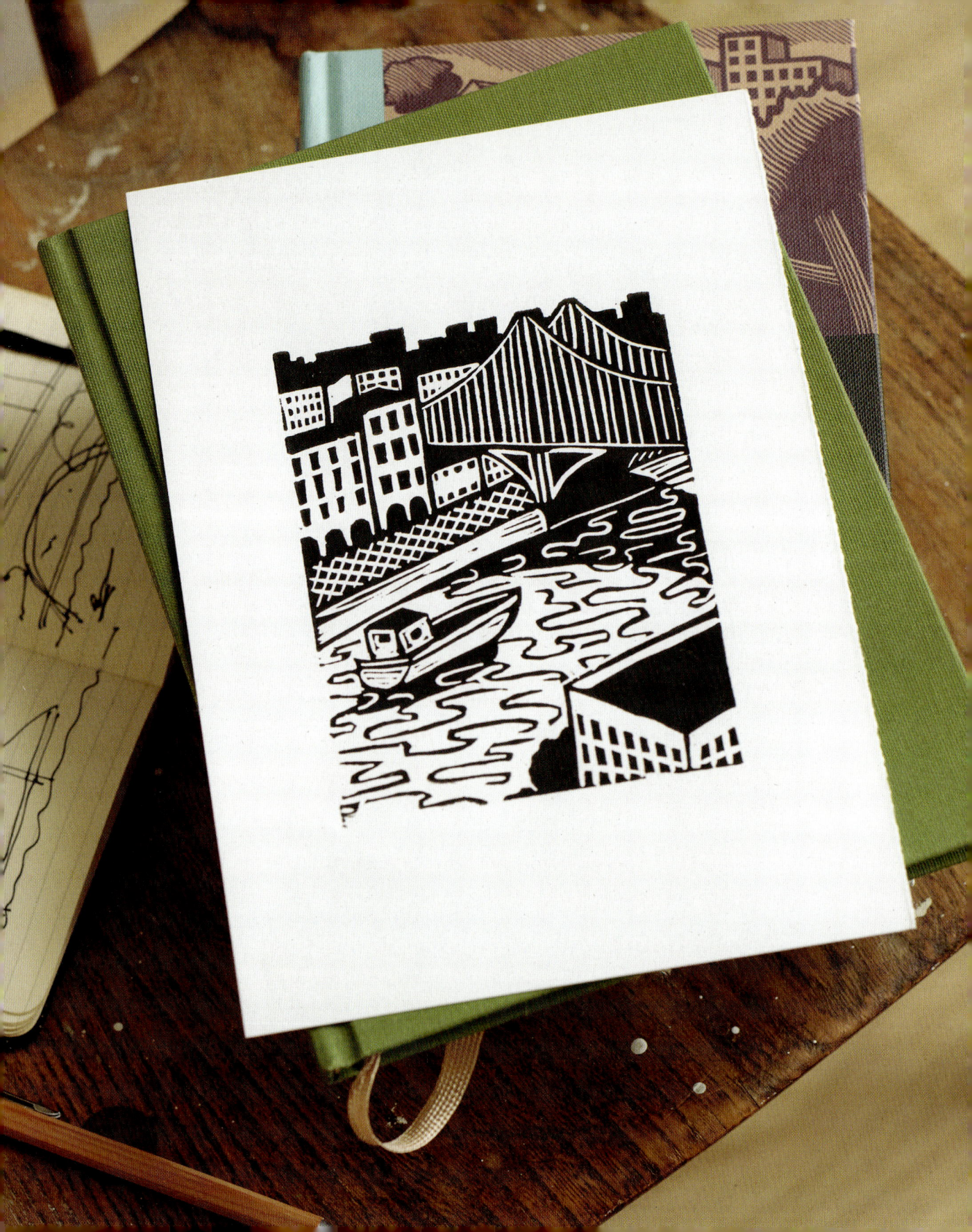

RIVERSIDE

Whether rural or industrial, a tiny stream or a major river, adding water into your prints is another way to add pattern, movement, and visual interest. This print introduces a key technique for carving water, which can be adapted to suit any future watery scenes.

SUPPLIES

Tracing paper

Pencil

Pen

Acrylic paint and brush

Narrow cutter

One sheet of lino
9 x 12cm (3½ x 4¾in)

Ink of your choice

Brayer

Baren

A5 card

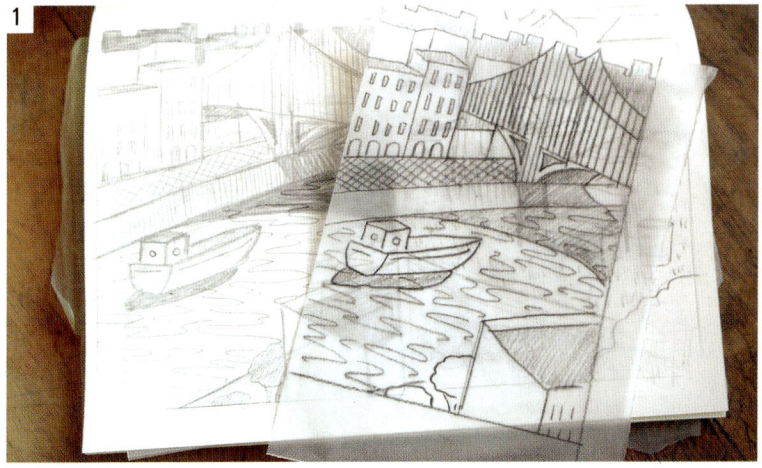

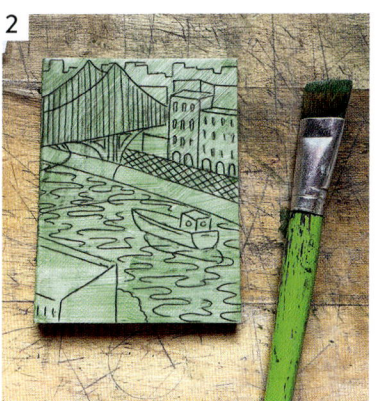

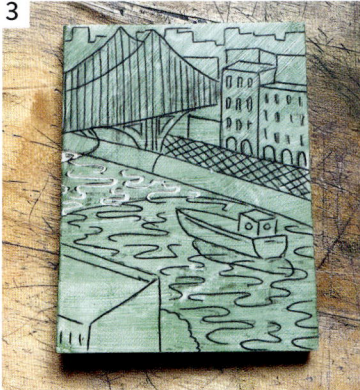

1 Begin with your sketch. This example uses a high vantage-point to make the river the central feature of the print. When you are ready, transfer your drawing to the block (using the techniques described in the Tools and Techniques chapter).

2 Add a layer of acrylic paint to provide contrast, which will help especially when carving the smaller details of the water.

3 Begin by carving the water in the shadow of the bridge and the boat, carving fluid, wiggly lines into the solid area.

47

4 For the rest of the water, carve away the area around the ripples, in the inverse of the water in the shadows. A guide for this technique for carving water can be found in the Pattern Guide in the Carving Tips section of the first chapter.

5 Begin adding details to the surrounding area. Roughly carve both the sides of the boat and the riverbank wall to suggest wooden boards and concrete. A grid pattern can suggest the tiles of a pavement (sidewalk).

6 Add some details to the buildings in the foreground using the same technique as in the City Skyline project. Make sure to align your windows with the perspective of the building.

7 For the bridge, carve the parallel lines for the supporting wires – this keeps the majority of the structure solid while suggesting the key defining features.

8 Add the details of the buildings in the background, reducing the detail as you get further back, so that the buildings right at the back are silhouettes.

9 Once you are happy with your design, add ink to check the balance of the print. As there are fine lines on this block, make sure not to add ink too thickly and build it up gradually.

10 Now your block is ready to print. Be careful when applying pressure to the details of the water, as they may be fragile on the block. This block could be used as the key block for either a multi-block or a chine collé print. These two techniques are explored later in the book.

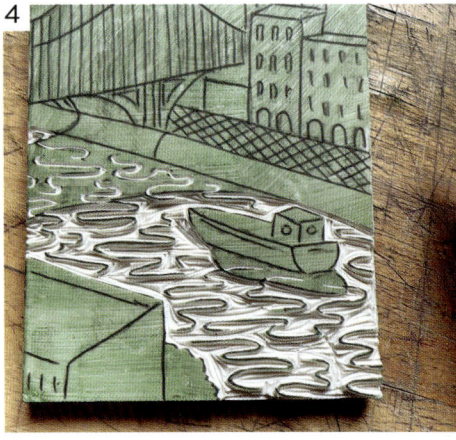

4

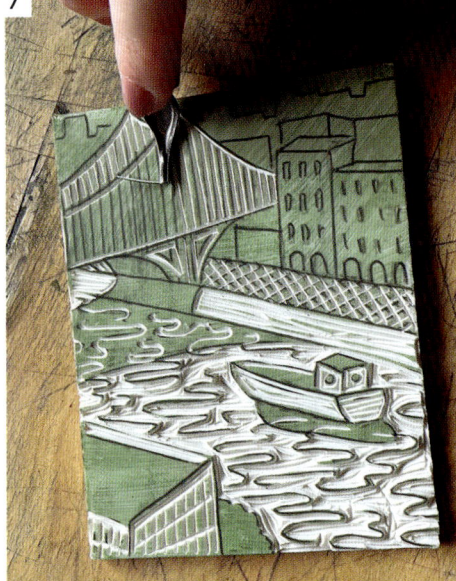

7

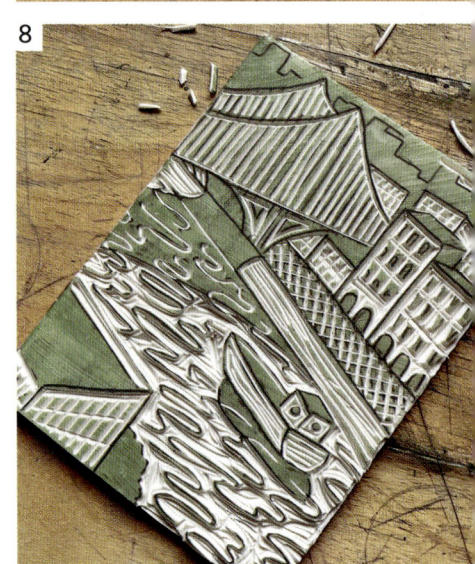

8

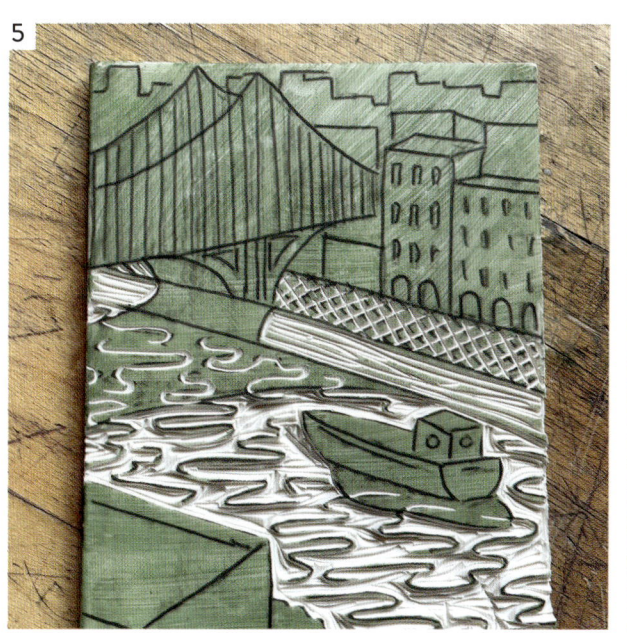

5

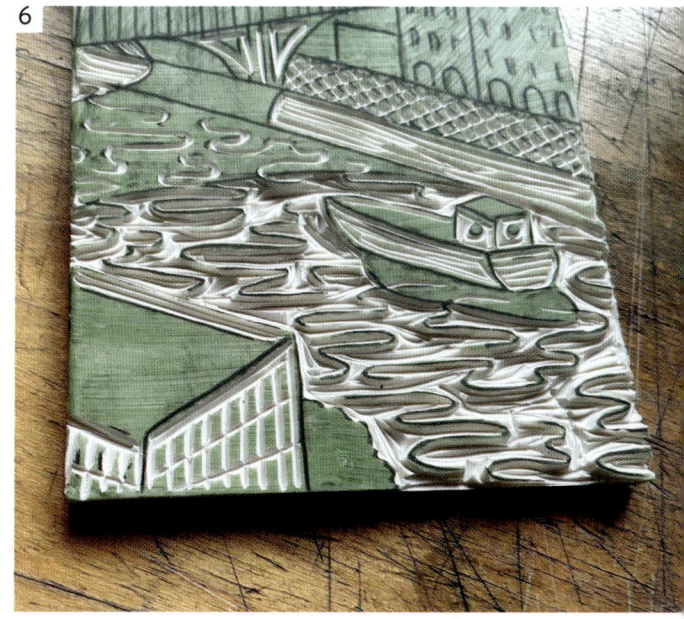

6

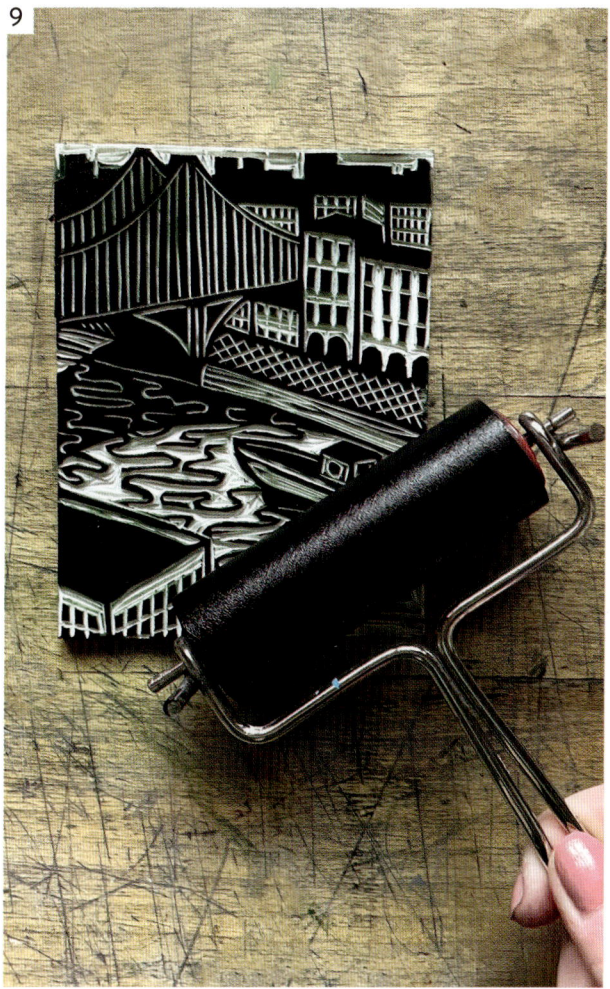

9

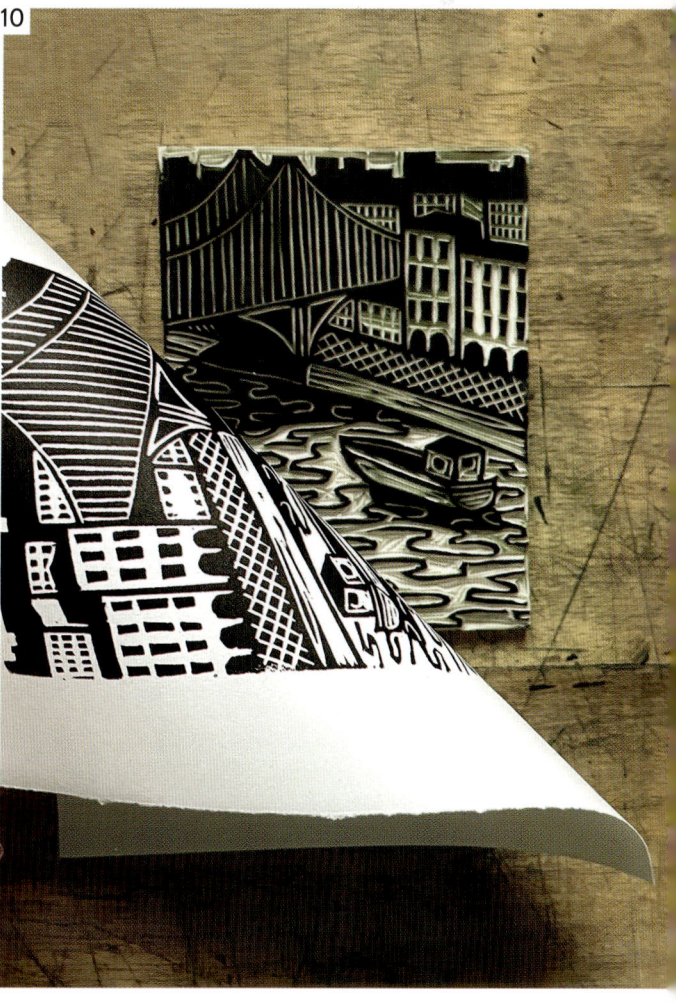

10

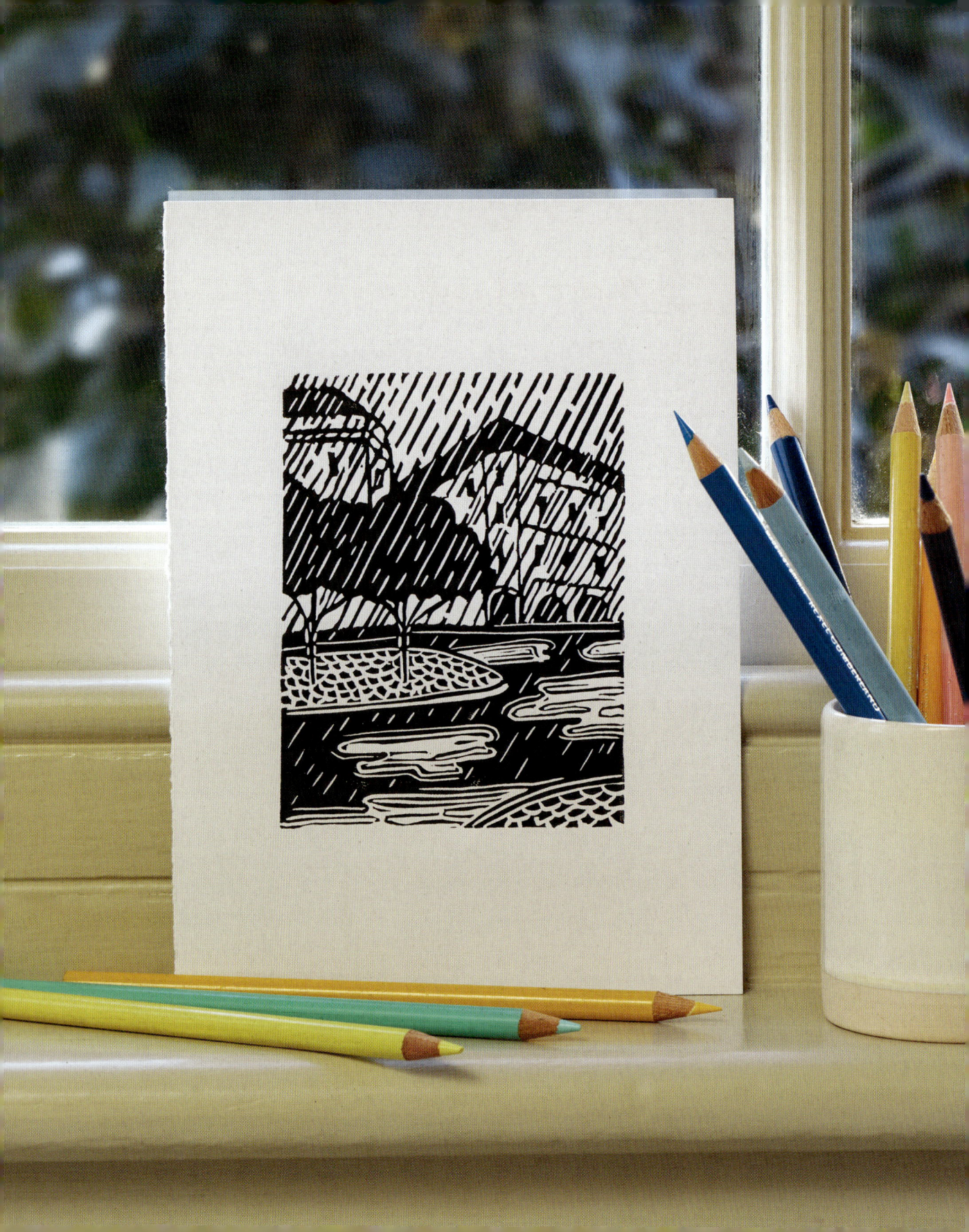

RAINY SCENE

Introduce the elements into your prints with this scene of a rainy day in the city. It's perfect for adding some extra visual interest and narrative into your work. This technique could also be adapted for snowy scenes too.

SUPPLIES

Tracing paper

Pencil

Pen

Ruler

Acrylic paint and brush

Narrow cutter

One sheet of lino
9 x 12cm (3½ x 4¾in)

Ink of your choice

Brayer

Baren

A5 card

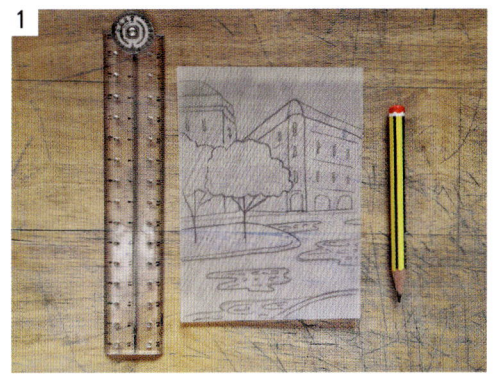

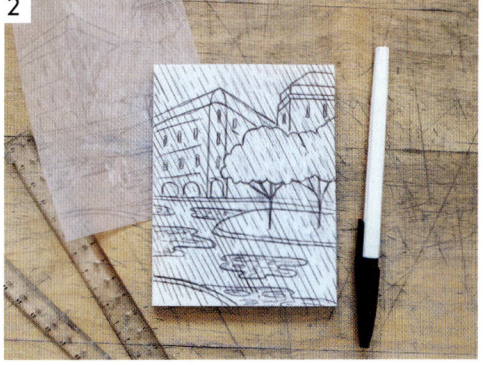

1 Begin by drawing a simple street scene. Keep details to a minimum, as these may become lost with the addition of rain, and focus on varying areas of light and shade. To add the rain, draw a series of parallel lines at an angle across the image. These will provide a guide later on for carving.

2 Transfer your drawing onto the block using the techniques described in the Tools and Techniques chapter. When reinforcing the lines with pen for the rain, you can either mark them as solid lines (as they appear on the original drawing) or break them up to indicate individual raindrops. Add a thin layer of acrylic paint to the block.

51

3 For the sky, where the rain is most visible, carve away the areas between the lines. You can then carve across these lines to create smaller raindrops or leave them solid to represent heavier rainfall. At this point, decide whether to carve around the roofs, which will make them stand out, or to let the rain merge with them, to give the impression that the rain is falling in front of the buildings.

4 To keep the balance of light and dark in your print, and to create visual contrast, keep some areas of primarily solid colour. For these areas, carve along the rain lines rather than around them.

5 For the background details, use the same technique as you did for the sky, carving around the lines to create a contrast with the trees. To define doors and windows, either use breaks in the rain or carve a line around the outside of these details.

6 Add some puddles on the ground by carving uneven shapes across the road. To create ripples, use the same technique of carving water as demonstrated in the Riverside project.

7 Distinguish between the pavement (sidewalk) and the road by adding cobbles. To do this, carve a row of 'U' shapes, alternating the rows so that they overlap. It may be easier to turn the block 180 degrees to do this.

8 To finish the carving, add some final lines of rain across the road – but not too many, or else the foreground details could become lost.

9 Your block is now ready to ink. As there are some finer lines in this print, make sure not to over-ink the brayer or press too hard during inking to prevent the ink from getting trapped in the details, which could lead to a blurry print.

10 Your block is now ready to print. This technique could be adapted for a snowy scene by swapping straight lines for small dots or circles, removing the ripple lines from the puddles, and adding snow to the tops of the trees. You could also try adding in some pedestrians with umbrellas too.

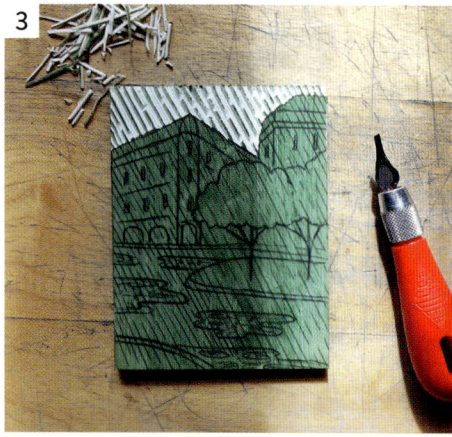

3

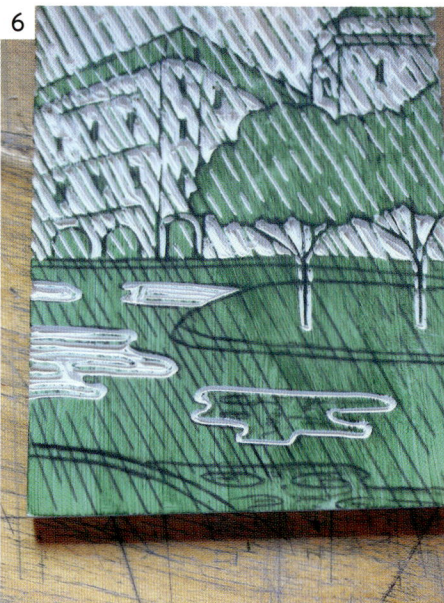

6

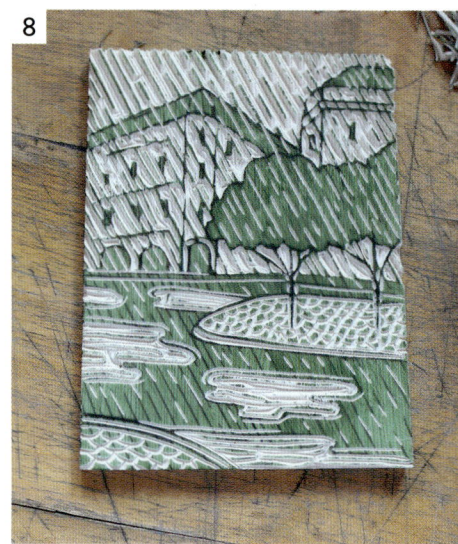

8

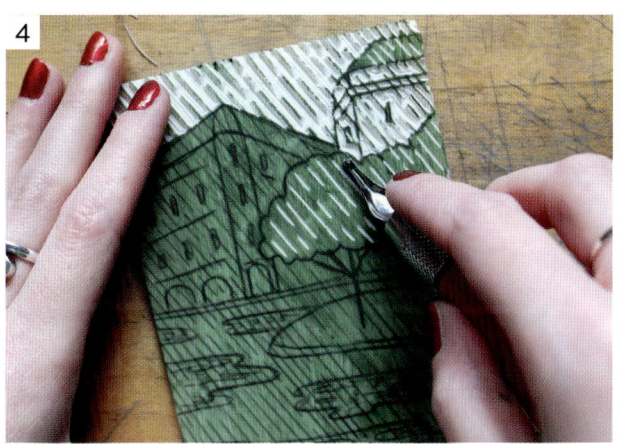

4

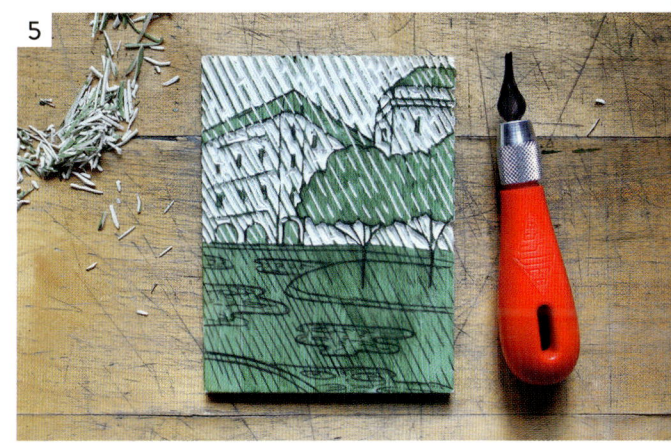

5

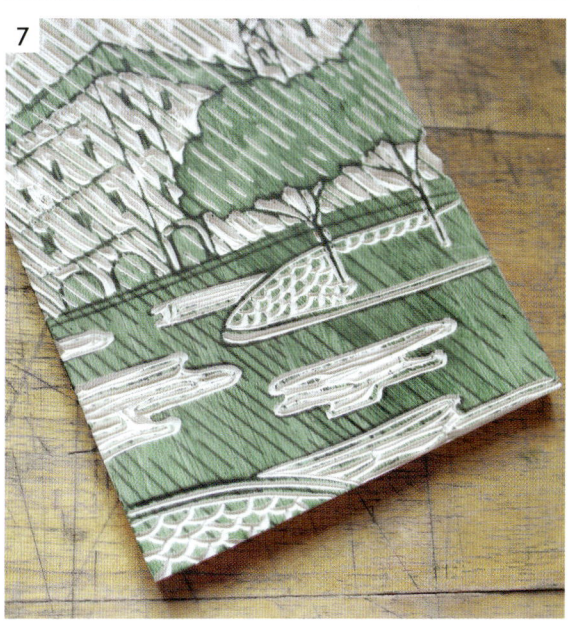

7

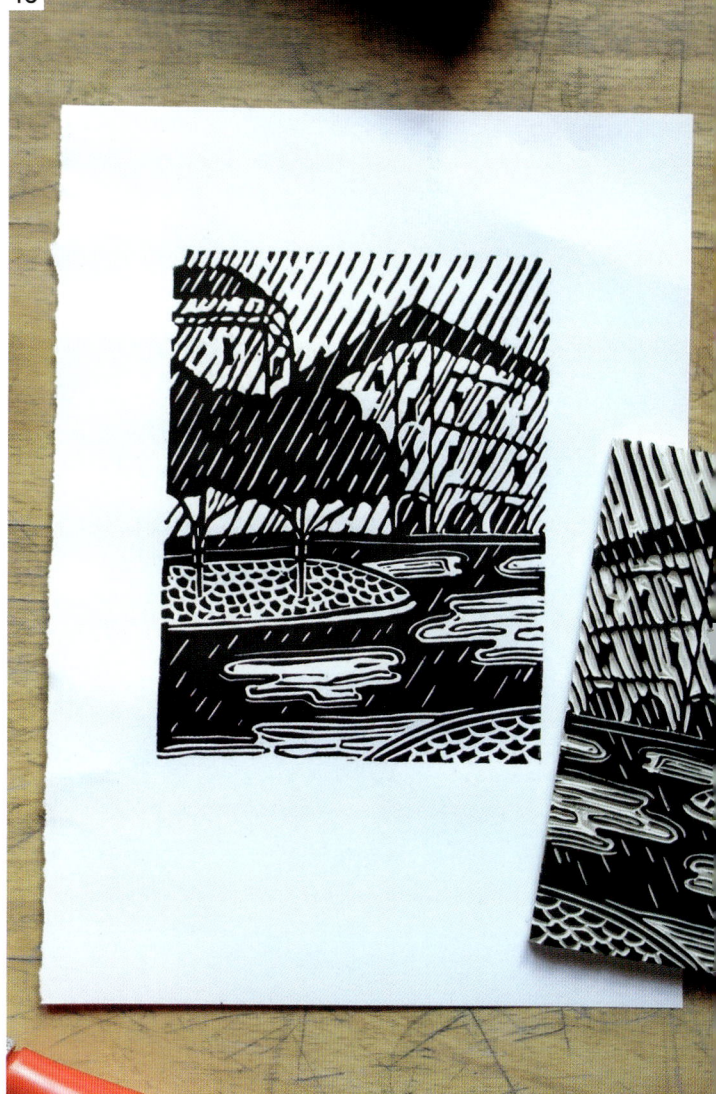

10

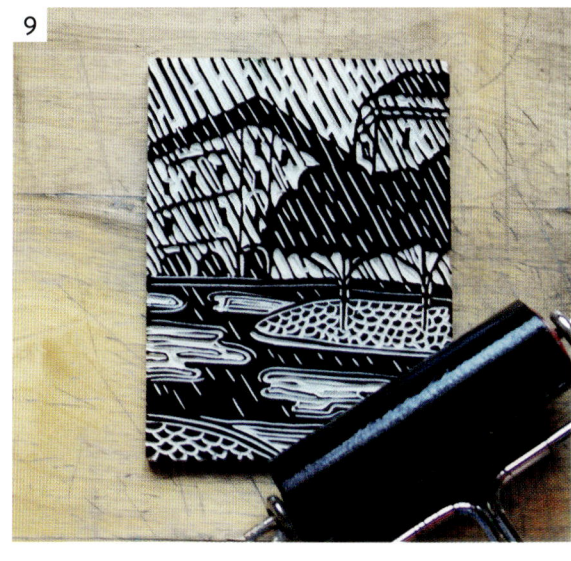

9

MINI STAMPS

Transform offcuts of lino into mini stamps of street furniture to get the most out of your materials and minimise waste. These stamps are great for creating patterns, scrapbooking, or for adding the finishing touches to other prints.

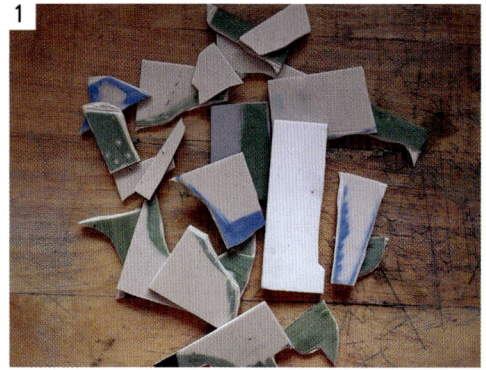

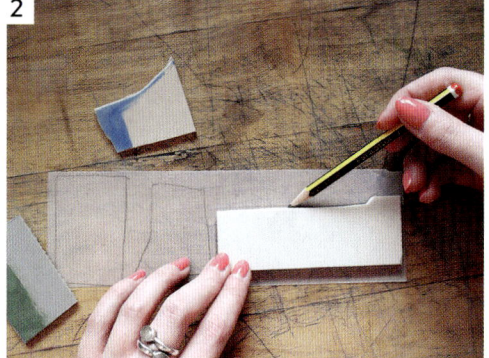

1 Begin by selecting the offcuts of lino you want to use. Some scraps will be too small to add a new design onto, so these can be used to practise carving techniques instead. Larger pieces are more useful for creating stamps – look for pieces that match the shape of what you want to carve to maximise how much you can use.

2 Once you have selected your scraps, trace around the edge of them so that you know how big your drawings need to be. If your lino is not double-sided, make sure to place it carving-side down onto the paper to account for flipping the drawing when transferring the print.

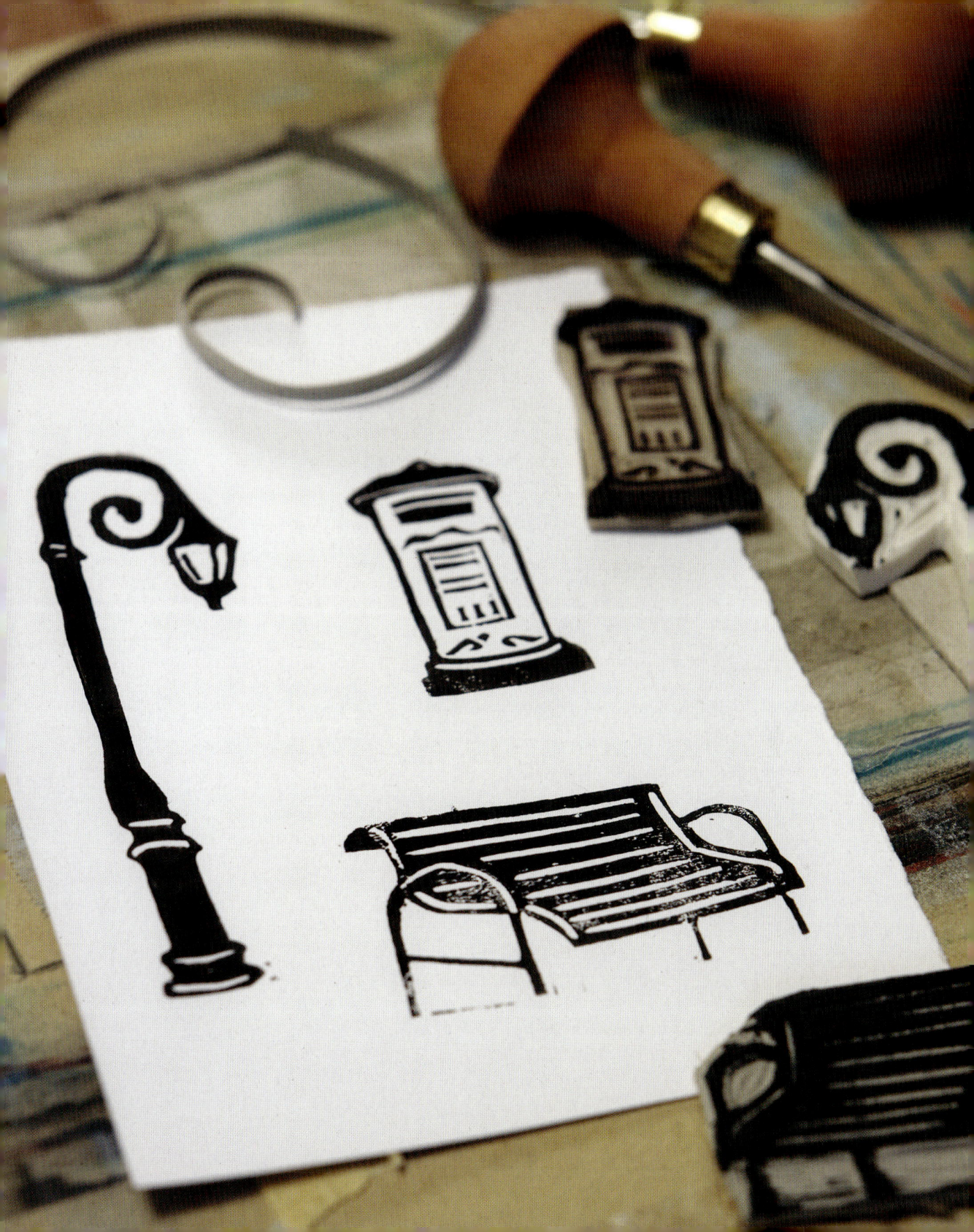

3 Create some sketches for the scraps. Make use of all the available space and consider what objects would suit the shape of the offcuts. For example, here a longer, thinner piece has been used for a street light.

4 Once you are happy with your drawings, transfer them onto the blocks and add a thin layer of acrylic paint (using the techniques described in the Tools and Techniques chapter).

5 As these are smaller pieces, carving can be a delicate task because your fingers will be a lot closer to the edge of the block and the carving area. Keep your carving slow and steady to minimise slips.

6 For some scraps, such as the street light design, your drawing will not fill the whole space. A craft knife can be used to cut away this excess lino and create more scraps for future projects. A craft knife can also be used to trim around your design to give a cleaner edge and minimise 'chatter' (unintentional raised areas that can catch ink).

7 For these smaller prints, an ink pad is a great alternative to using a brayer, which can be tricky to use on small blocks. Ink pads come in a range of colours and are just as durable as other types of block printing ink. They work best on soft linos rather than hard, grey lino.

8 When printing stamps, it is easiest to place them on top of the paper and press down, rather than placing the paper on top. This is so that you can see where you have placed them. Press down firmly, being careful not to move the block, which can result in smudging.

9 Repeat the process until you are happy with your design. Small stamps can be used to create wrapping paper or card designs, or alternatively could be transformed into individual mini prints and stickers.

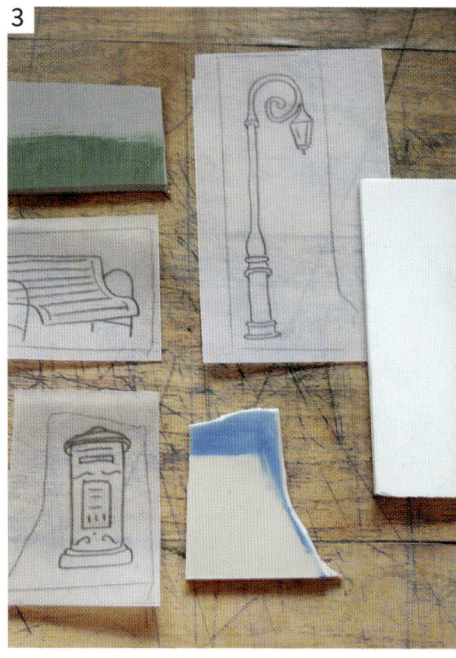

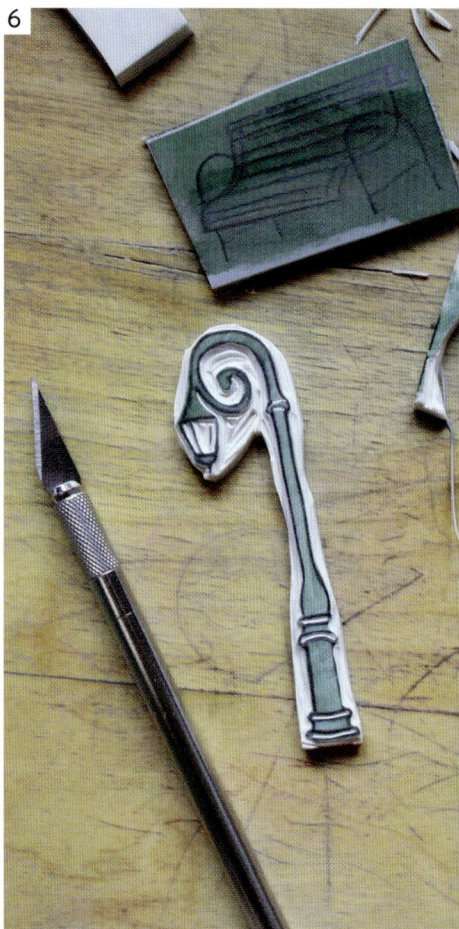

4

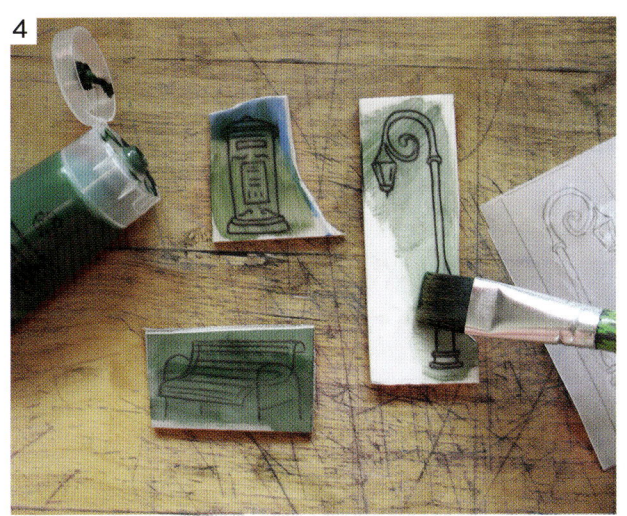

5

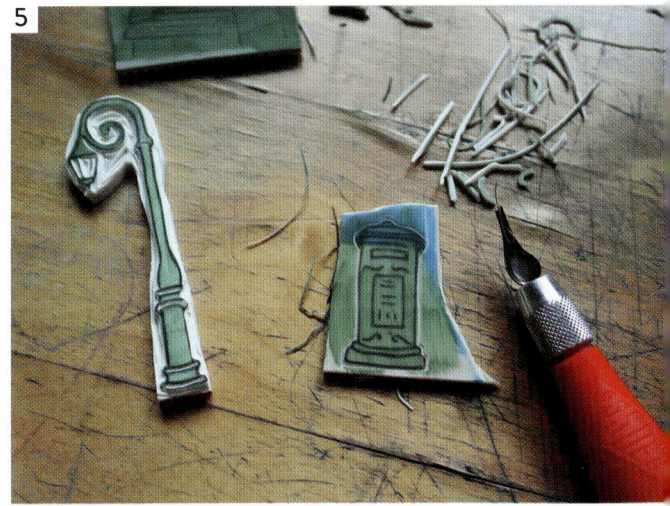

7

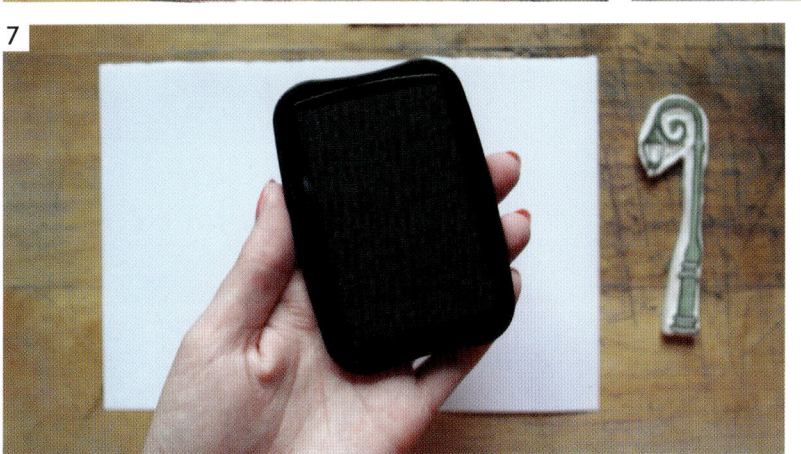

8

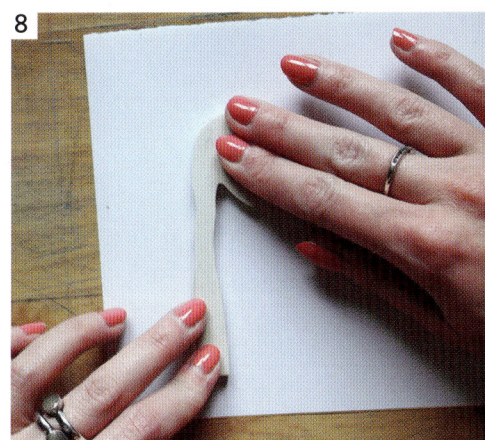

9

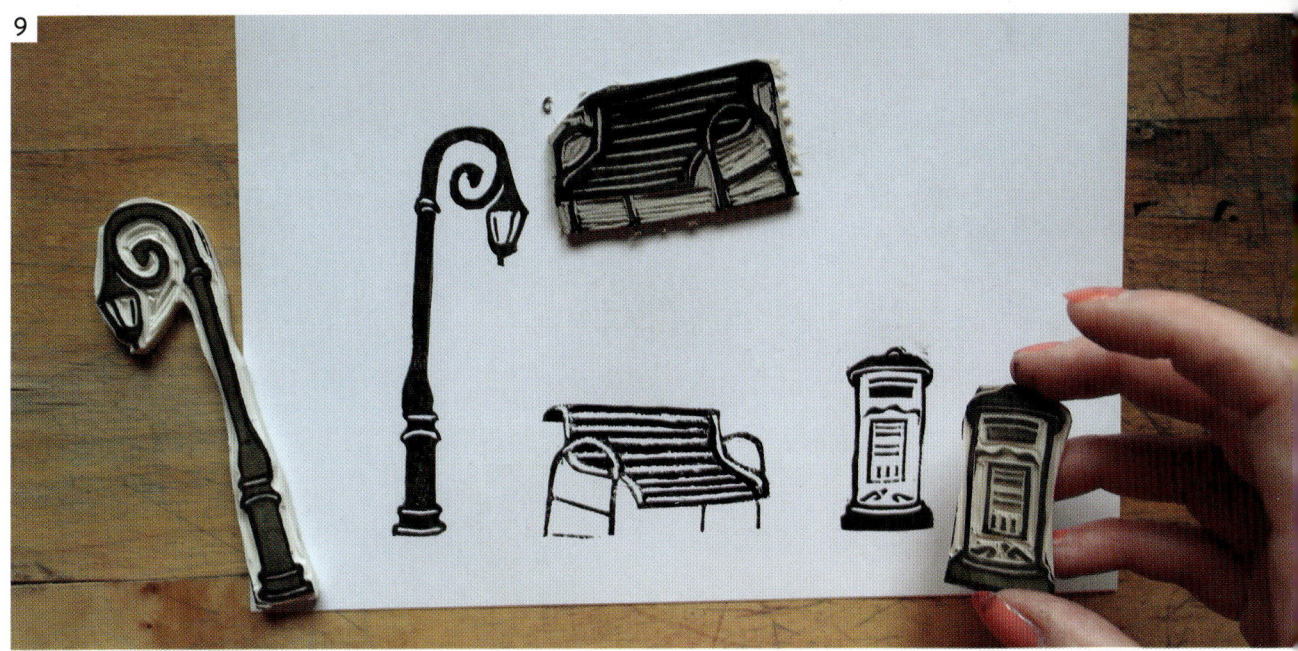

INSPIRATION FINDER

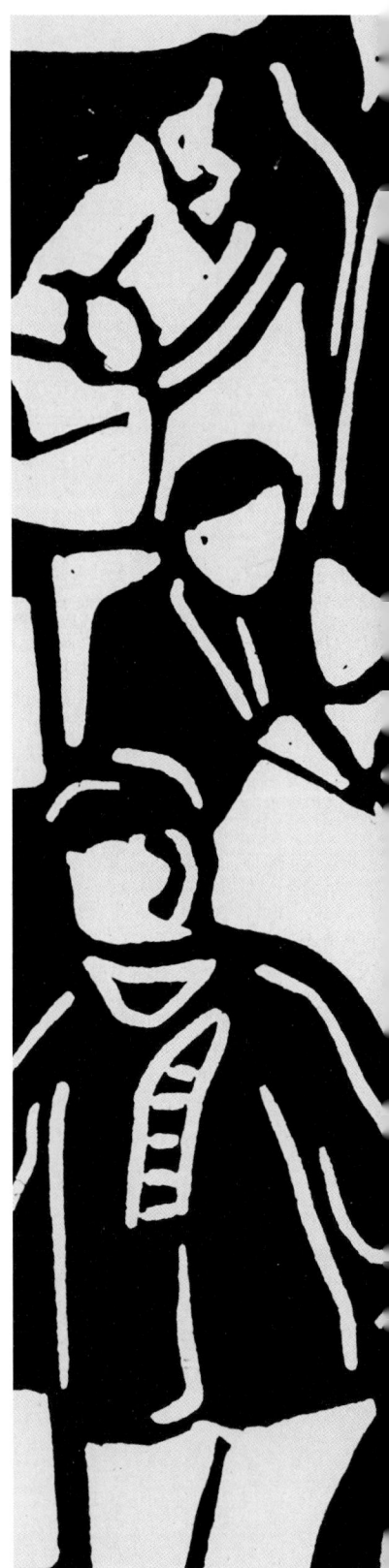

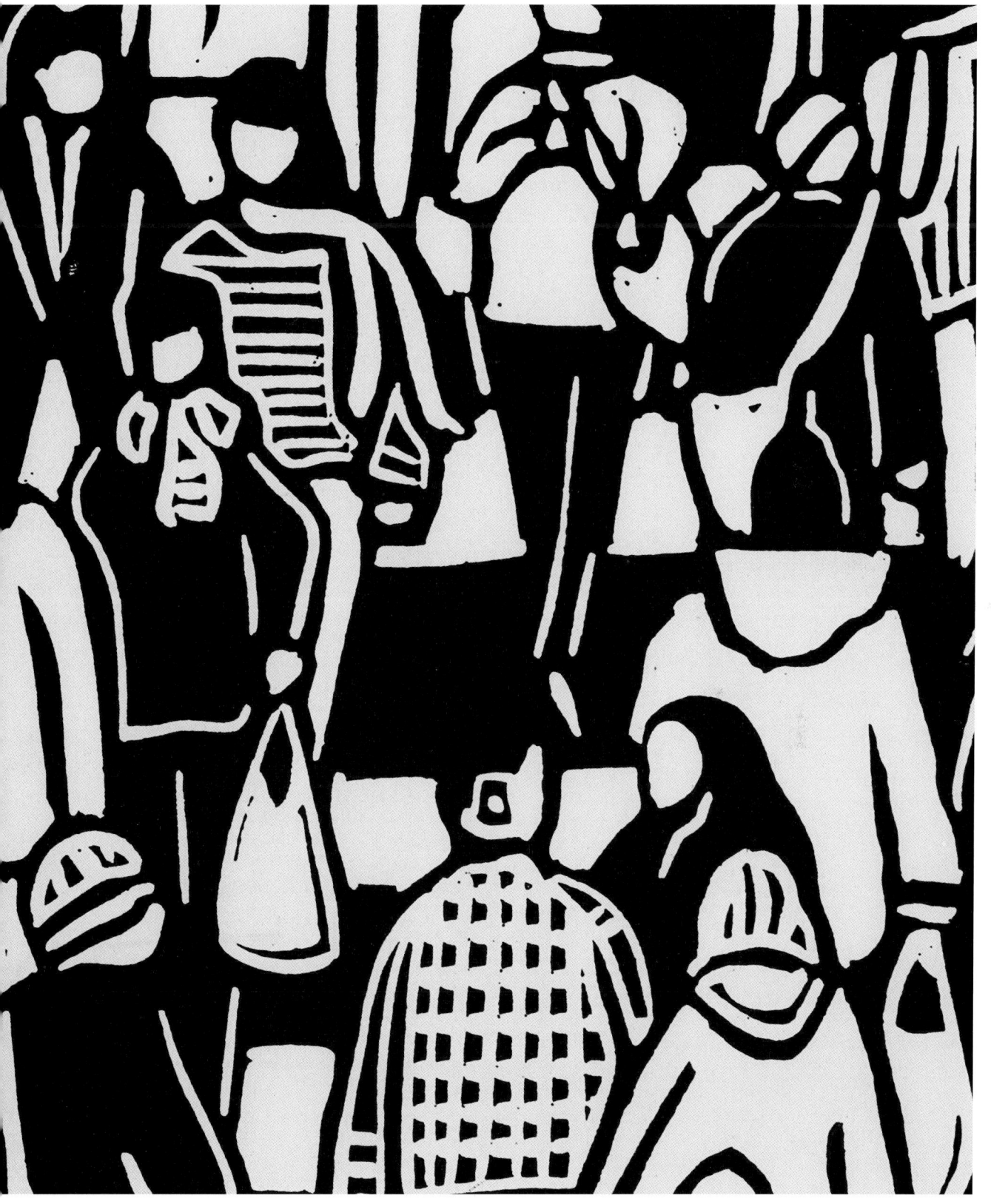

SOURCES OF INSPIRATION

Linocut printmaking is an incredibly versatile artform and lends itself to lots of different subjects – from animal studies to portraits, wild, rural landscapes to the urban cityscapes explored in this book. Because of this, it can be overwhelming when faced with so many sources of inspiration. With so much choice, it can be hard to know where to start! Over the next few pages, we'll explore some of the subjects I often turn to when in need of inspiration, discussing how I approach these different sources, how they can be translated into print, and providing some visual examples.

Whether walking down the street or surfing the internet, keeping a record of anything that catches your eye will help when planning future prints. Keeping a sketchbook is one of the best ways to record your ideas, because it allows you to begin to think about composition and the way your image is constructed. These sketches don't have to be perfect but can be used to capture the main shapes, textures, and spatial arrangement. Taking photographs that can be sketched or traced later on is just as useful. It is also a good idea to take sketches or photos from multiple angles so that you have a variety of sources to work from.

Once you are ready to plan your print, it's time to think about composition. Sometimes it may be necessary to change the angle, scale, or position of buildings and objects to make your print 'read' better – which could be to make details more visible, draw attention to certain things, or to remove things that might clutter your print with too many small details. The composition can also be used to tell a story, change the mood, or guide viewers through your print.

Printmaking can be a very personal activity – your subjects might reflect places of personal significance, such as local landmarks or memories of holidays. Over time, you will begin to develop your own personal style. Using your preliminary sketches as a place of experimentation is a good way to test out your ideas before committing to carving.

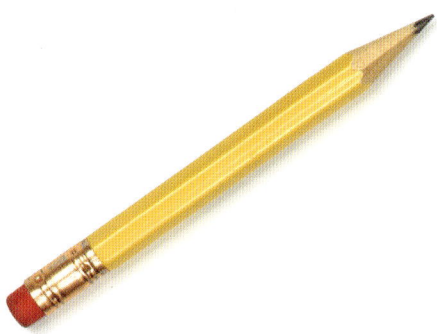

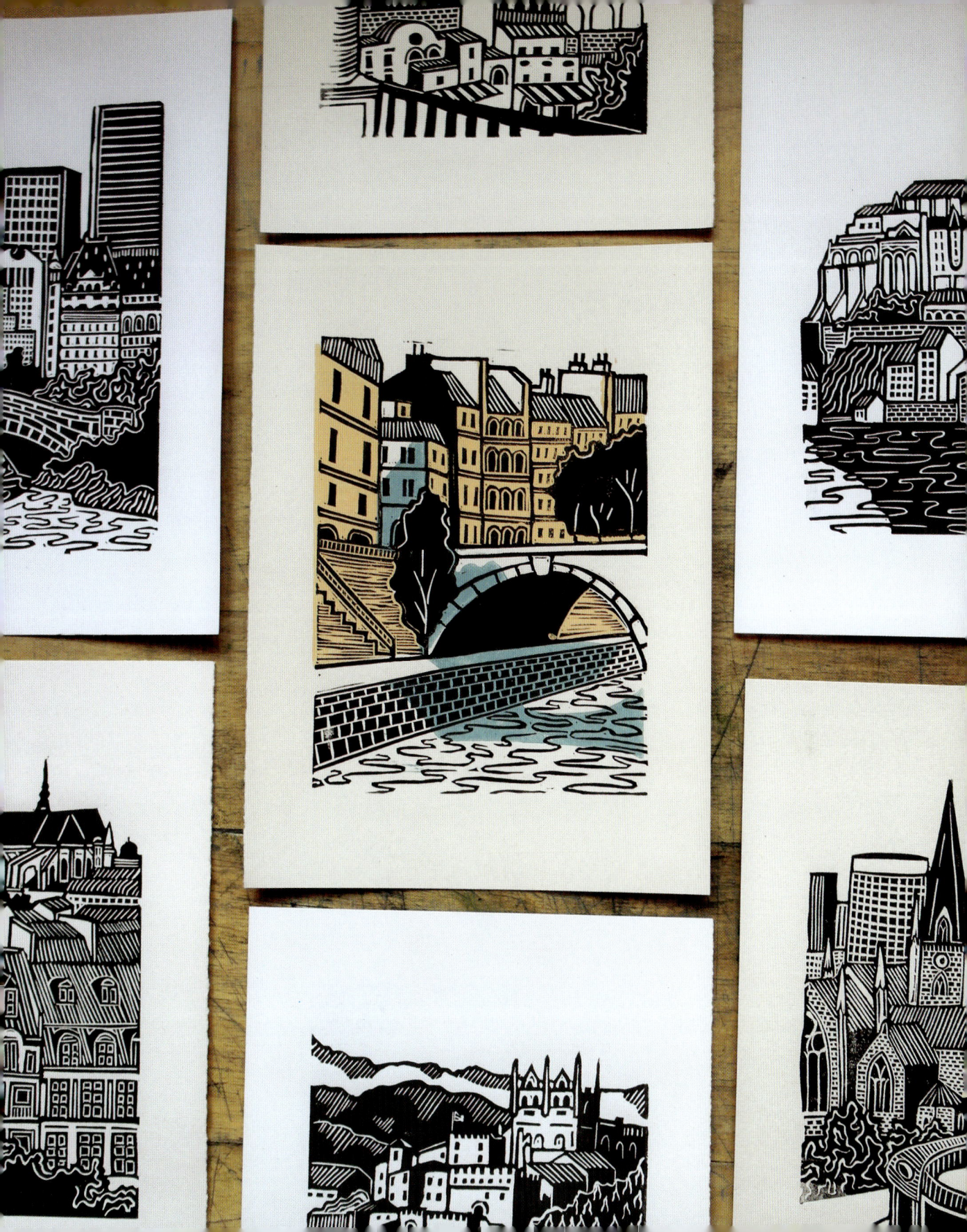

CITY ADVENTURE

The urban environment has so much to offer that it can be quite overwhelming to know where to begin. One of the best ways to get a feel for a city is to take a walk through it, to experience its different areas and to uncover its hidden gems. Taking a walk around a city – or just your local neighbourhood – is a great way to gather inspiration for your prints, whether that's through photographs, sketches, or just experiencing the urban environment first-hand. A similar effect can be achieved by exploring a city online too, through photos, walk-through videos, or street-level style maps.

While the images you collect on these adventures can be made into individual prints, the walk itself can be transformed into a work of art, by collaging together snapshots from your journey. These can either be random images collected along the route, or a more thematic selection. You could even tailor your walk to make it a treasure hunt for specific things, such as interesting signs, unusual public art, or specific details like doorways and windows.

This method is also a great way to test out print ideas on a smaller scale, or to practise different methods of creating pattern and texture. You can either work on one large block divided into smaller sections, or use smaller, individual blocks, which would also allow you to take your lino with you to work on.

Whether a random or curated selection, this exercise is a good way to get out of a creative block, as it encourages you to focus on smaller details and scenes. It takes some of the pressure off planning a larger scale print and, as they can be done relatively quickly, are perfect for when you only have a short amount of time.

Alternatively, you could explore a single scene at different times of the day, in different seasons, or in different types of weather. This could be a view from your home, workspace, or even your favourite spot in the city. This would work especially well with colourful prints, showing the change from the bright flowers of springtime to the orange and brown leaves of autumn (fall), or how sunlight changes with the seasons.

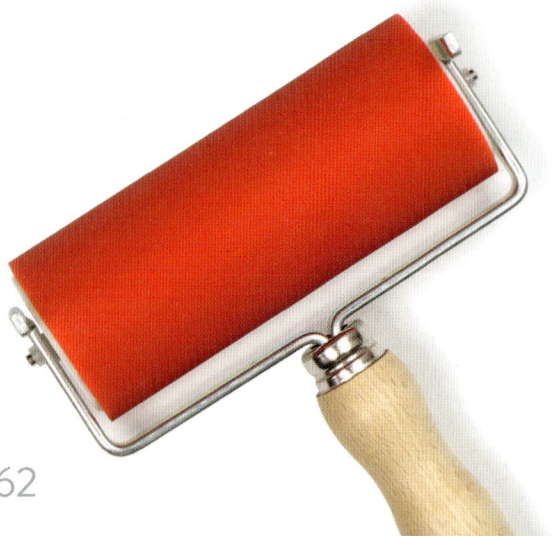

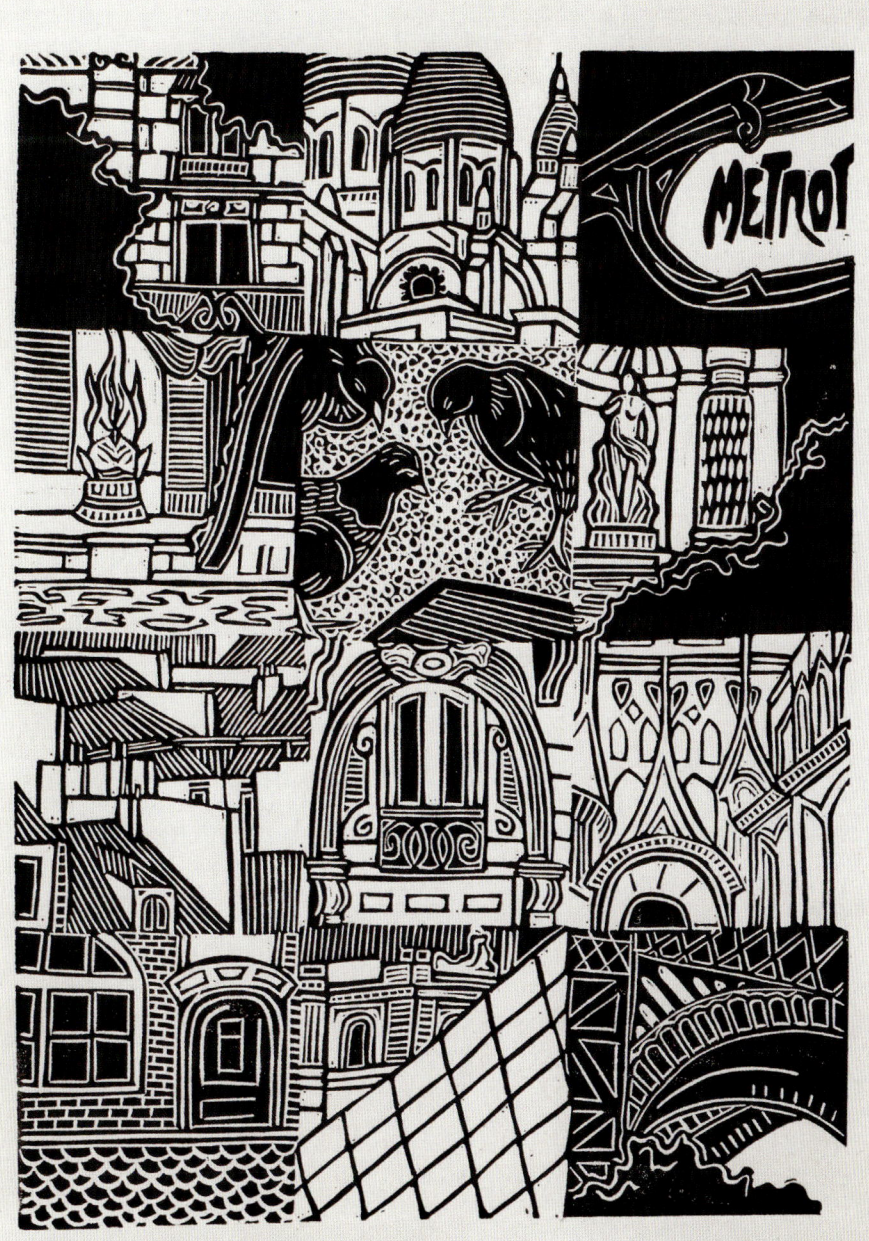

CITY ICONS

For centuries, printmakers have turned to culturally significant buildings and locations as a primary source of inspiration for their prints. In the 17th and 18th centuries in particular, a trend grew for prints made to commemorate big, historic events or important places that were sold as tourist souvenirs and commemorative mementos. This tradition continues to this day, with many printmakers using their work to highlight places that have both personal and historical significance. There's a reason why these places are so attractive to printmakers – they offer the perfect combination of interesting or intricate architecture with the bonus of often having a great story to go with them.

Although these buildings may be very familiar, they can still make unique and beautiful prints, whether you find a new angle to look at them from, or whether you carve them in your own personal style. Part of the fun is working out how to translate your subject into print or finding new ways to approach a very familiar subject.

Historic buildings also offer a range of patterns and textures that are perfect for prints, such as the delicate stonework of Gothic cathedrals, the worn wood and brick of old houses, or the textured, concrete surfaces of modernist masterpieces. These textures translate really well into linocut, or in some cases can even be used to make texture rubbings to collage into your prints (see Texture Rubbing in the Mixing Media chapter of this book). These details are often worthy of becoming prints in their own right. Focusing on one element of a building – for example a particular area of carving, or the pattern created by windowpanes – can be a great way to shed new light on these places and to make elements of them that are often overlooked into the focus of your image.

These places provide great opportunities for storytelling in your prints and can be used to represent both historical and contemporary events – such as a reimagining of a medieval castle filled with its original inhabitants, or a scene of bustling tourists vying for photographs. Even without these figures, the buildings themselves can be used to tell a story, to take a peek back into the past, or to show how historic buildings and sites now exist in the modern urban environment.

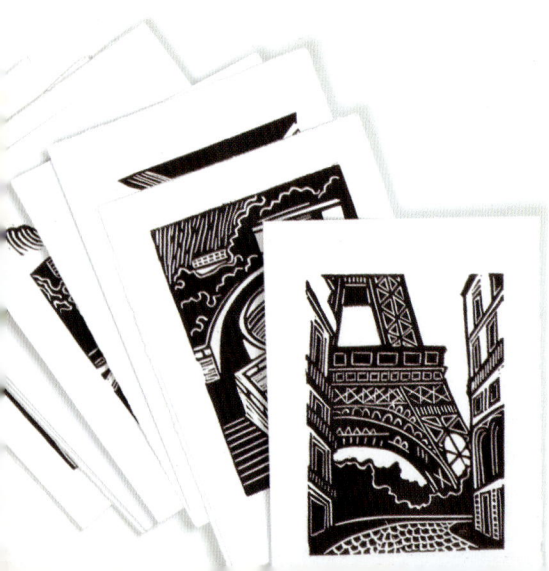

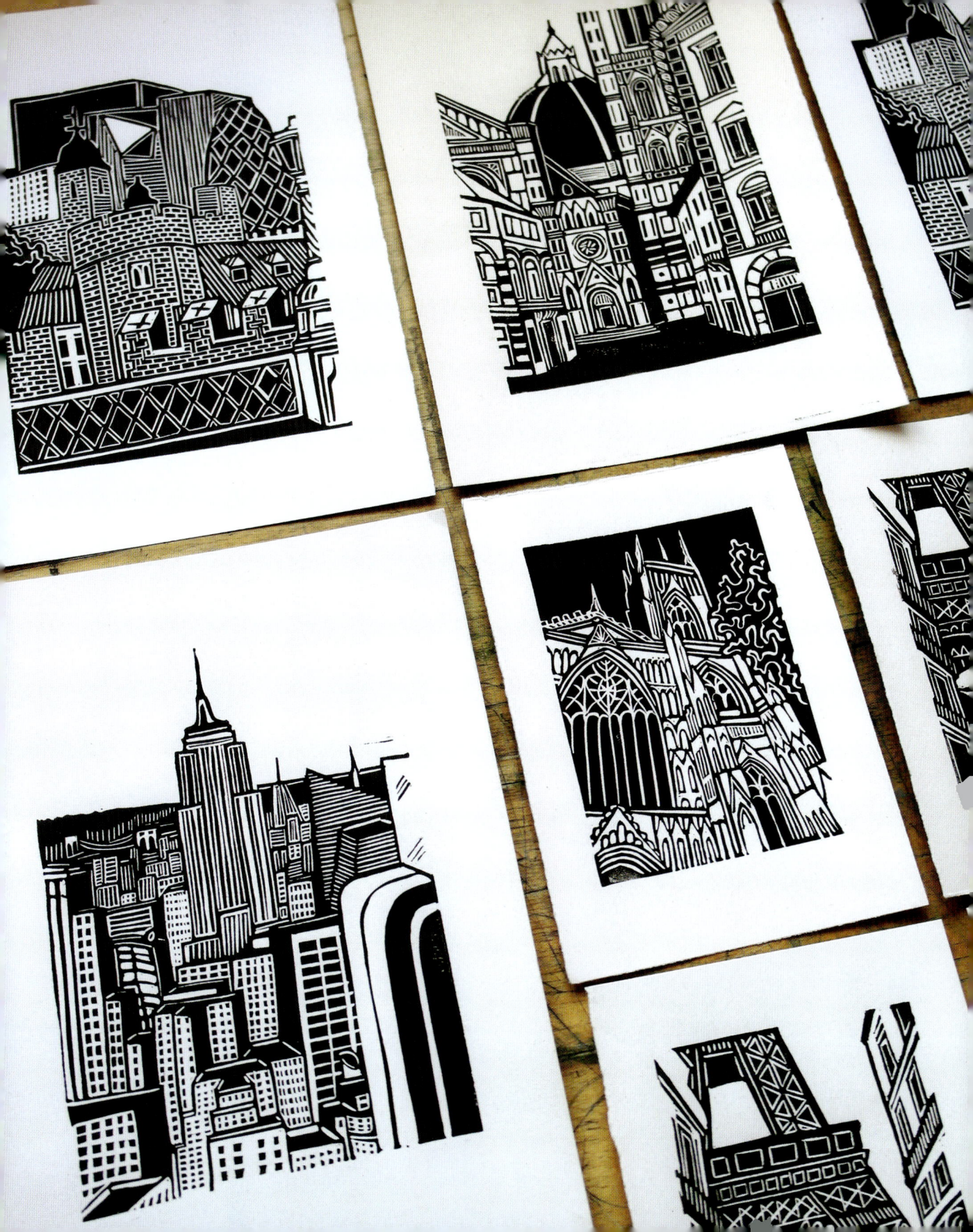

PERSONAL STORIES

While city icons are a primary draw for artists and printmakers, those places that hold a special, personal significance are also important sources of inspiration, and can make truly beautiful and unique works of art. These might be places from your childhood that hold special memories, places visited with friends and family, or locations where big life events have happened that you want to commemorate – or even little life events, like your favourite place to get coffee. These prints also double as great gifts for friends and family!

Sometimes the things that we see every day become so familiar that we stop noticing their beauty. By using them as the focus for prints, we can rediscover the amazing things hiding in plain sight around us or shed light on overlooked gems that are worthy of more attention.

As we study objects to draw them, the way we look at them changes too as we consider space, volume, light, and shade. The same new way of looking happens when translating them into print, with the added consideration of thinking about pattern, texture, and graphic contrast (when working in solid colour especially). Making prints of these familiar places can be doubly rewarding, not only to create your own works of art, but to also have the opportunity to discover new aspects of things you see every day.

Keeping a visual diary can be a good way to both practise drawing and to record your daily activities, again changing the way you look at the world around you. This visual diary could be in the form of quick sketches, or even small stamps or prints, perhaps using scraps of lino saved from bigger projects (see Mini Stamps in the First Projects chapter). These visual diaries could also be used for special events and holidays as unique souvenirs. In turn, these can be great mementos to look back on later, as gifts to share, or as a way to experiment with printmaking on a smaller scale.

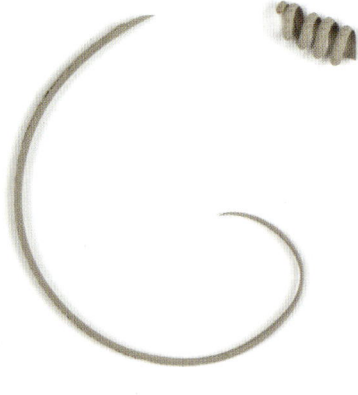

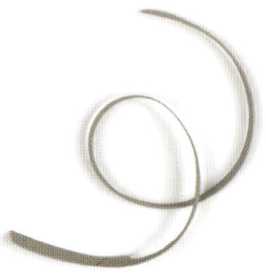

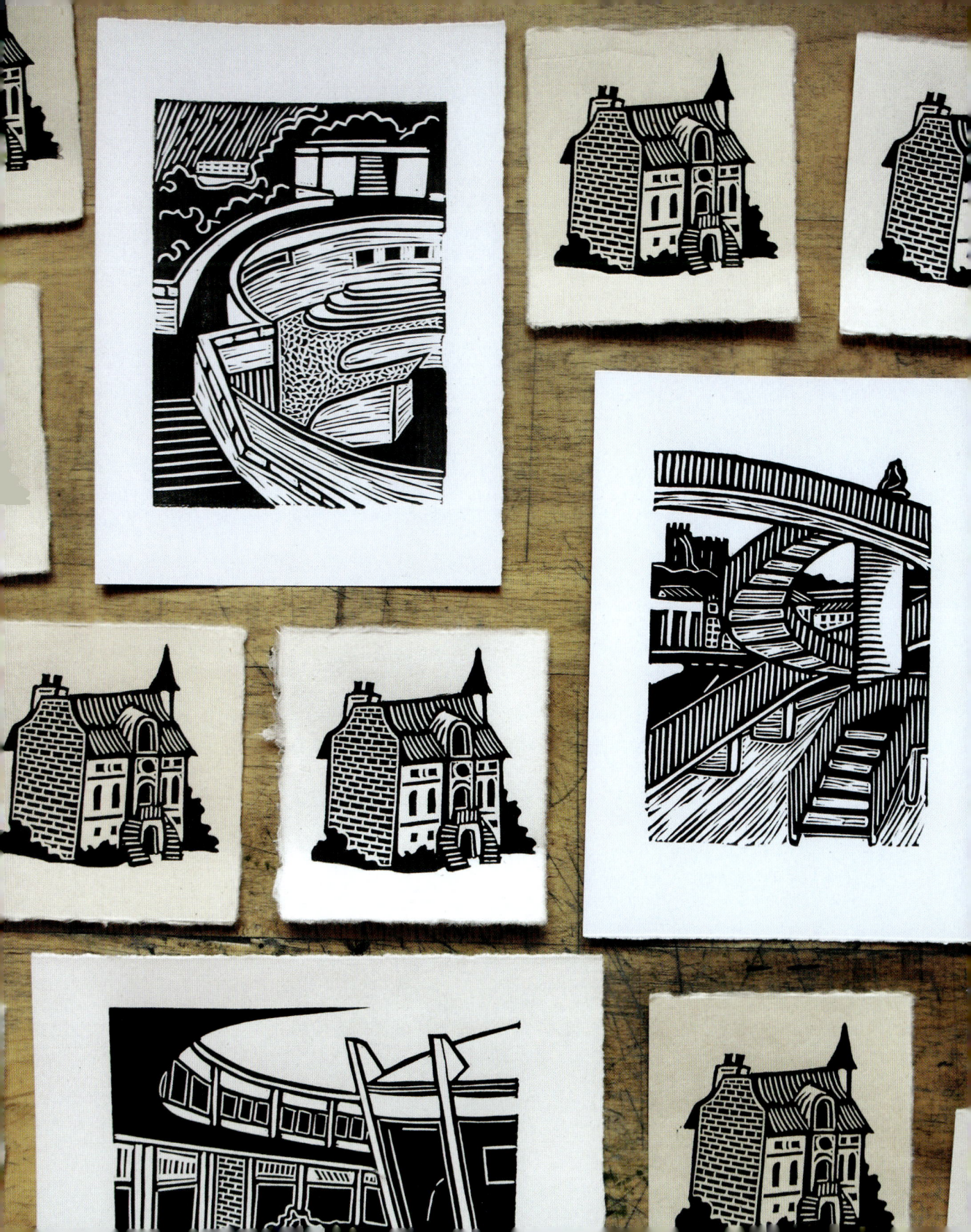

FANTASY CITIES

Sometimes the best source of inspiration is your own imagination, and printmaking is a great form of escapism! Creating a fantasy world filled with fantastical, impossible, or unusual architecture allows you to experiment with different carving techniques and subjects. And the best part is that your fantasy world works entirely to your rules – whether that's through defying gravity, futuristic buildings, or a trip into a magical medieval realm.

Books, films, and television shows are a great source of fantasy inspiration, as is visiting places with old or unusual buildings, such as ancient castles or industrial locations that have interesting architectural elements. You can combine different sources to create surreal landscapes too, like the paintings of Giorgio de Chirico (1888–1978), a Surrealist artist who combined ancient monuments and statues with elements of modern life to create eerie, dreamlike cityscapes. He also played with scale to add to the drama of a scene, making objects either much larger or much smaller than they would be in real life – something that you can also do in your fantasy prints.

If you are unsure where to begin, a good exercise is to gather together objects like boxes, jars, and bottles from around your house and arrange them together. Now, focusing only on the basic shapes and volumes, you can create a skyline that can then be transformed into a futuristic or fantasy city, depending on the details you choose to add. For example, adding an elevated roadway with unusual vehicles immediately creates a futuristic, sci-fi scene with lots of potential for further details. Elaborating on these basic shapes and rearranging your objects is a great way to get those creative juices flowing!

The fantasy element does not necessarily need to be about the buildings. It could be the weather, the people, animals, or mythical creatures that inhabit your world that transform your print from the everyday into a world of imagination. Playing with colour will also add a fantasy element to your work, even in prints of otherwise normal scenes – adding a fluorescent pink sky or bright blue trees can instantly transform the scene from the everyday to the otherworldly.

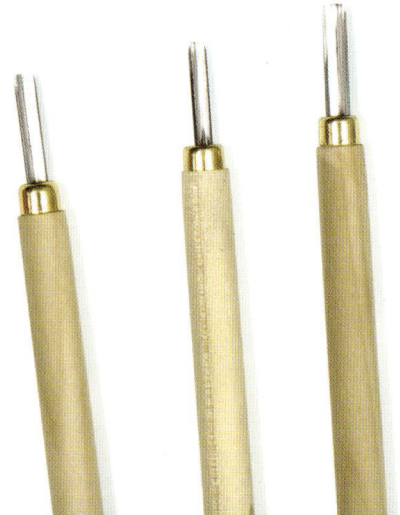

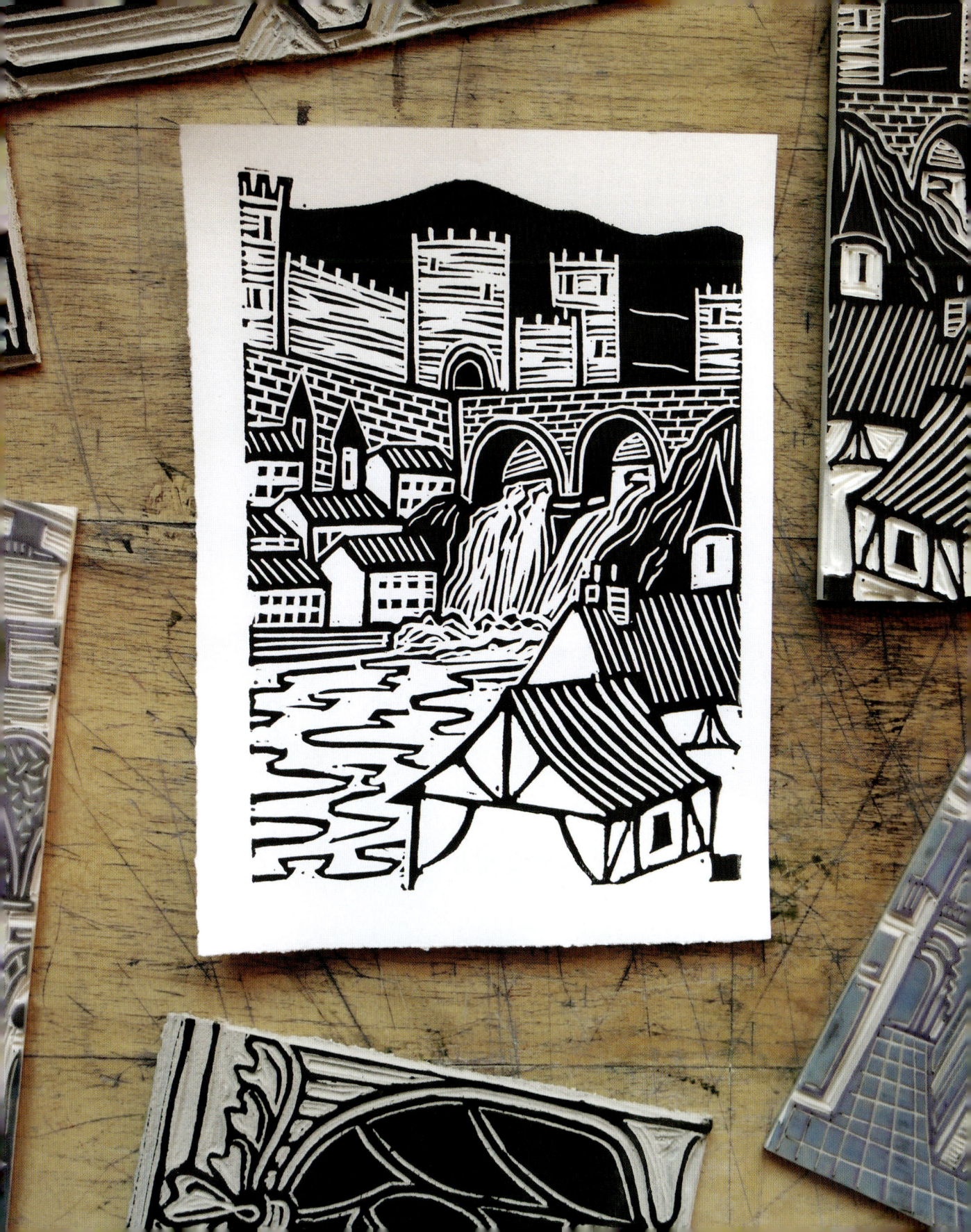

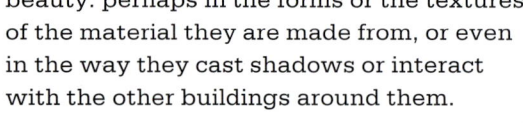

UGLY BEAUTY

For a printmaker, beauty and inspiration can be found everywhere, and that includes in those places and things that are usually overlooked. From suburban streets to factories, roads, and bridges to utilitarian structures, places that are considered to be less picturesque can actually offer a range of interesting textures, shadows, and patterns that create really striking prints.

Just like using personal stories as inspiration for your prints, finding these overlooked or under-appreciated places can encourage a new way of looking at the world around you. Things that you might see every day – for example, a footbridge over a road, or a car park (parking lot) – may at first glance appear ugly, or even boring, and not worthy of our attention as artists and printmakers. Taking a second look, however, can reveal their hidden beauty: perhaps in the forms or the textures of the material they are made from, or even in the way they cast shadows or interact with the other buildings around them.

A contrast between the old and new can be particularly striking in a print and can offer a range of different textures to work with when translating them into print – smooth concrete against rough brick, or shiny metal against old wood. Industrial landscapes, as discussed in more detail in the Engineering section, are also wonderful sources for printmakers. They offer a range of textures (such as corrugated or rusted metal), and there is often a contrast of the human-made and the natural world that can be especially exciting to explore. The contrast of the geometric with the soft lines of nature works especially well in print form.

Almost anything can be transformed into something of visual interest through your prints, just by changing the way you approach them – sometimes literally, by changing the angle or the perspective, which can be enough to make the ordinary something extraordinary. This way of looking and printmaking is a good challenge too, to turn the everyday into something new and exciting. A simple way to do this would be to change the colours, adding vibrant ink to create a Pop Art twist to your scene. For guidance on different ways of adding colour, see the Watercolour and Chine Collé projects in the Mixing Media chapter, and the Multi-Block Print project in the Further Studies chapter.

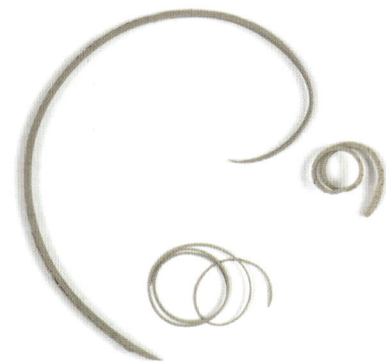

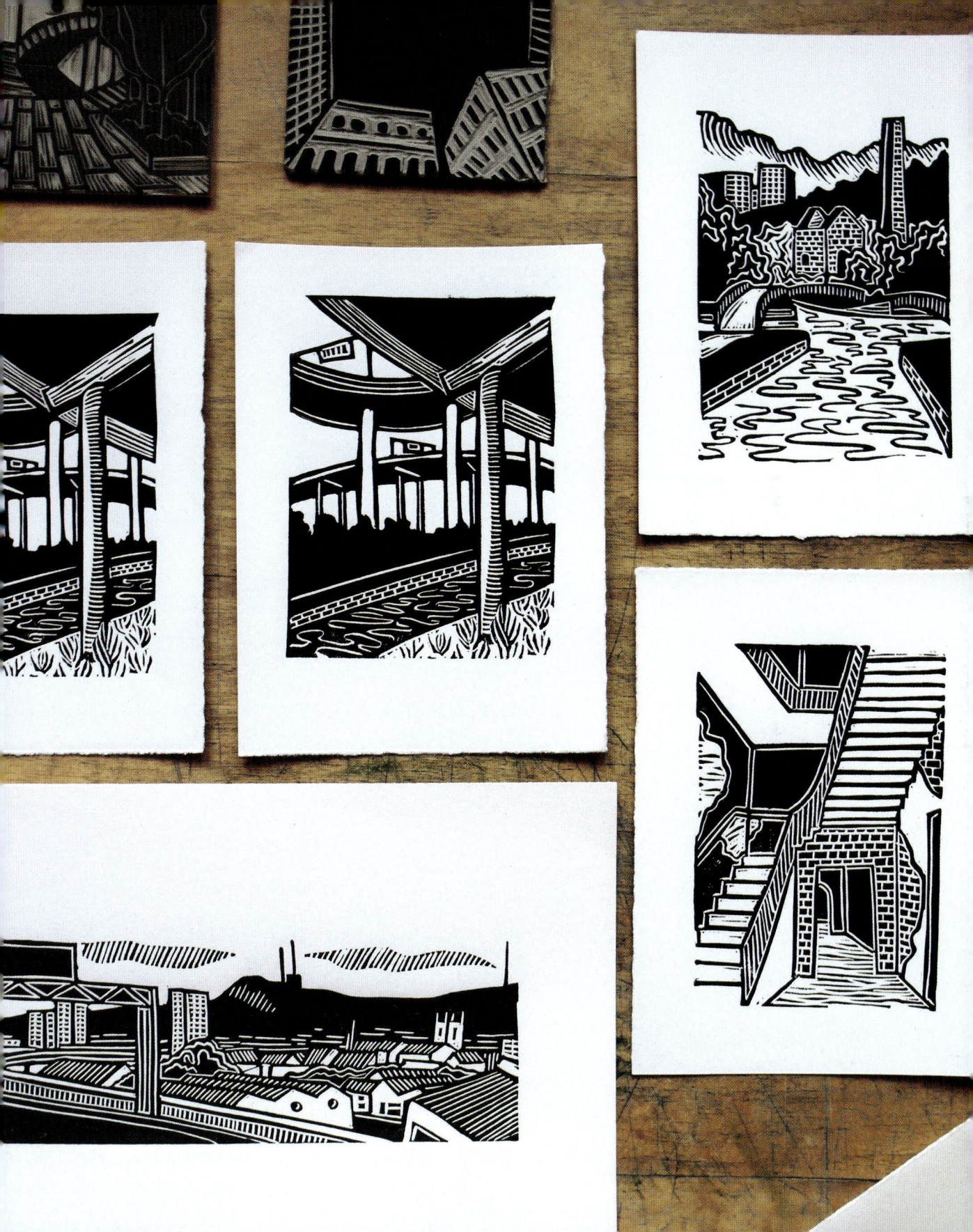

ENGINEERING

Sometimes, the things that aren't instantly visually appealing can make for the most interesting prints. Just as the previous section on Ugly Beauty suggested, industrial landscapes and examples of engineering offer the printmaker plenty of opportunities to create visually striking prints, with a focus on graphic contrast and the play of light and shade.

The contrast of human-made structures with the natural world around them is a particularly interesting element. The mix of strong lines with natural forms works especially well with linocut, which suits both bold forms and more delicate carving. Using softcut lino would work especially well for this, as it can hold a lot of minute detail. The contrast of the manufactured and the natural is also useful for adding a storytelling element to your prints.

Images of the natural world taking over human structures, or flowers growing in unexpected places, can be especially powerful for adding a sense of narrative to your prints.

Engineering can be a great subject on its own, however. Bridges are a particular favourite of mine, from the ancient bridges left behind by the Romans to the grand steel bridges that span major rivers. Although there is also the contrast here of the constructed and the natural in the form of the water below, the bridges themselves can dominate the composition of the print. The intricate supports of the bridge can be used to create interesting patterns or shadows. Zooming in to the shapes created by the bridge or focusing on a particular area of the construction can be used to make a more abstract print or to create a repeating pattern (see the Repeat Print project in the Further Studies chapter).

Engineering as a subject can take many forms and isn't limited to utilitarian structures like bridges. Soaring, ultra-modern skyscrapers, large glasshouses in botanical gardens, and ancient feats of engineering (such as the pyramids or Stonehenge) are all great subjects. They offer a range of textures and patterns, from the reflections in glass to the rough surface of historic monuments. Additionally, construction sites can make a great subject and offer the potential to introduce figures into your work and to show the scale of the new building. Scaffolding and the other elements of construction work can add an extra layer of texture, pattern, and shadow to your prints.

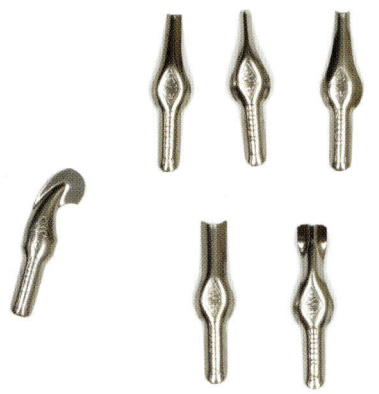

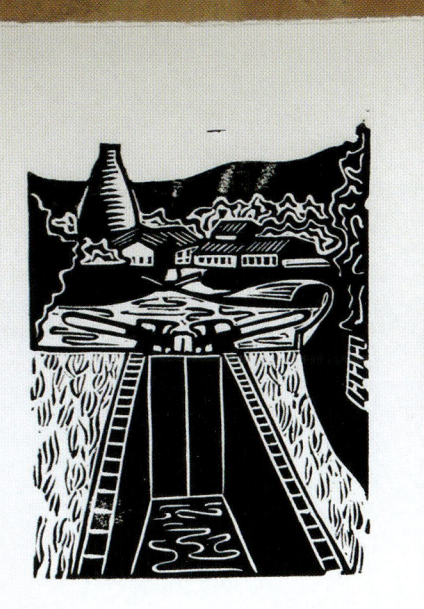

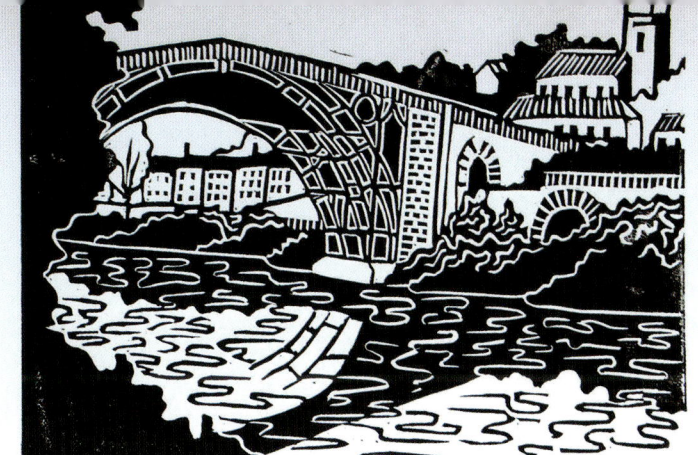

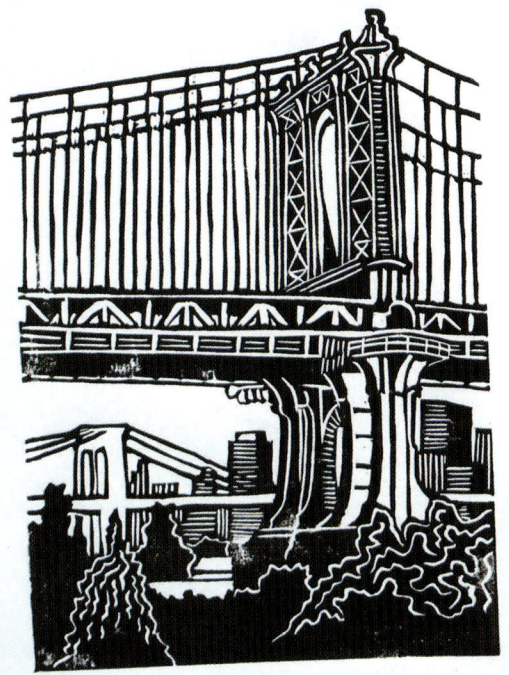

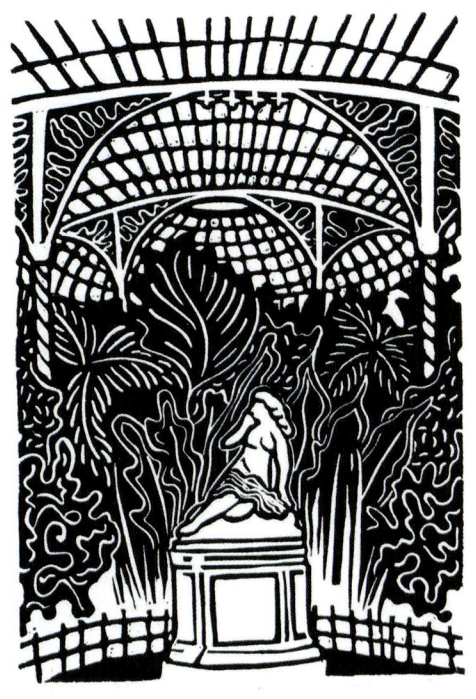

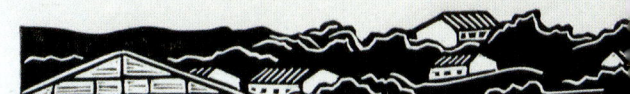

NIGHT

One of the best ways to explore light and shade in your prints is to change the time of day, with nighttime especially offering the potential for dramatic contrast. At night, shadows are elongated, light shines a little harsher on surfaces, and the gradual tonal variations of daytime are replaced by a strong contrast of black and white, which is perfect for monochrome prints.

The quickest way to indicate nighttime in a linocut is to keep the sky on your block solid, and then to print using a dark ink – black or navy blue works best. This solid sky immediately changes the time of day and the feeling of your print too. Carving details into this solid sky can further indicate nighttime – adding a moon and stars, or smoke from chimneys, can all be used to reinforce the setting of your print.

Shadows will add drama to your nighttime prints. Lots of different things can be used as light sources: street lights, the light from windows, and even candles and fires (all of which also work as scene-setting elements). For example, using candles as your light source may suggest a festive time of year or can suggest that your print is set in the past.

Different light sources will also cast different types of shadows. Electric lights create stronger, more defined shadows while fire and candles create more of a glow, so shadows will be softer and more mysterious. These can all be used to add a narrative element, or create some extra visual interest.

Switching the time of day in your prints is a quick way to change the mood. Setting your image at night adds a whole new narrative element without needing to change the scene too much – by simply changing the colour of the sky or adding shadows, your design takes on a whole new meaning! Whether mysterious and spooky, or festive and fun, the night-time setting can totally transform the meaning and emotion of your print.

The addition of colour can add an extra element to your night-time scenes – watercolour is especially good for adding the glow of lights to prints, as you can vary the tone to create softer light as it dissolves into the darkness around it (see the Watercolour project in the Mixing Media chapter).

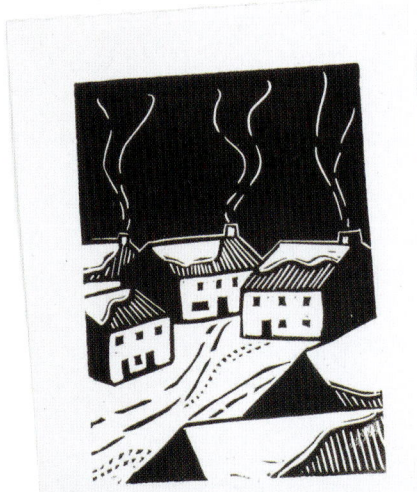

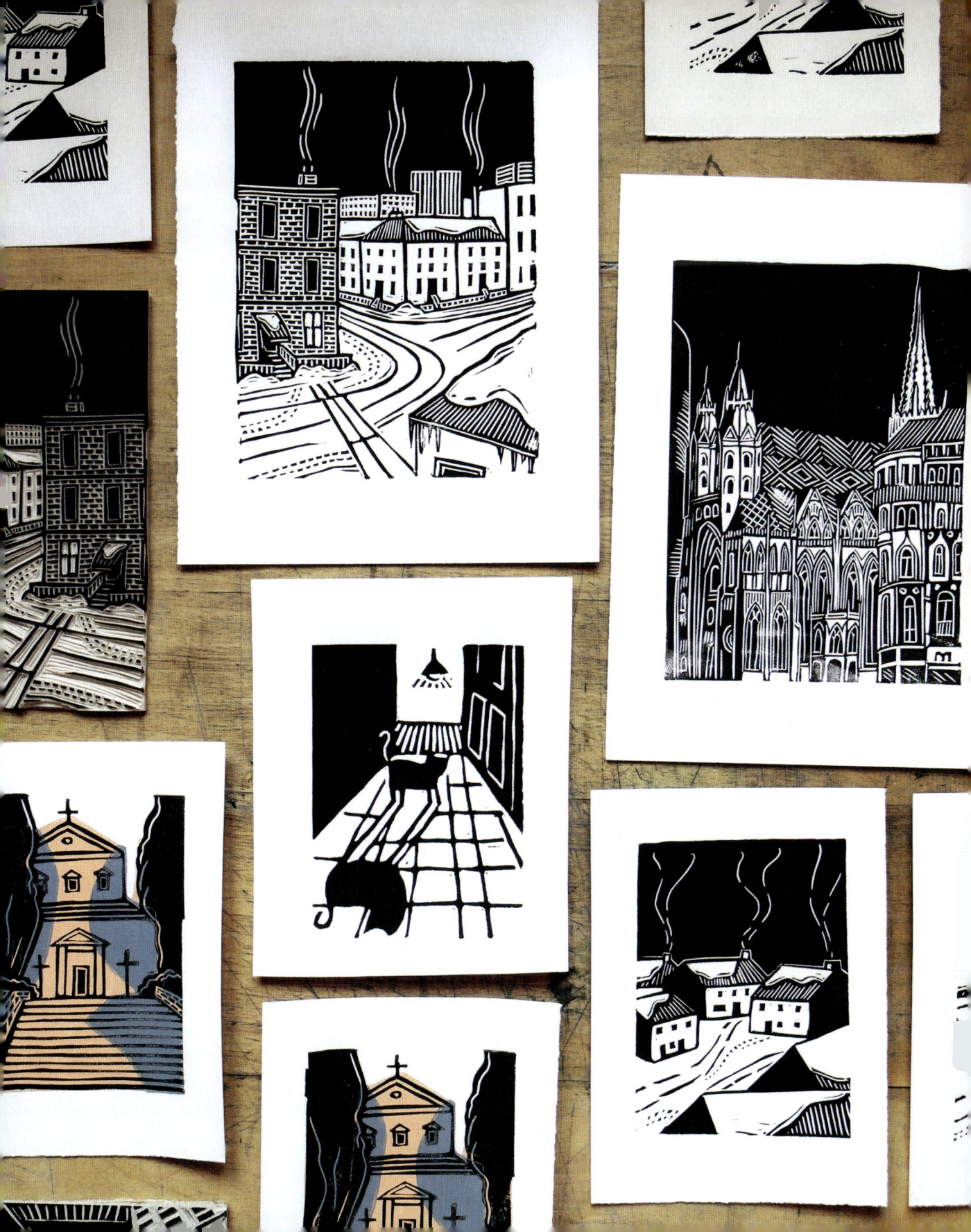

DETAILS AND ABSTRACTION

Linocut is a medium that lends itself to detail. No matter what carving surface you use, it is always possible to add intricate detail to your prints. Details can be part of a larger print or can sometimes be the subject of the print itself, as the Close Detail project in the Further Studies chapter demonstrates. Focusing on a particular element of a building or a scene and using that as the basis for your print can be an interesting way to explore your topic or to show it in a new light – zooming in really closely to details can make your print appear almost abstract.

Increasing the level of detail in your prints will require specific tools and – depending on the carving surface – different methods of preparation. Using a narrow-gauge cutter (the smaller the better) is best for when adding areas of small detail. A V-shaped cutter is especially handy for this, as it can be used to create very thin lines and smaller marks.

Softcut lino holds lots of fine detail, and I would generally recommend this type for when you want to create prints that require delicate work. Traditional grey lino can also be used, as long as your tools are kept sharp. This type of lino may also need to be warmed before carving, either on a radiator, with a hair dryer, or using a heating pad, as this will make the surface more malleable, easier to carve, and less prone to cracking.

Detailed prints, although they take a lot of time and concentration, are incredibly rewarding to work on, and can really capture your chosen scene. Studying a building for that long encourages you to discover hidden elements or parts you have never noticed before. As well as creating a beautiful print, you also gain a new appreciation for your subject and the work that went into its construction and design.

Detail can also be used to create more abstract designs, either by eliminating any extraneous detail and focusing on the bare shapes of your subject, or zooming in really closely to a single element, which transforms the representational into the abstract. Looking past the overall scene and focusing on its basic elements (such as the shape of buildings, trees, or figures, the colours, or the patterns and textures) can be used as the starting point for abstract prints. While works of art in their own right, abstract prints also make for excellent repeat patterns (see the Repeat Print project in the Further Studies chapter).

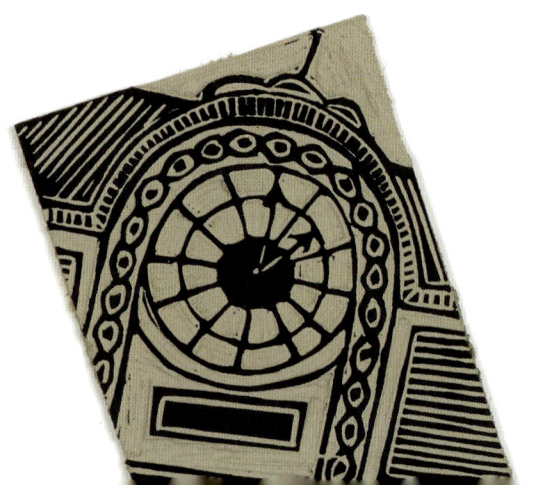

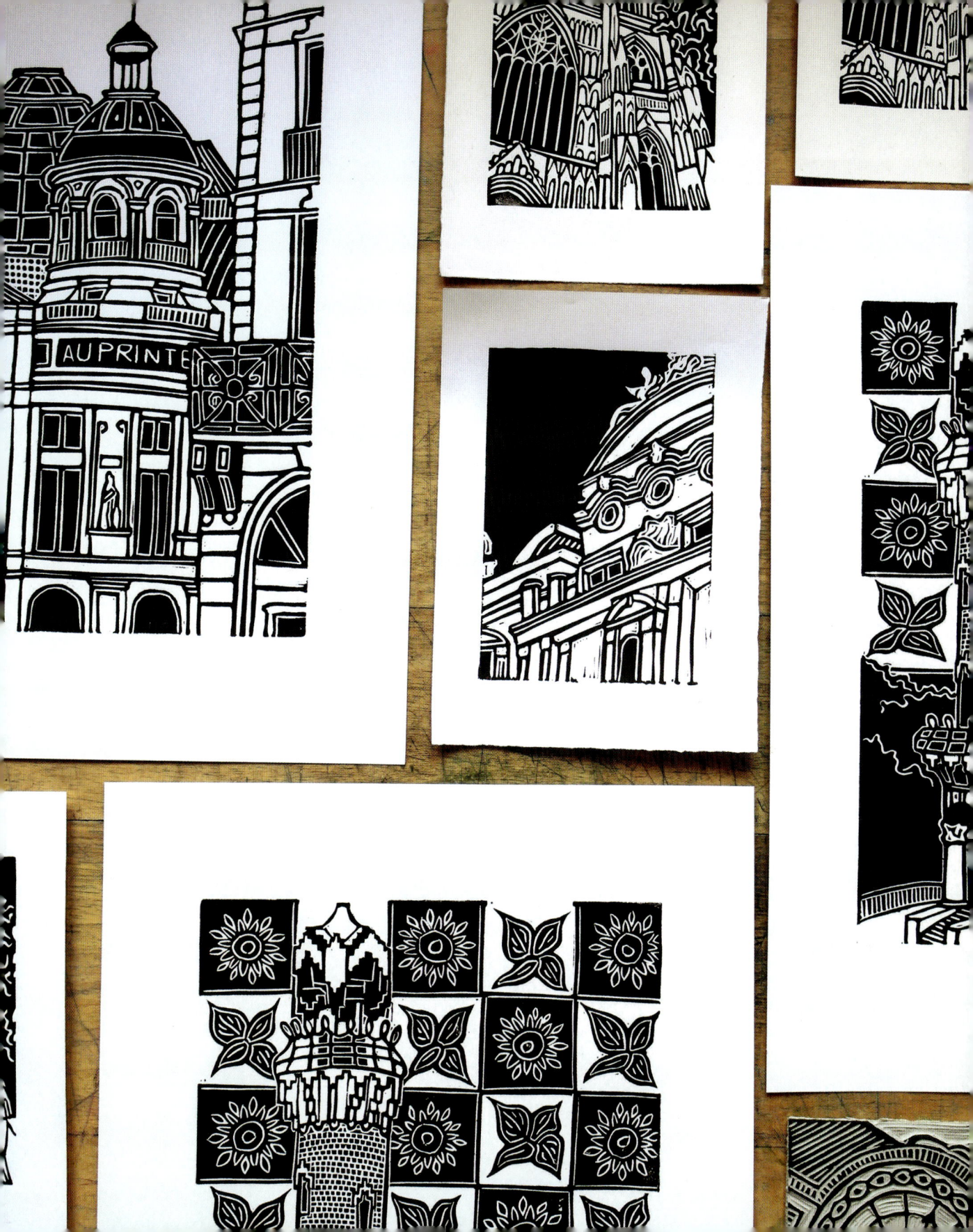

CROWDS

Crowds are a great way to practise carving figures from a variety of angles and in a range of positions, from sitting to standing, in motion and at rest. Figures can add an extra narrative or contextual element to your prints, indicating weather, season, or an event just by changing the way people are dressed or the way in which they are reacting to the environment around them. Dressing your figures in warm clothes and adding shopping bags suggests a festive city centre, while sun hats, sunglasses, and the occasional ice cream create a summertime vibe. Changing how you dress and arrange your crowd provides lots of contextual information to the viewer.

Crowds are, then, the perfect storytelling feature for a print, indicating much more than just the location, time of year, and weather. The way in which your figures interact with each other, their positioning, their body language, and facial expressions can all be used to indicate emotion and to guide your viewer through the narrative.

If you are not confident with drawing figures (particularly faces, which can also be tricky to carve), you can simplify your figures to the basics of either their silhouette or to more abstracted, stylised representations that focus on gesture, arrangement, and positioning. Simplified figures also work well when you have a lot of other detail in the print, or for when your figures are in the background. This prevents the overall image from being overwhelmed with detail and, on a practical level, means you don't have to worry about carving very small faces in the distance.

Added visual interest can come from colour and pattern on clothing. These can either be incorporated into the main block or added afterwards using a new block or smaller stamps carved to fit specific areas of the print.

While inspiration for your crowd scenes can come from your own experiences of busy urban environments, sketching either on-the-go or from photographs, TV is also a great source to take preliminary sketches from, especially as it presents a range of figure types, costumes, and arrangements. A good exercise to practise figure drawing is to sit with a sketchbook while watching TV and sketch along to the programme – the fast pace can help you to capture the main outline and gestures in a concise way that you can then work up later into finished drawings.

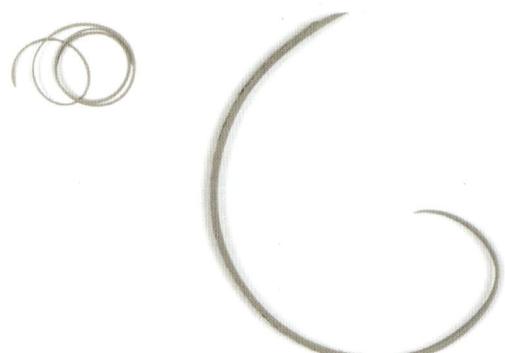

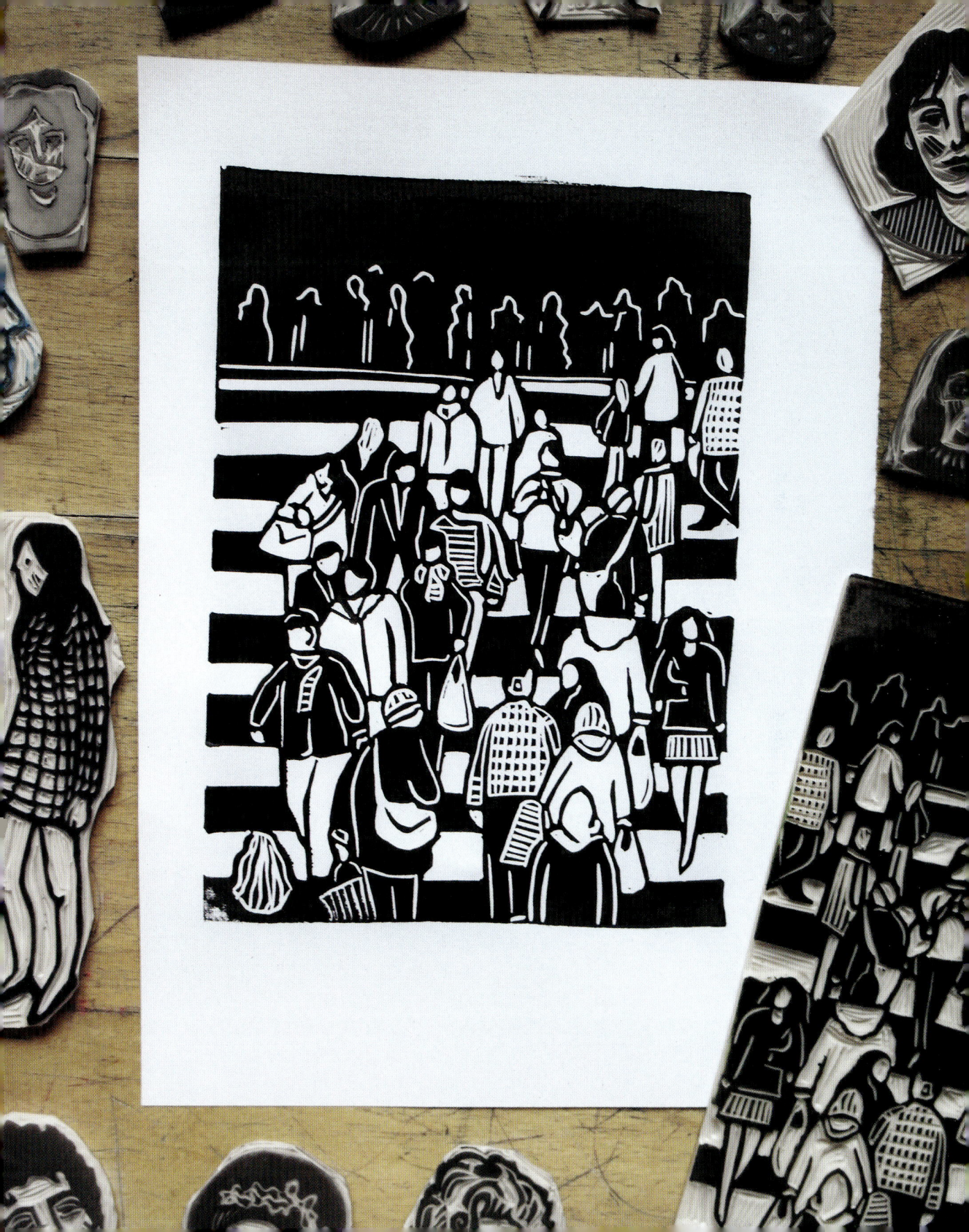

MIXING MEDIA

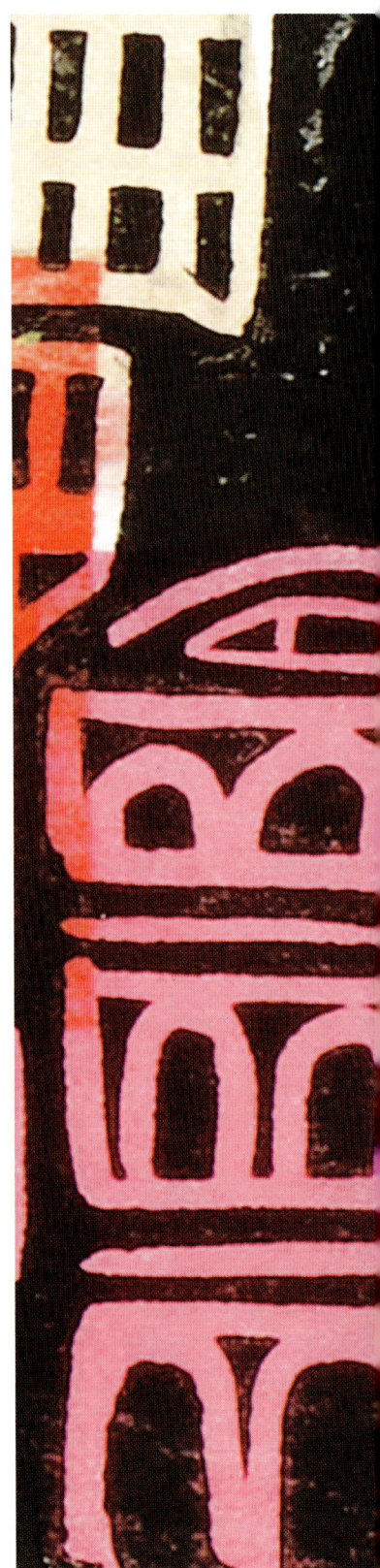

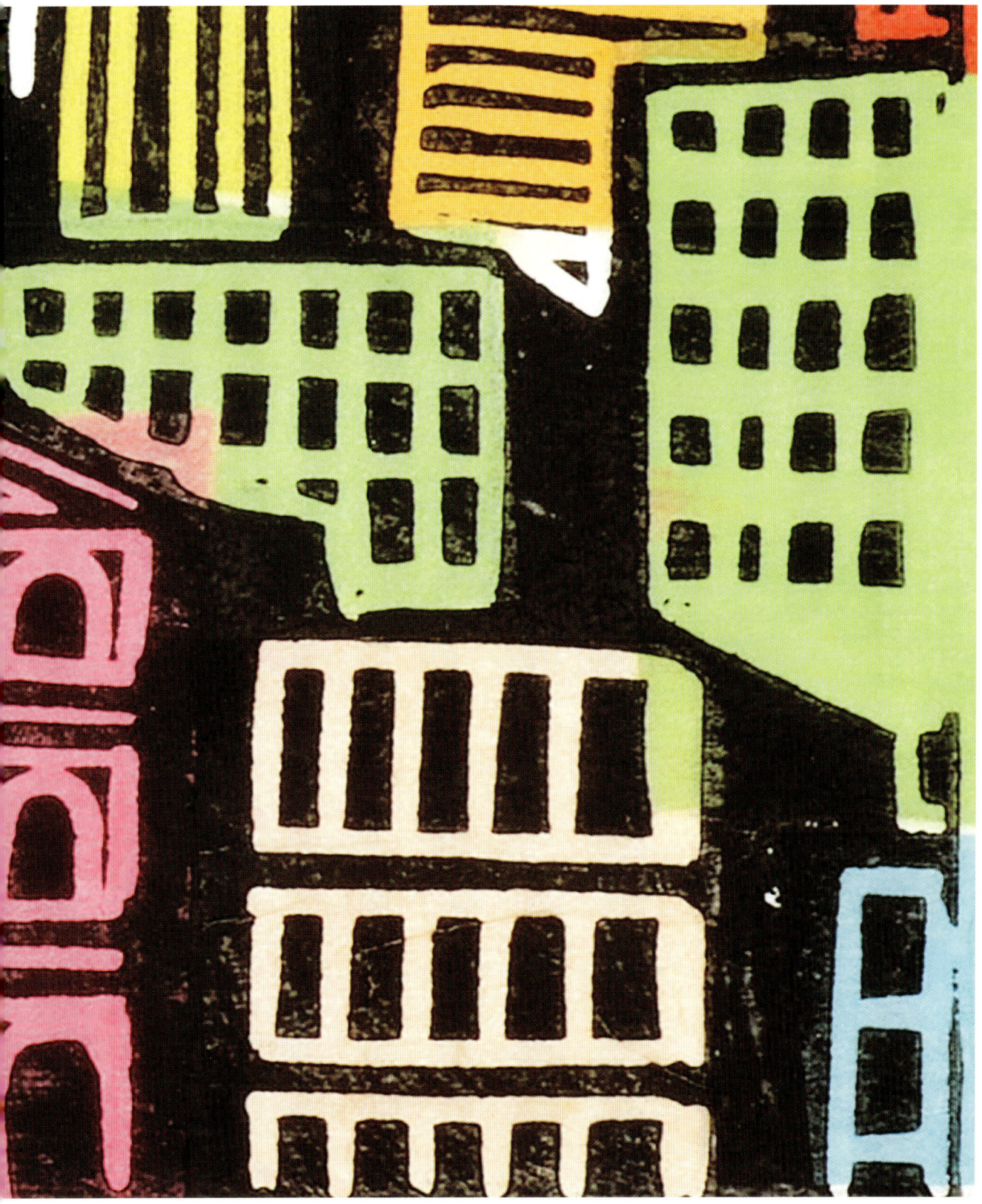

CHINE COLLÉ

The chine collé technique is a great way to add colour or extra decorative elements to your prints, without the need to carve extra blocks. Chine collé involves printing onto two layers of paper – a thinner layer, usually tissue paper, and a thicker base layer, usually a thick card. While there are lots of different methods to achieve this technique, the one described here is a great introduction to using collage in conjunction with your prints.

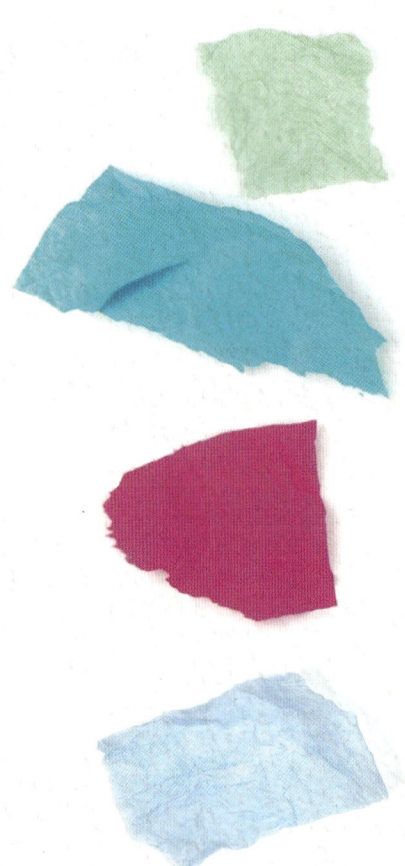

SUPPLIES

An existing lino block
of your choice

The original tracing
for the lino block

Thick card bigger than
the size of your block

Pencil

Ink of your choice

Two brayers

Baren

Scissors

Tissue paper or
decorative scrap paper

Old paintbrush

Rice starch glue
or PVA glue

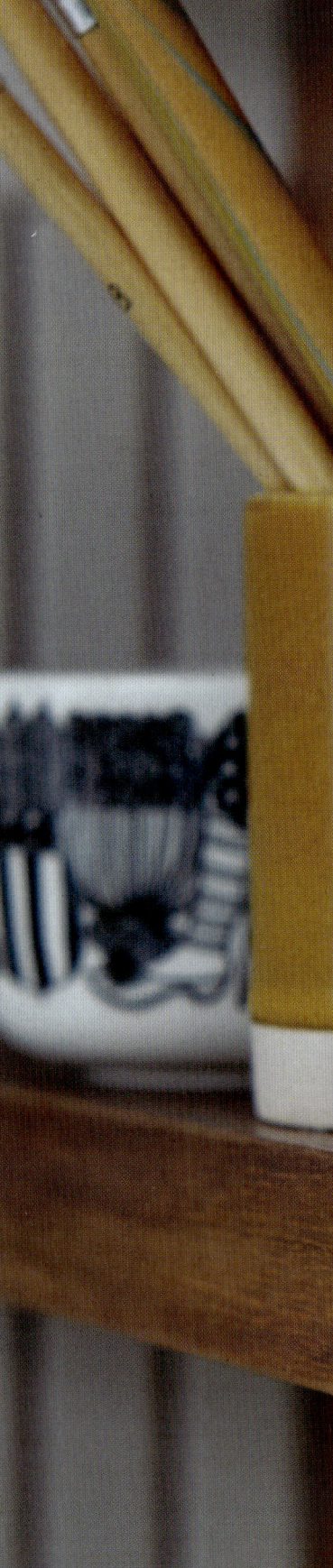

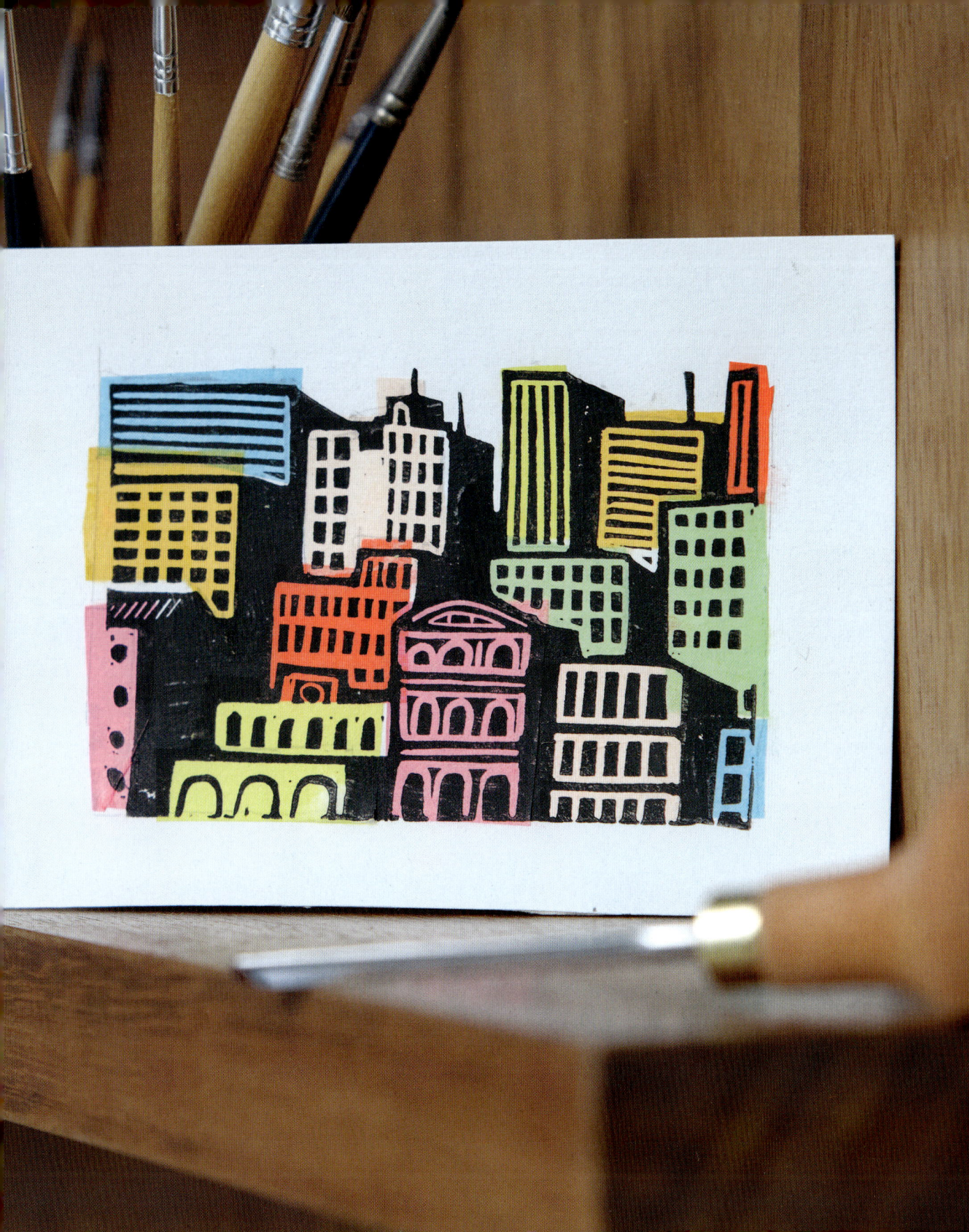

1 Using the original tracing of your block as a guide, cut tissue paper to fit the sections you want to add colour to. Blocks with larger areas of lino cut away work best for this technique, as the tissue paper below will show through. You can also try decorative, patterned paper instead of tissue paper.

2 On the card that you will be printing onto, re-trace the original image so that you have a faint outline – this will function as a guide for when you stick on the tissue paper. Make sure that you reverse the image so that it aligns with the print. Draw around the outside of the sketch too so that you can line up the block later on.

3 Using an old paintbrush, paint on a thin layer of glue on to the card. Rice starch glue, which is available from many printmaking suppliers, is perfect for this as it creates a strong bond. PVA glue can also be used but may take longer to dry.

4 Using the pencil lines as a guide, paste on the tissue paper. Make sure it is completely stuck down, and add more glue if necessary.

5 Once you have pasted on all your tissue paper, leave it for a few hours. Make sure the glue has completely dried before continuing.

6 Ink your block as usual. A colour that contrasts with the tissue paper works best.

7 Carefully lay your inked block on top of the tissue paper, using the drawing as a guide. Using a clean brayer or a baren, press down firmly to transfer the print. Make sure the block does not slip during this step.

8 You can now reveal your print. The tissue paper will show through as if you had coloured the print itself.

1
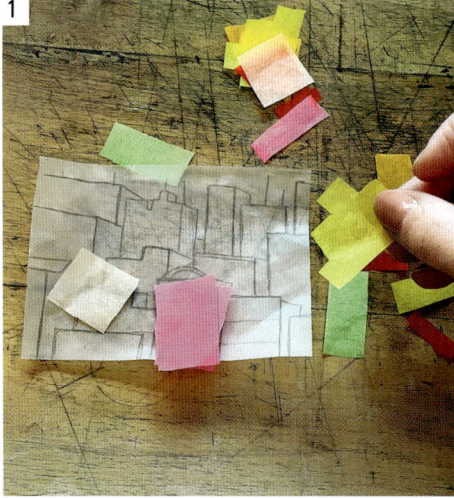

4
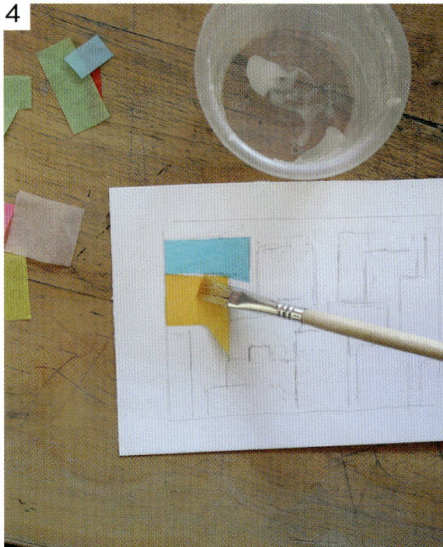

6
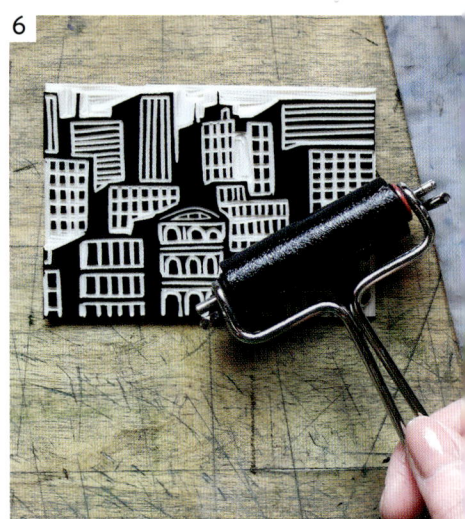

2

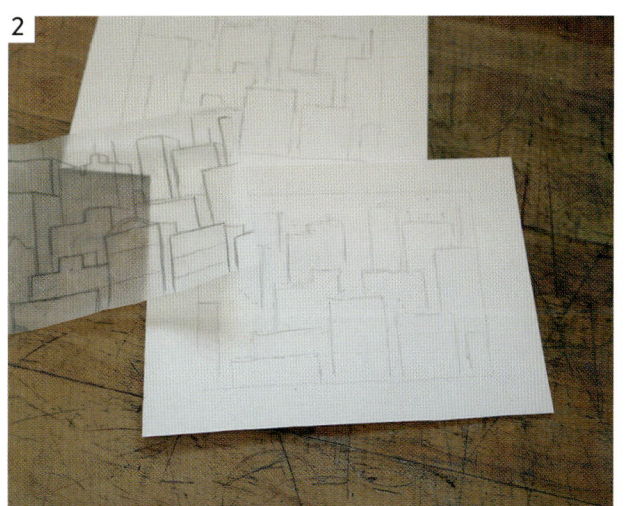

3

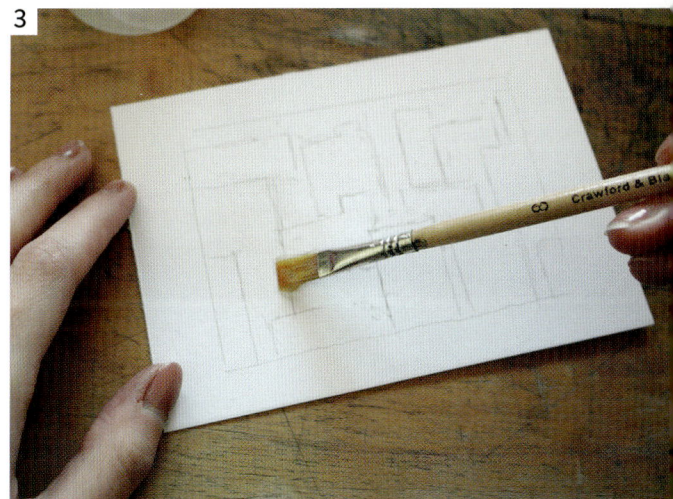

5

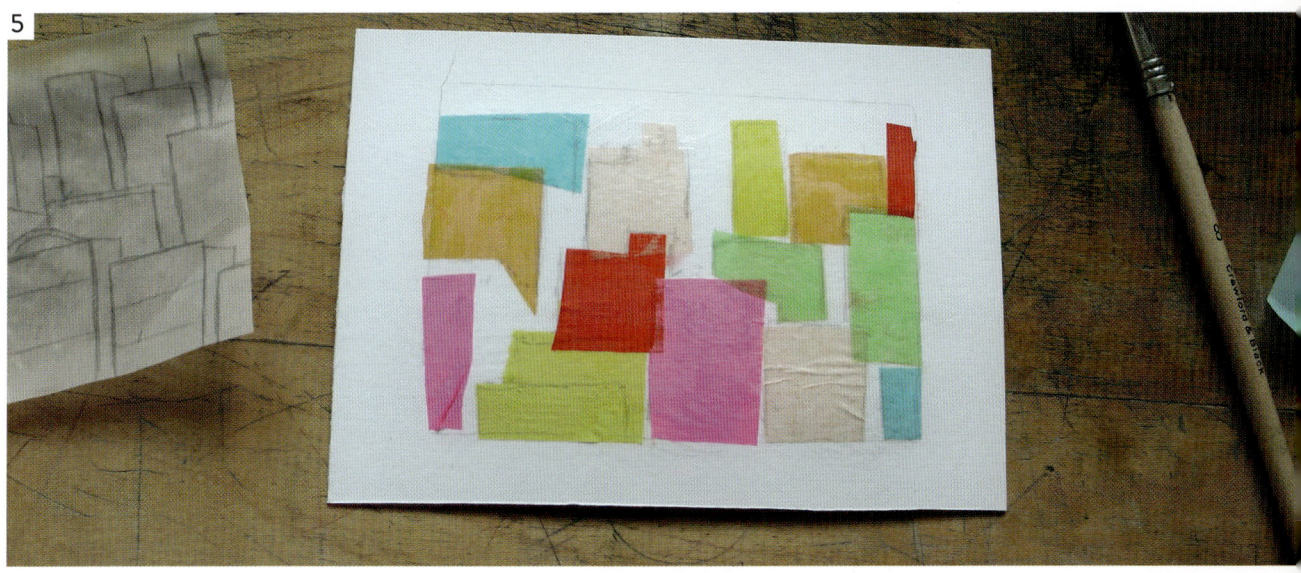

7

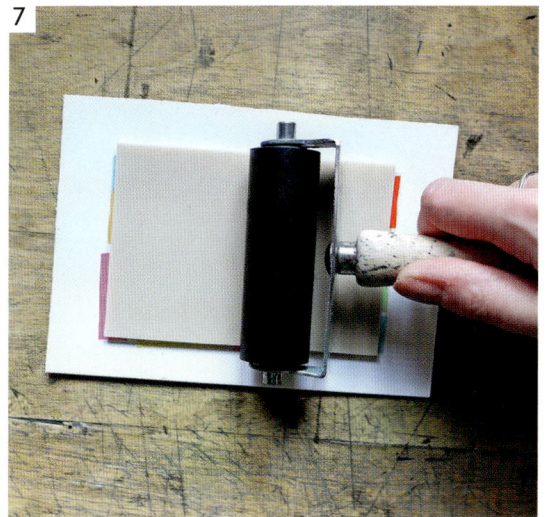

8

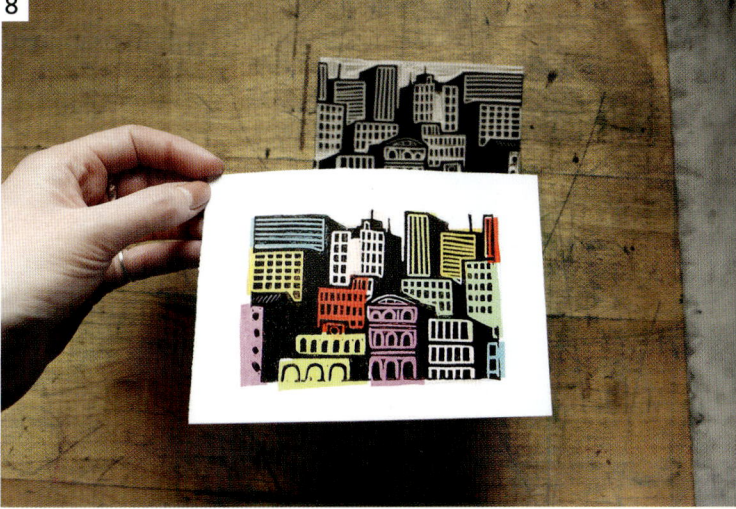

Mount board

Card bigger than the size
of your mount board

Pencil

Baren

Craft knife

Parcel tape

Masking tape

Paper towels

Ink of your choice

Old toothbrush or stiff-
bristled paintbrush

COLLAGRAPH

Collagraph printing uses a mixture of different surfaces and textures to create a grainy, gritty image. It's perfect for high-contrast designs and for capturing the urban environment. Unlike linocut, these blocks can only produce a few prints, with no two being the same!

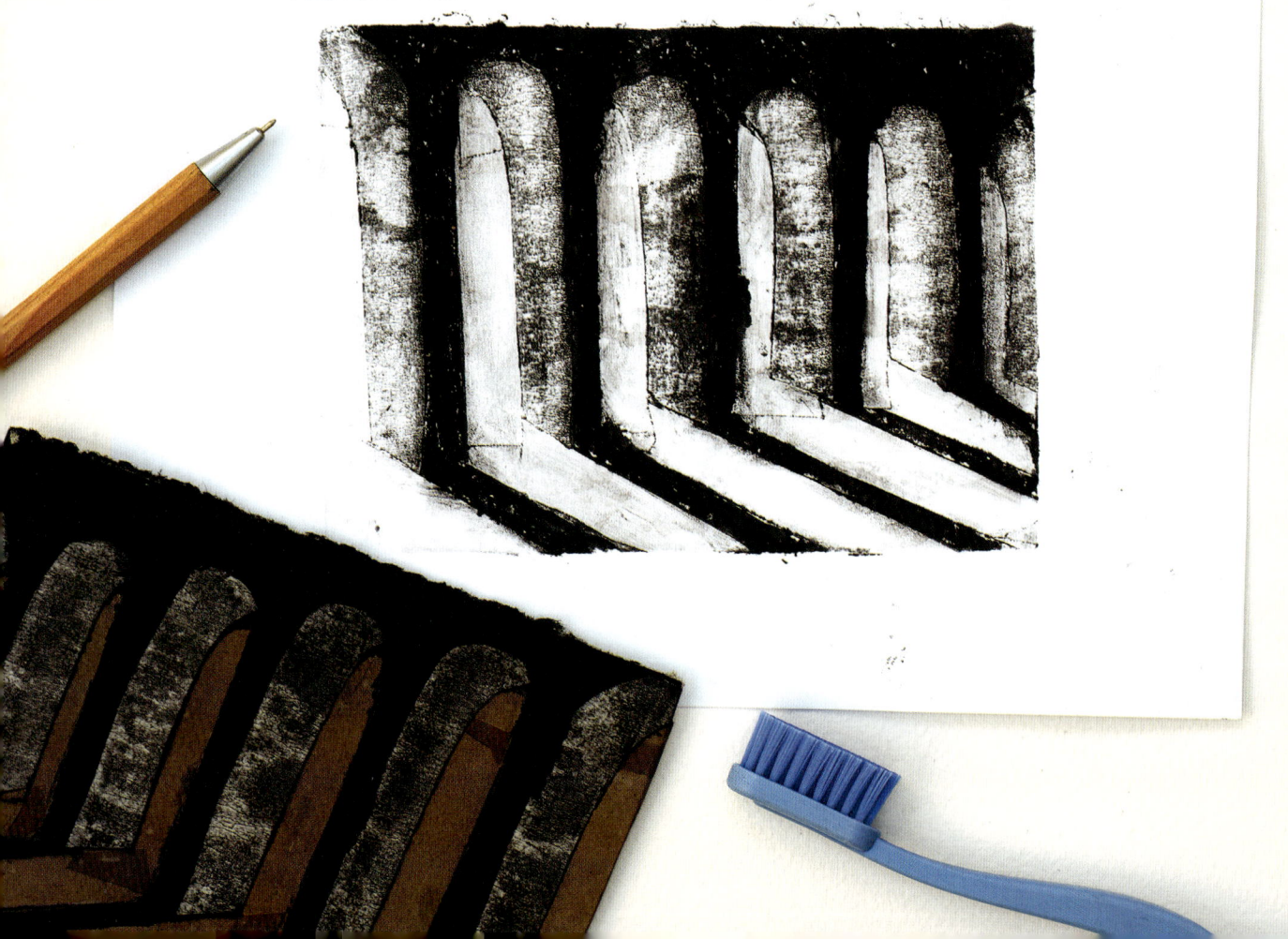

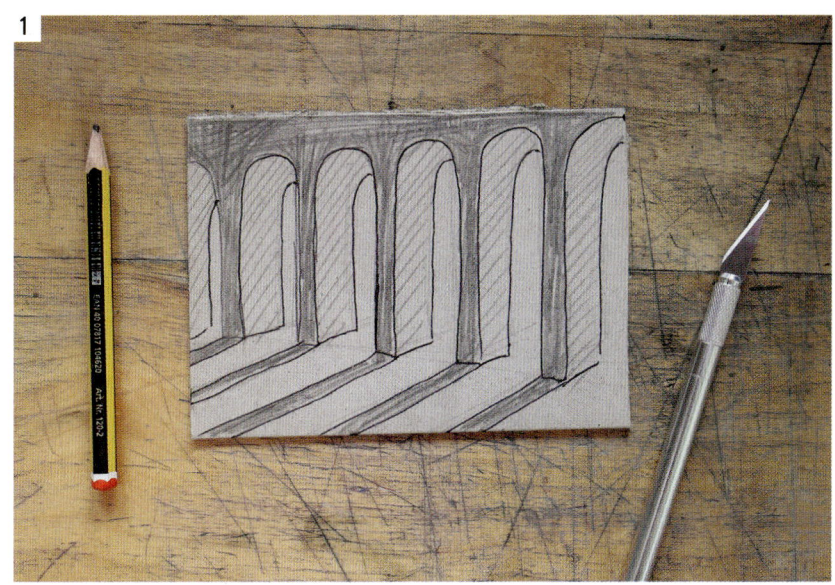

1 Begin by sketching your design directly onto the mount board. For collagraph, the simpler the design the better your print will be – too many small details will easily become lost. Mark out the different tonal areas (white, grey, and black) to make the next steps easier.

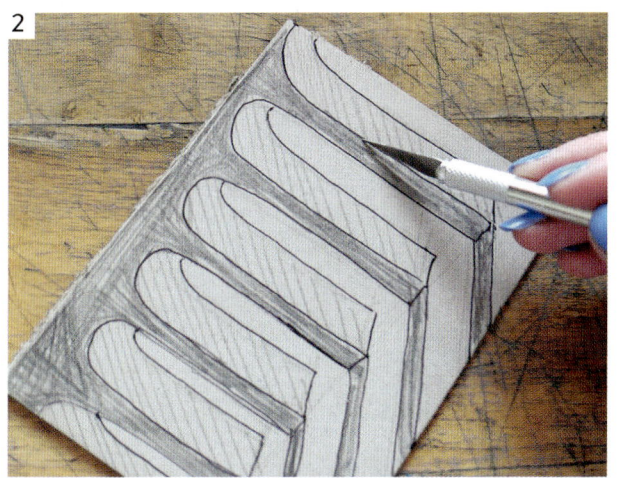

2 For the areas of your print that you want to appear black, use a craft knife to score the mount board around the edge of your chosen area – be careful not to cut all the way through.

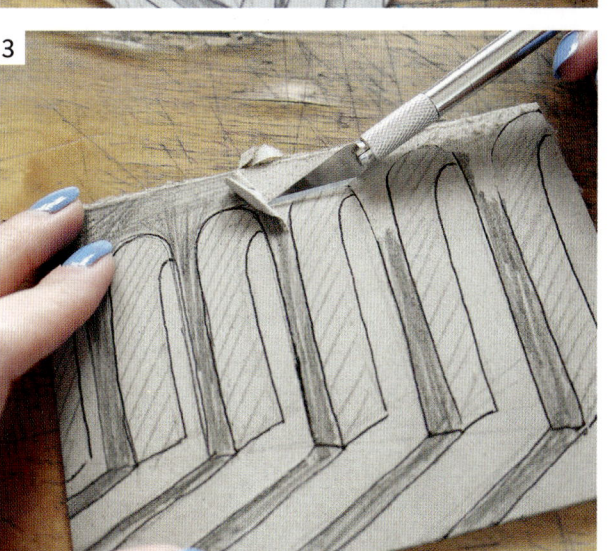

3 Using the tip of the craft knife, gently peel the top layer of the mount board away from where you scored it. Underneath is a fibrous, fuzzy surface that will hold lots of ink for printing the darker areas.

4 Now add the parcel tape to areas you want to keep clear of ink in your final print. Use a craft knife to cut away any excess and shape the tape to fit your desired forms.

5 Repeat this process with the masking tape. The slightly rough, porous surface of the masking tape will retain some ink during printing, creating a mid-tone.

6 Before inking your block, place your card between two pieces of damp – but not soaking wet – paper towel. Dampening your card will help draw the ink from the block and will help the printing process.

7 Using an old toothbrush or stiff paintbrush, gently work your ink into the block. Load up the ink quite heavily, as this will stop it drying out too fast and will give you a deeper colour.

8 Using a clean paper towel, work the ink into the block by pressing down and twisting. Use the paper towel to remove excess ink from the masking tape, as well as cleaning away ink from the parcel tape, which you want to keep as clean as possible.

9 Your block is now ready to print. Move the block onto a clean surface, or alternatively place it into a registration device to stop it moving (see Registration Blocks in the Other Tools section of the Tools and Techniques chapter).

10 Place your damp paper onto the block. You can print a collagraph in the same way as you would a linocut, but with extra pressure on your baren to make sure all of the paper makes contact with the surface. The damp paper may be more delicate than usual, so be careful not to tear it as you print.

11 You can now reveal your print. Every collagraph will be different, depending on how the ink is applied and rubbed away. If necessary, use a paintbrush to retouch any areas where the ink has not fully adhered to the card.

4
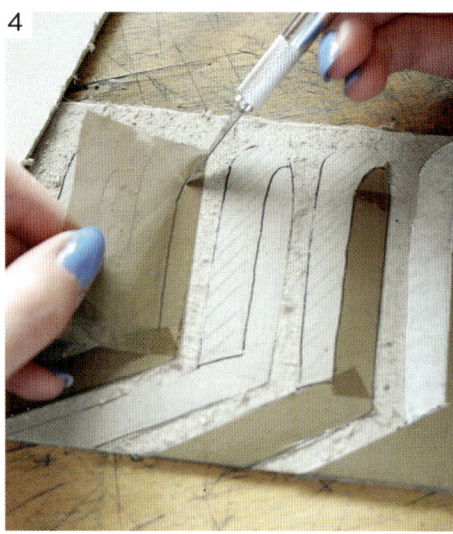

7
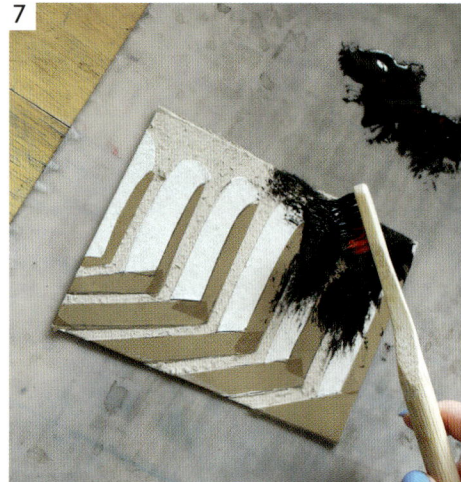

10
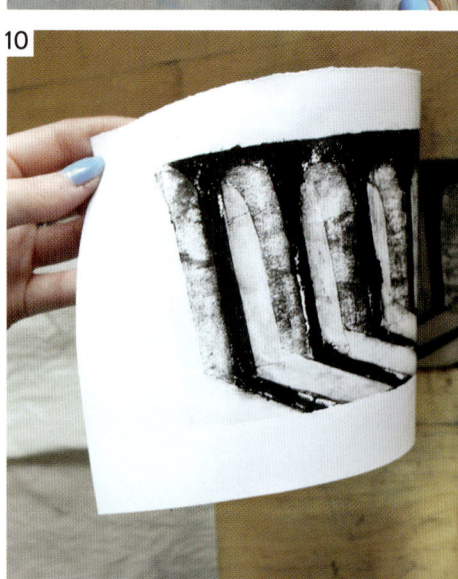

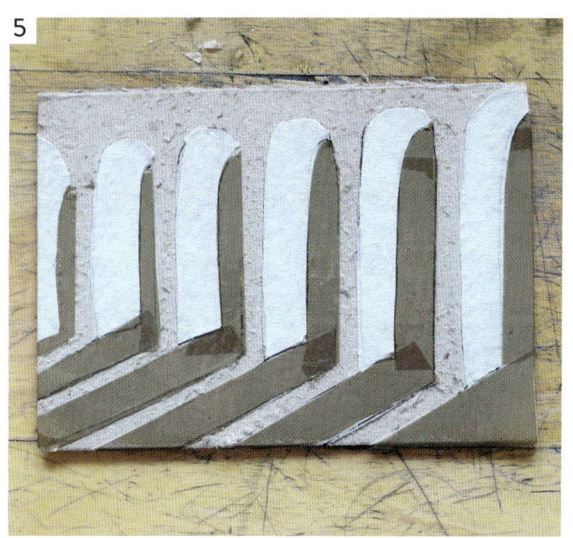

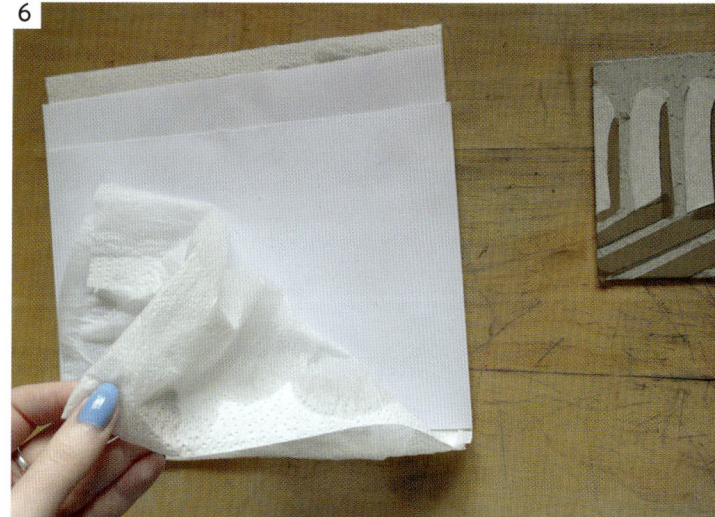

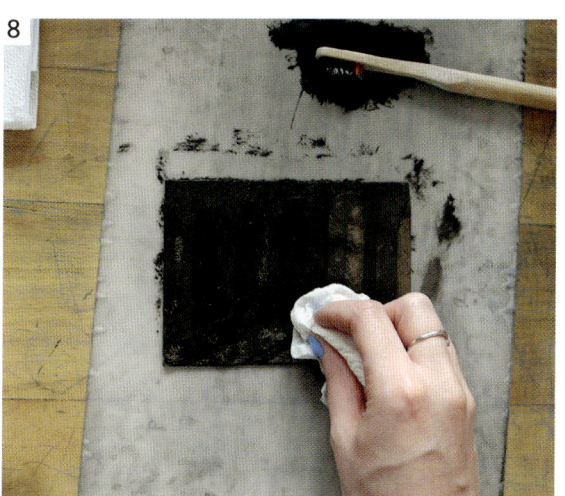

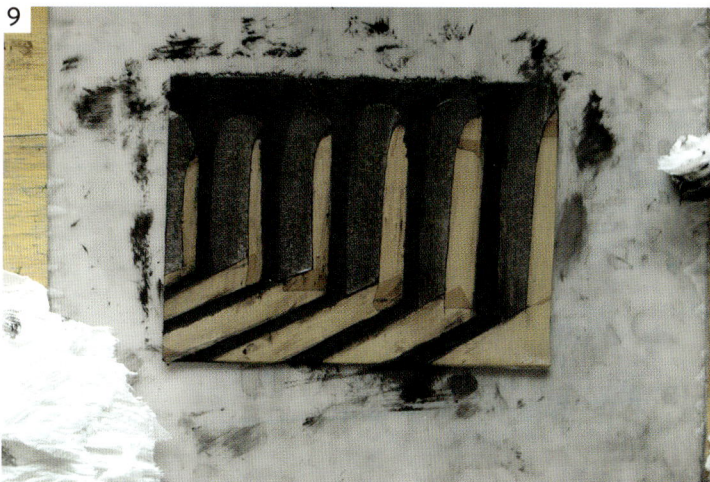

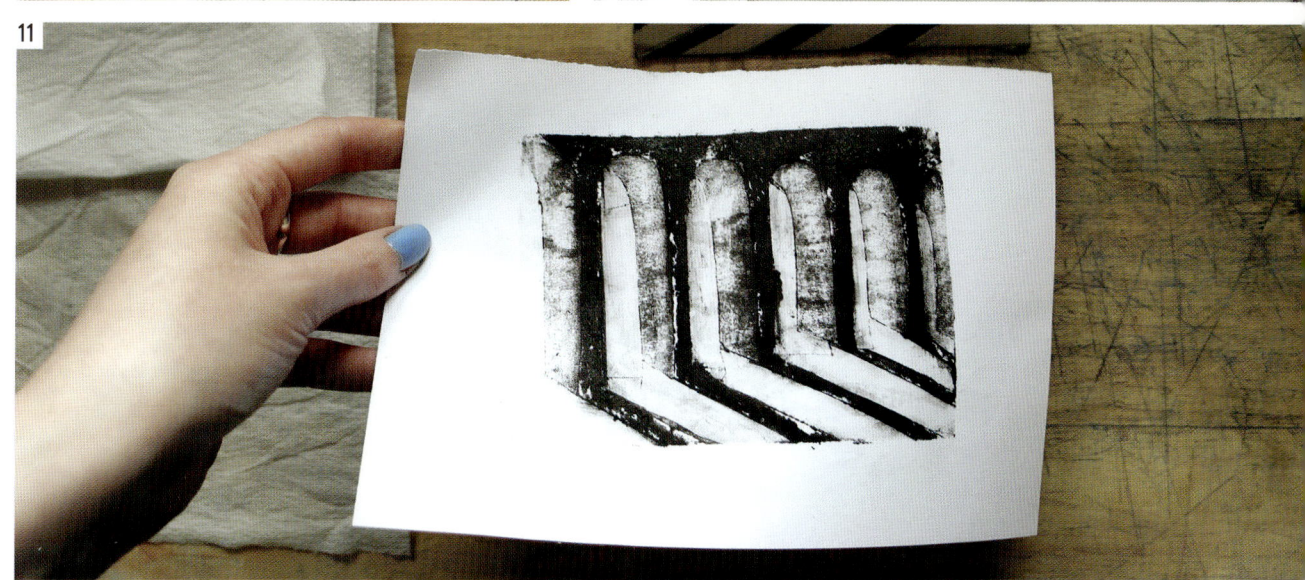

SUPPLIES

Coloured pencils

Textured surfaces

Thin paper (household printer paper works best)

Scissors

Rice starch glue or PVA glue

Old paintbrush

Card

Ink of your choice

Inking plate

Brayer

TEXTURE RUBBING AND MONOPRINTING

Texture rubbing is a great, low-mess way to create prints and to collect different textures from the urban environment that can then be used as inspiration for your linocut prints. This project also demonstrates the monoprint technique, which can be used to add extra details to your texture rubbings to create unique, one-of-a-kind prints.

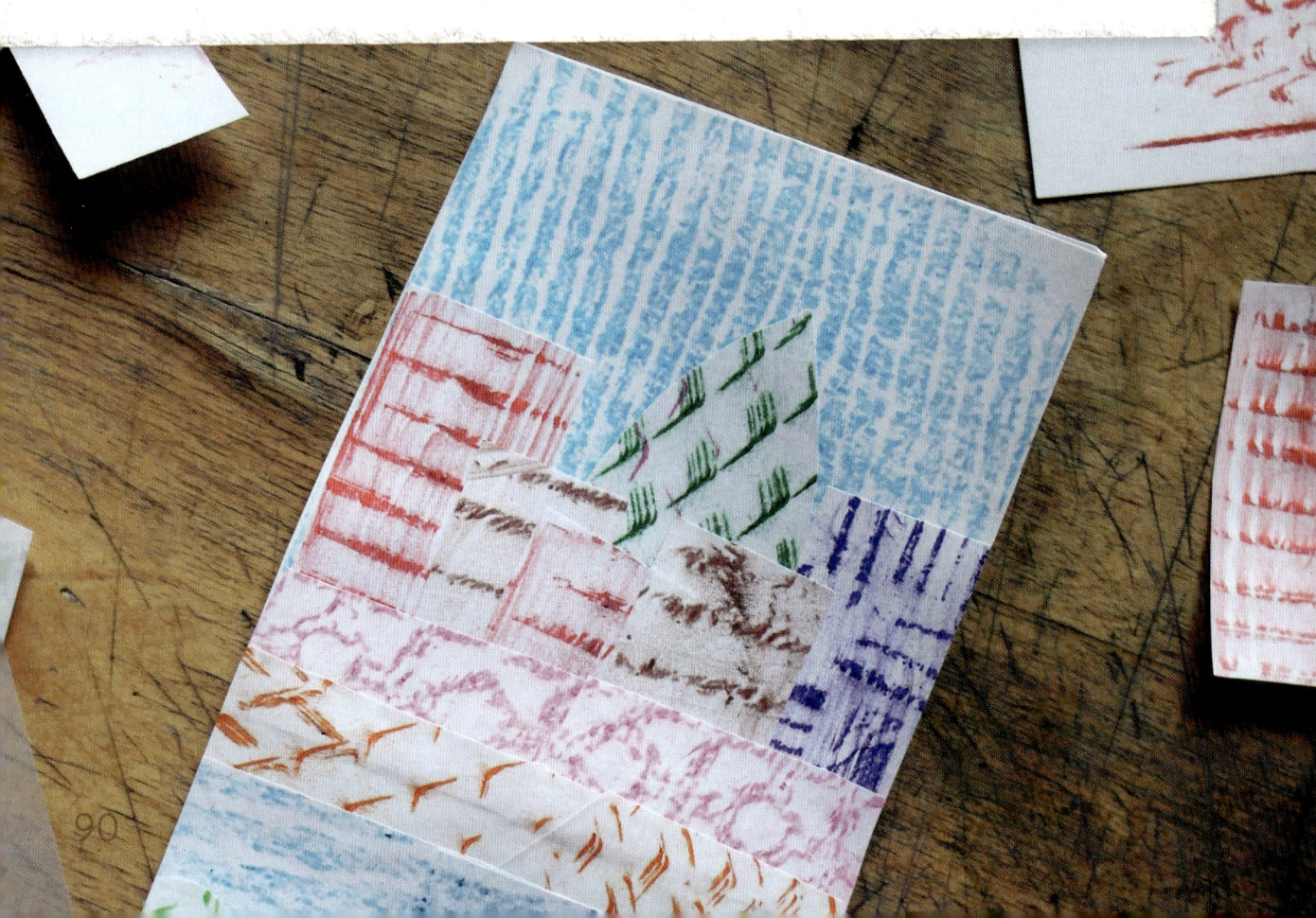

TEXTURE RUBBING

1 Begin by selecting your materials. These coloured pencil sticks work well, as they give a lot of surface area to use when rubbing – but standard pencils will also work. Don't use thick paper as it may not be able to capture all the texture.

2 Select objects outside or in your home that have an interesting surface design. Firmly rub the pencil on top of the paper. Adjusting the pressure and angle will achieve different results.

3 You can move the paper around on top of your object to change the shape or use multiple colours at the same time to enhance your rubbed design. Take rubbings from a variety of surfaces and in a variety of colours. Rubbing over embossed text can be used to add words into your prints.

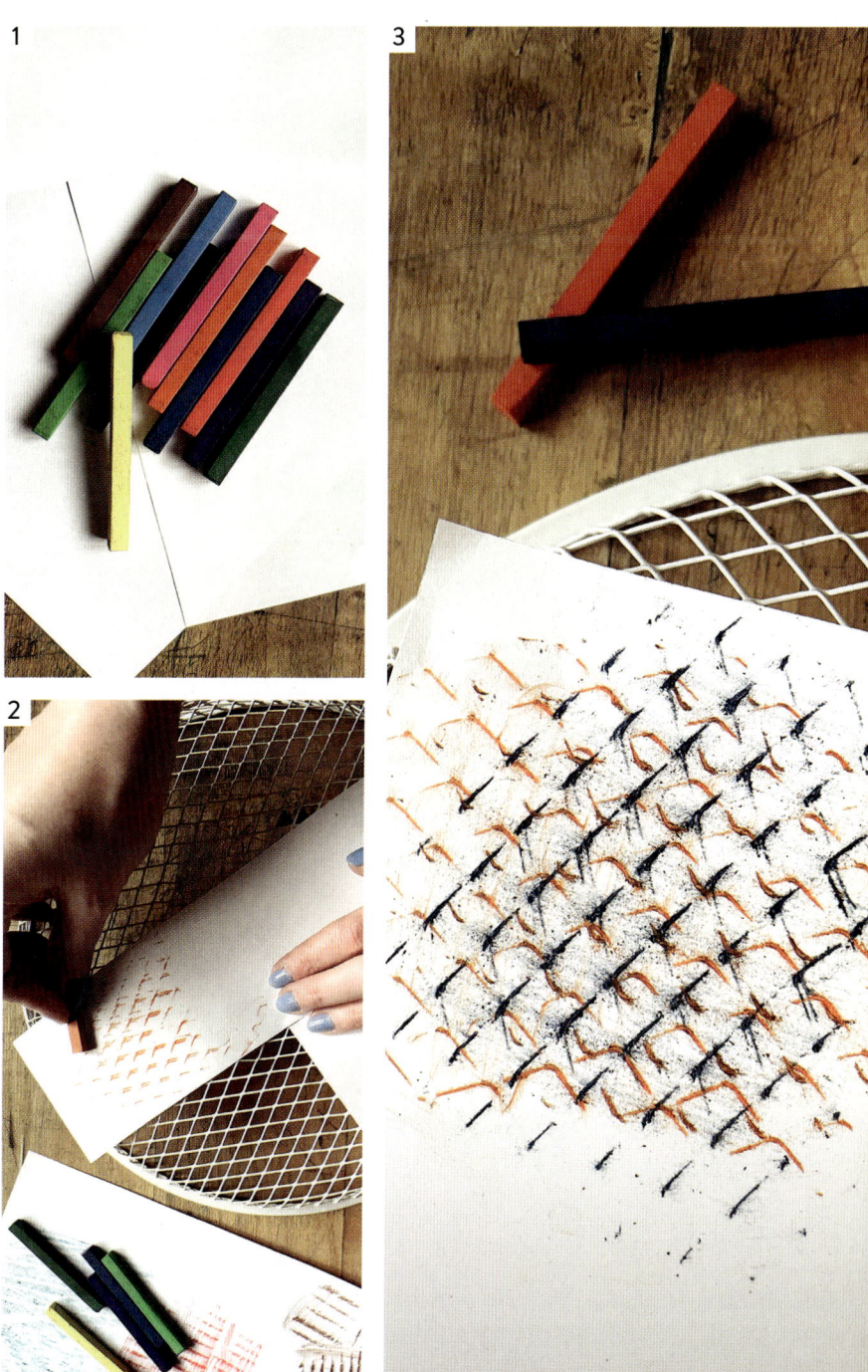

4 While these rubbings can be mini prints in their own right, you can also cut them up to use as collage elements. You can work to a sketch, or let your imagination run wild, turning the abstract designs into different aspects of a cityscape.

5 Keep arranging your pieces until you are happy with your design. Here, striped rubbings have been used for skyscrapers, while wood grain is perfect for suggesting water.

6 Secure your collage with glue onto a thick piece of card. Rice starch glue applied with an old paintbrush (as described in the Chine Collé project) works best, but PVA glue can also be used.

7 Once the glue has dried, trim your print down to neaten the edges.

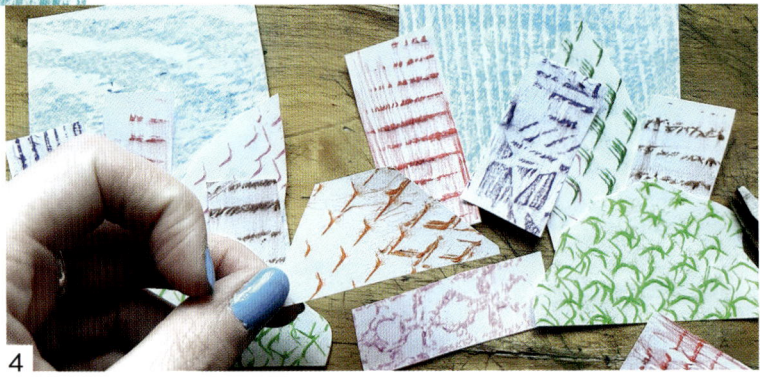

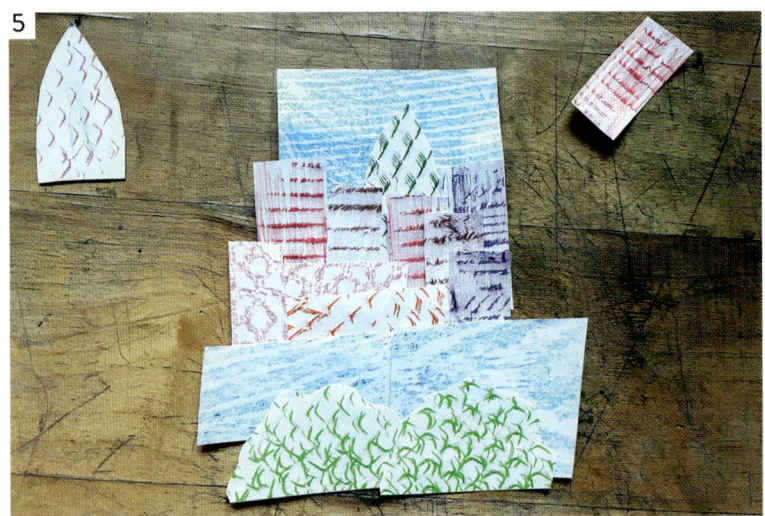

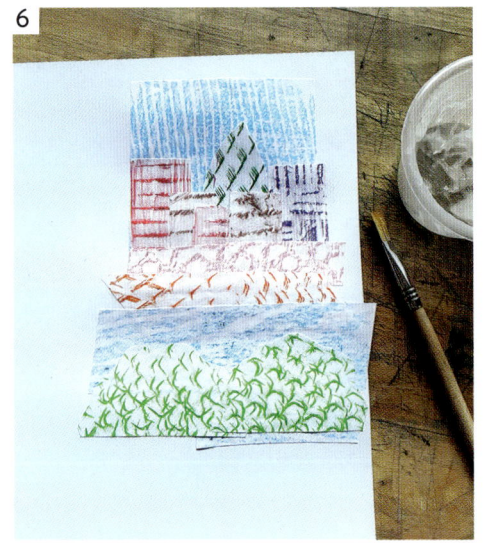

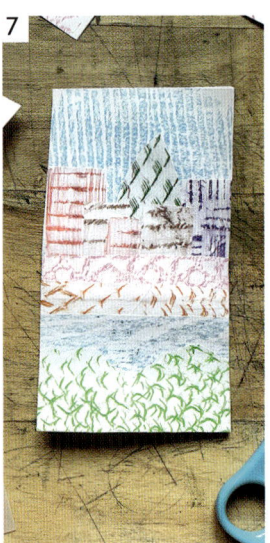

MONOPRINTING

Texture rubbings, on their own or even collaged, are perfect for monoprints – one-of-a-kind prints made by drawing on the reverse of your chosen paper.

8 Roll out a small amount of ink across your inking plate as thinly as possible, so that the plate is lightly covered. Take your selected rubbing and lay it lightly face down on the ink – do not press it down, as any pressure will cause the paper to be marked.

9 Using the end of a thin paintbrush or a pencil, trace any pattern you like onto the back of the paper.

10 Carefully peel the paper away from the ink to reveal your design. Do not worry if there are unexpected marks on the paper – the beauty of monoprinting is that these marks create a completely unique print every time!

11 This technique can also be used to draw images onto your texture rubbings.

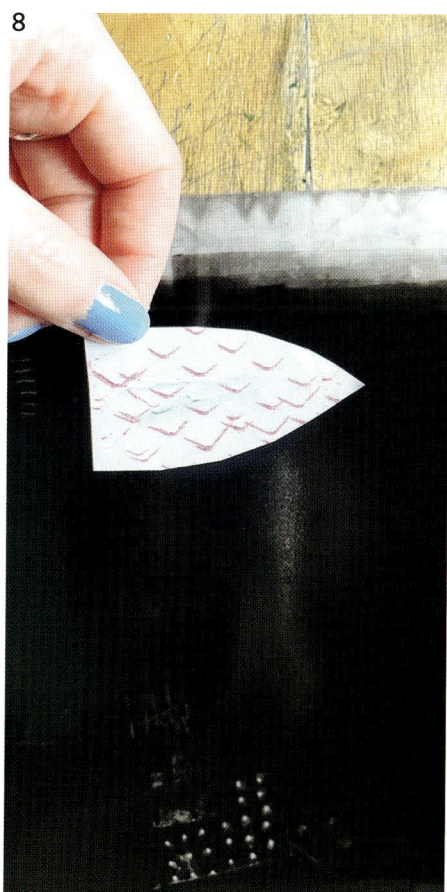

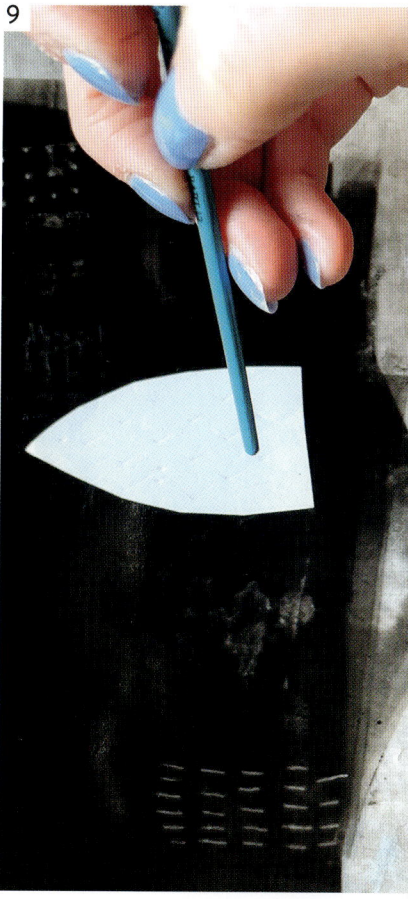

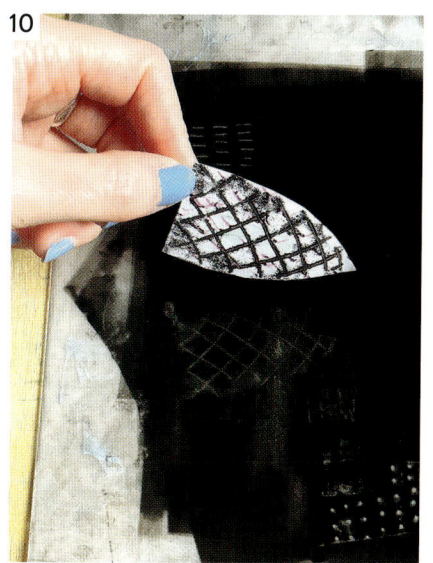

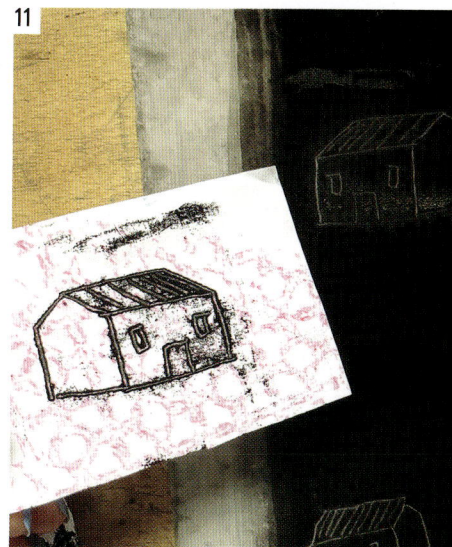

WATERCOLOUR

Watercolours can be used to add a unique, illustrative quality to your prints, providing a splash of colour, shading, extra details, or even a personalised touch. This project uses the blocks created for the Continuous Landscape project (in the Further Studies chapter) to demonstrate some of the key techniques for introducing watercolour into your print projects.

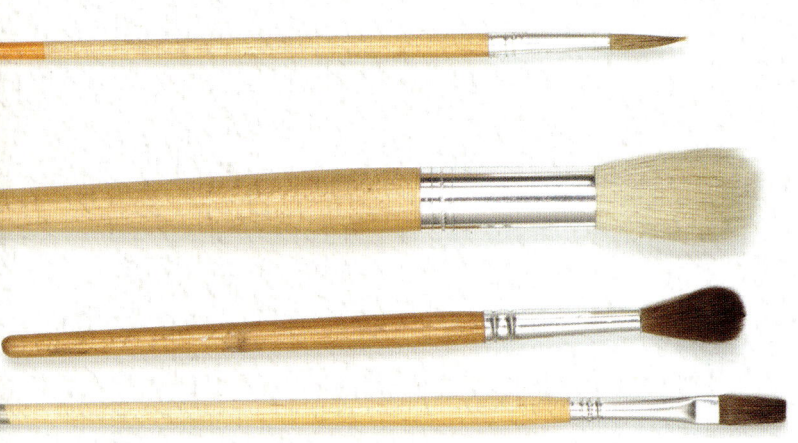

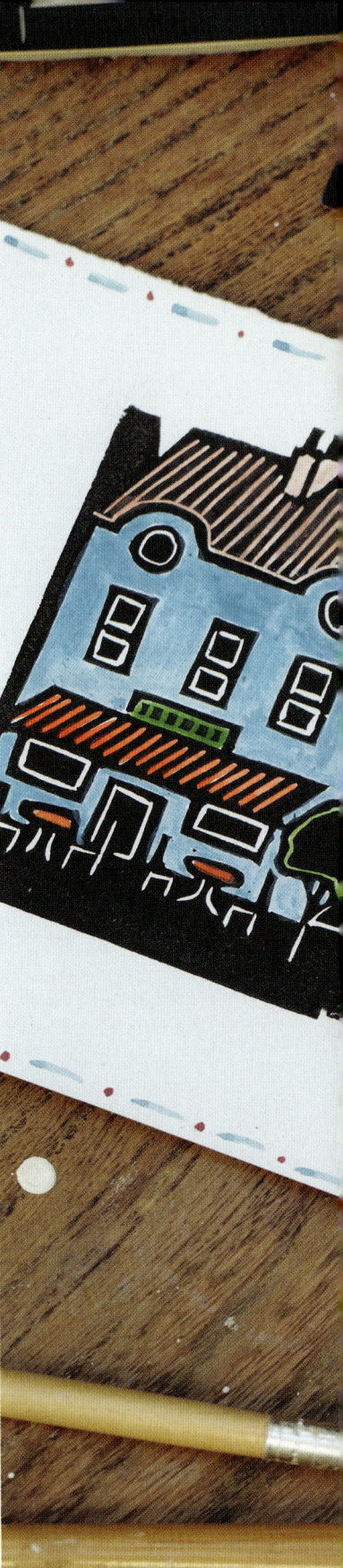

SUPPLIES

A dry print of your choice
....
A set of watercolours
....
A selection of
watercolour brushes
in different sizes
....
A jar of water
....
Paper towel
....

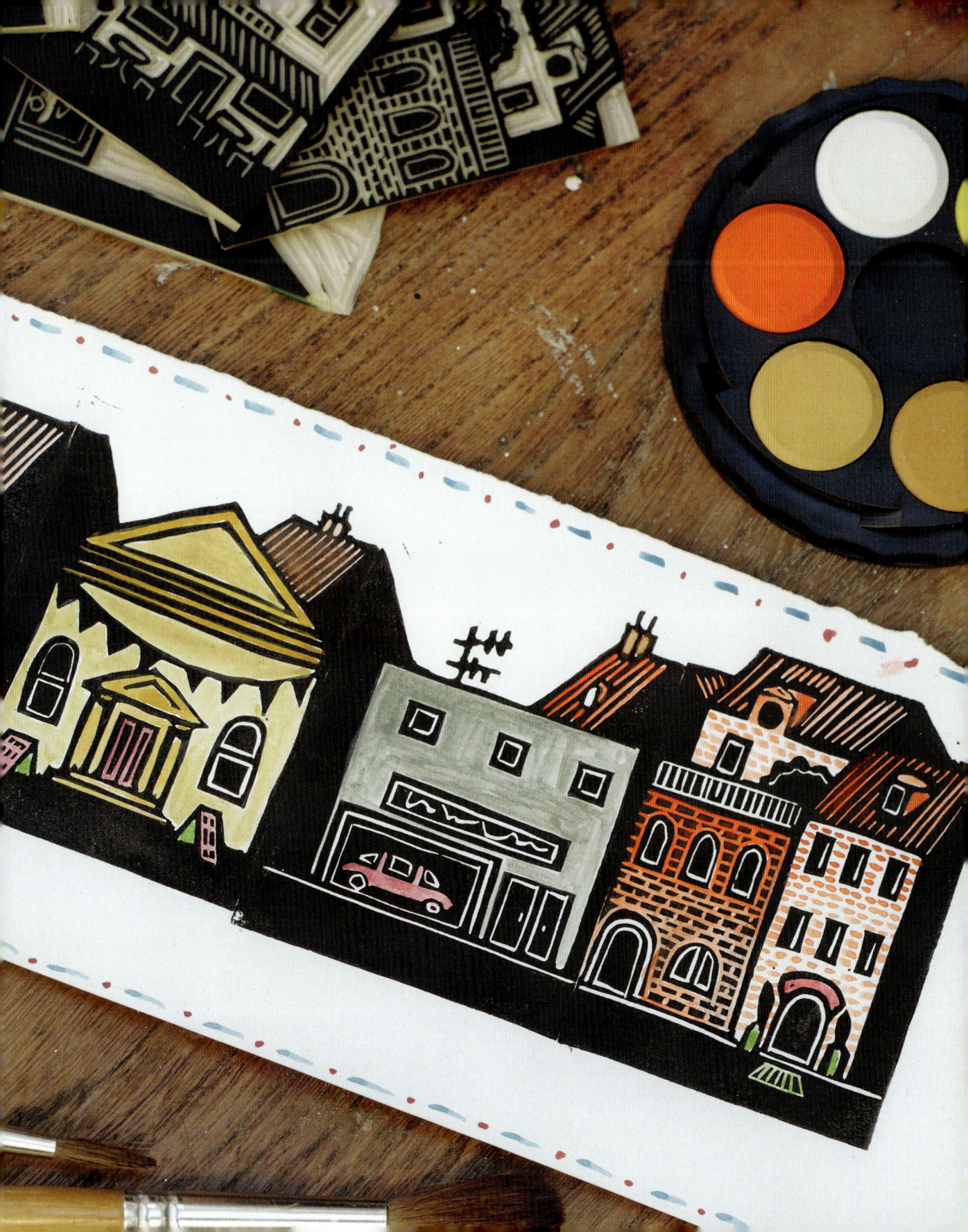

1 Start by selecting the print you want to add colour to. Watercolour paints work well with even the most detailed blocks, so you're free to choose.

2 You should be able to use watercolour in conjunction with most types of printing ink. However, make sure when mixing your paint not to add too much water as this could saturate the paper and risks causing your printed design to run.

3 Begin by painting the smaller details with your smallest brush. Starting with a smaller area can help test the consistency of the paint and how it interacts with the ink. If you go over the lines, do not worry as the ink is usually quite resistant to small amounts of water.

4 Working in one colour at a time, and cleaning your brush thoroughly between colours, will help keep your painting clear. You may want to leave areas to dry to prevent colours bleeding into one another, though this accidental mixing can also create a great effect!

5 Colour can be used to suggest what materials your buildings are made out of. Here, a warm yellow is used for the sandstone of the museum, while a grey is used for the concrete of the car dealership.

6 As well as using solid colour, bricks can be indicated by painting small dashes in a mix of orange and red. This same colour can be used for buildings where the bricks are part of the original print design.

7 Bold colours, such as this blue, contrast really nicely with the solid black ink and can highlight the designs you have created on your lino block.

8 Adding a decorative border with the paint is a great way to finish off your print design.

9 Once you are happy with your painted print, leave it to dry. Once dried, you may need to put the print under something heavy to stop the paper from curling due to the extra water.

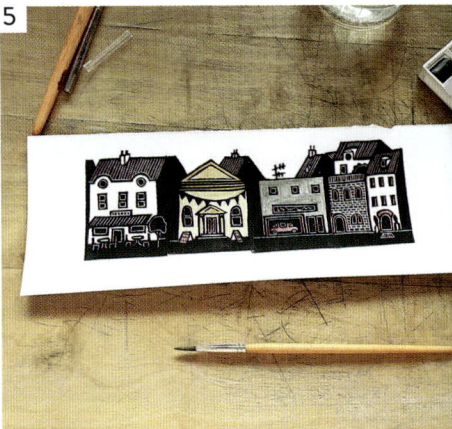

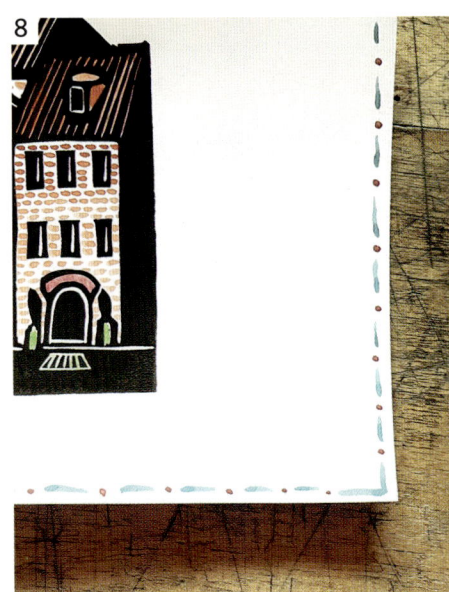

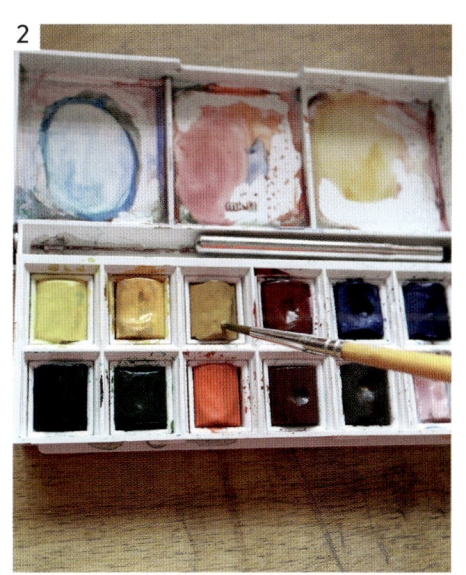

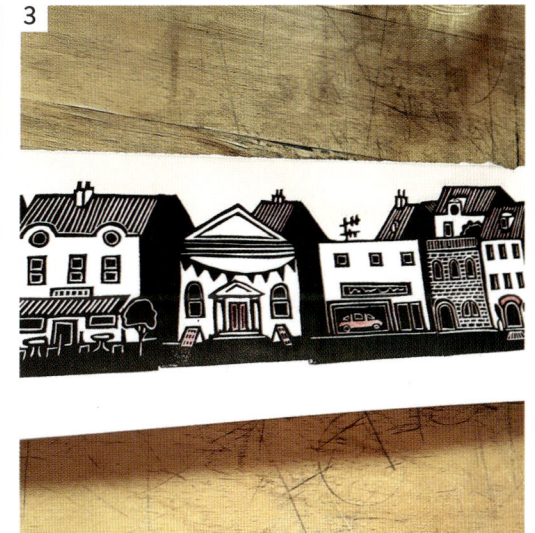

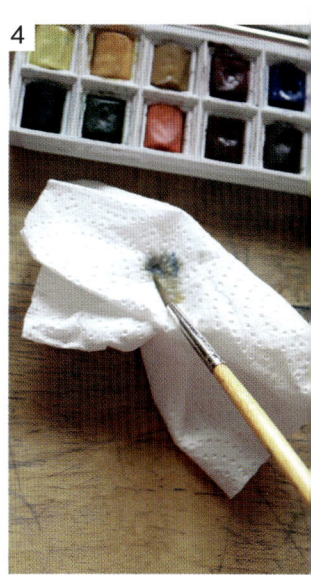

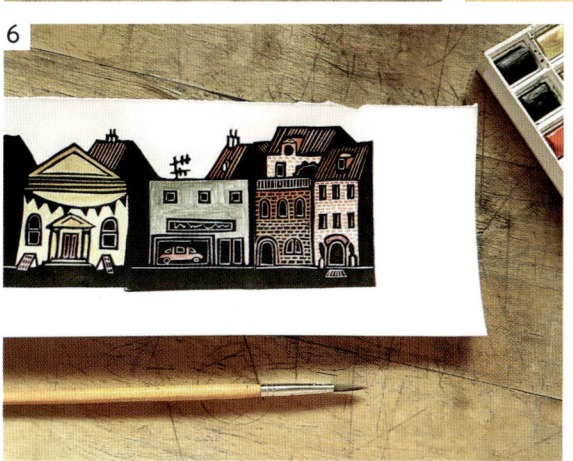

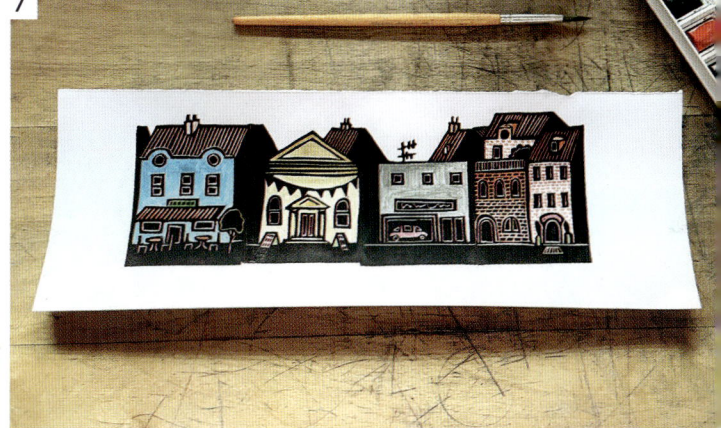

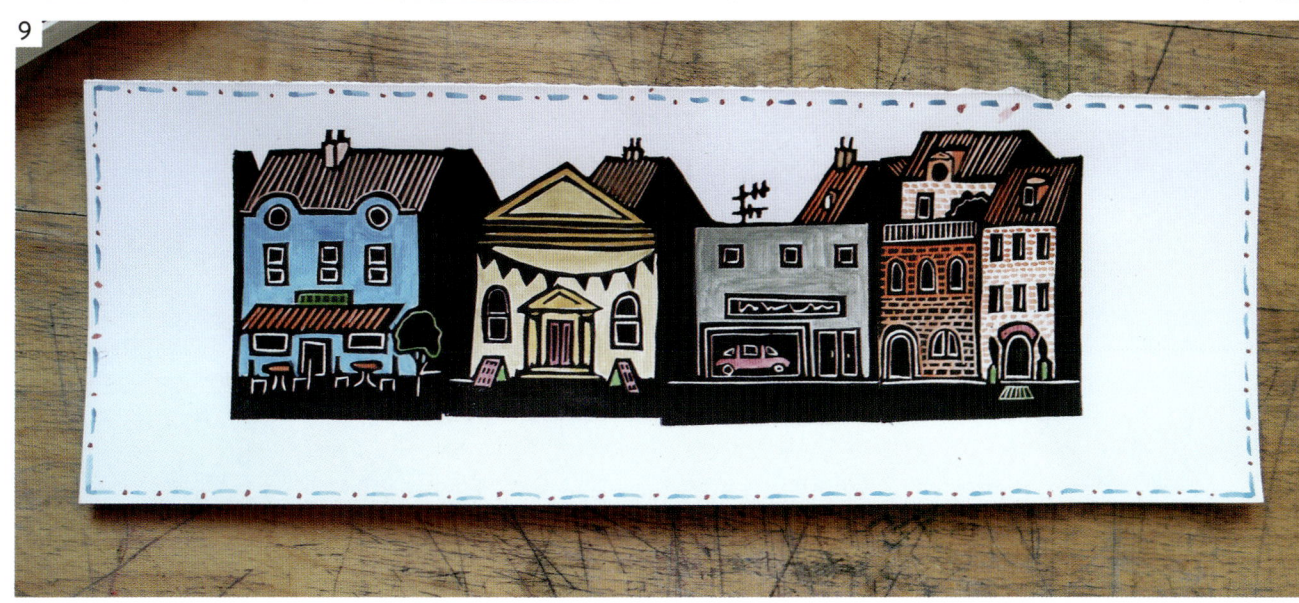

FURTHER STUDIES

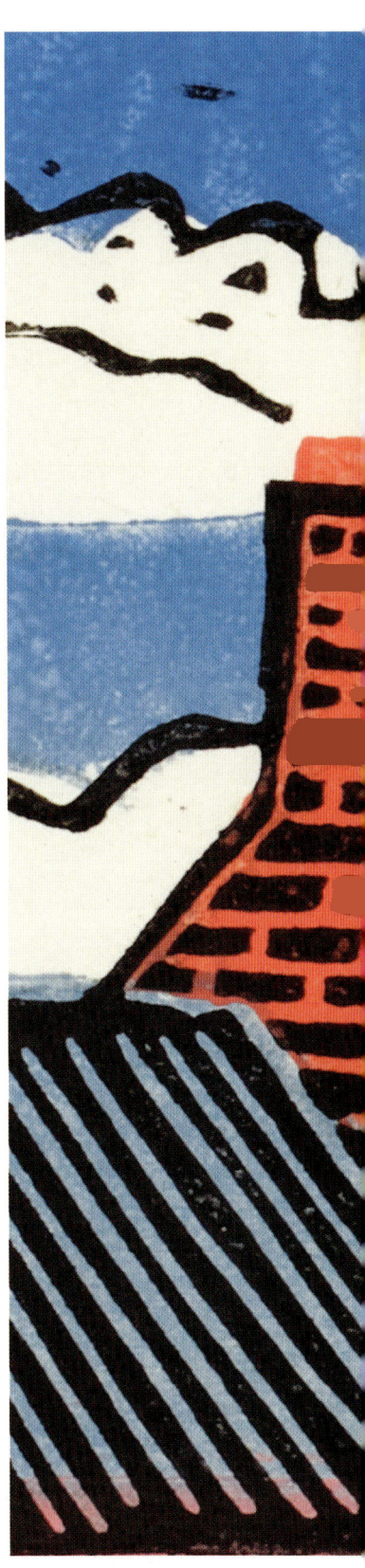

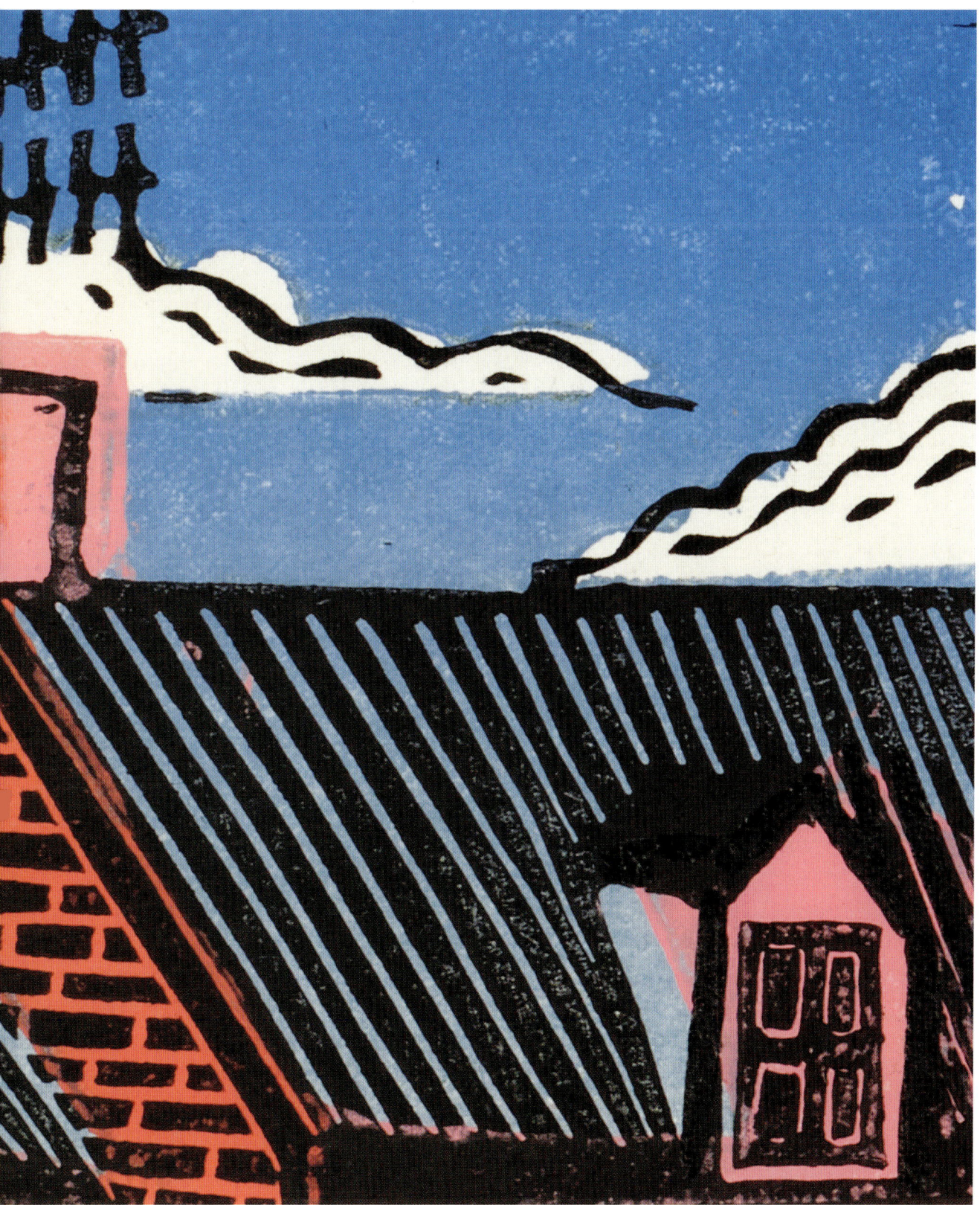

NARRATIVE

Prints are great storytelling tools, and using a comic book style layout maximises narrative potential. This project uses a comic book structure to capture snapshots of a walk around a town but can be customised to suit your own story, from a commute to work to a favourite holiday memory.

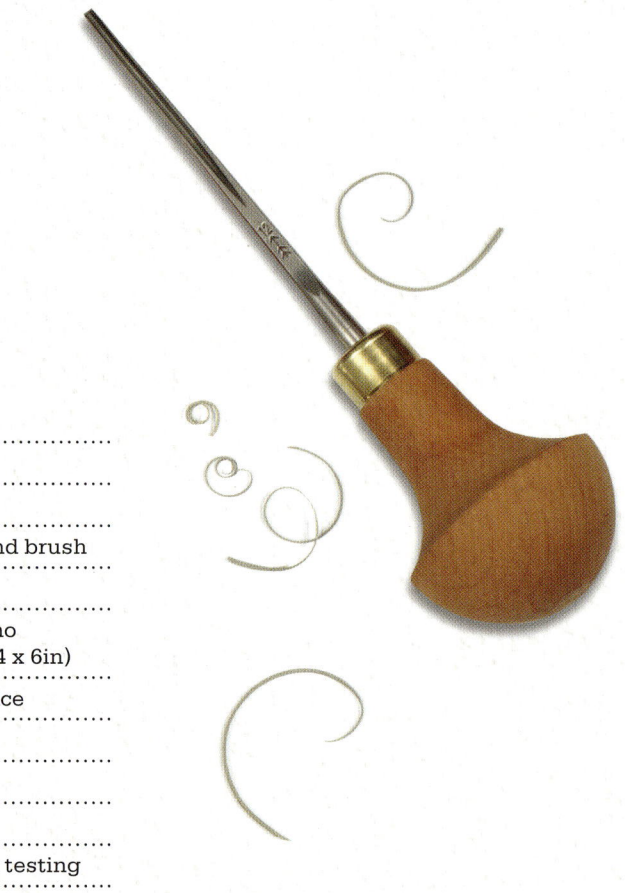

SUPPLIES

Tracing paper

Pencil

Pen

Acrylic paint and brush

Narrow cutter

One sheet of lino
10.5 x 14.8cm (4 x 6in)

Ink of your choice

Brayer

Baren

A5 card

Scrap paper for testing

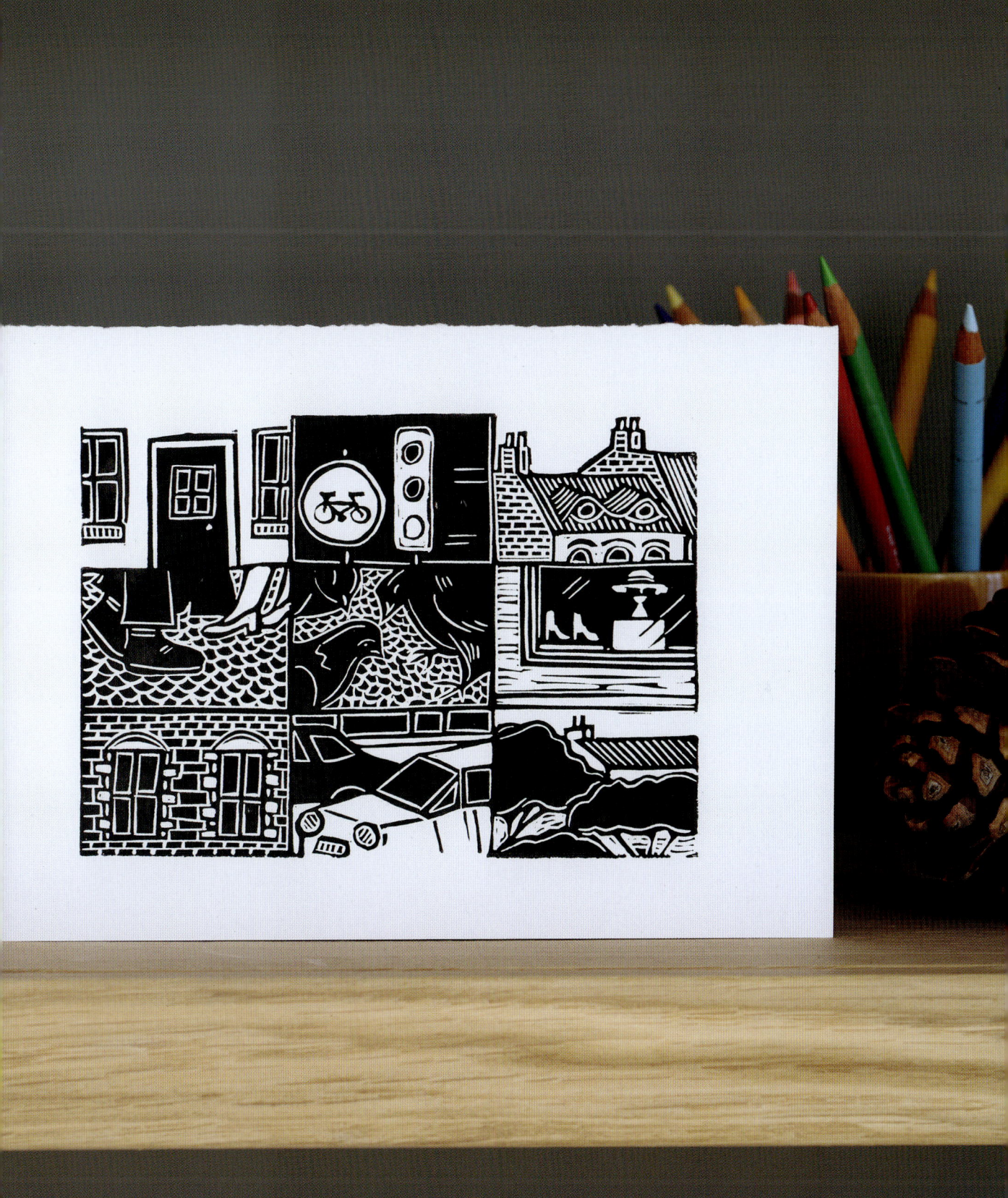

1 Create your drawing by dividing your paper into smaller sections. This block has been divided into nine, which creates enough sections to make a narrative but which are still large enough to include lots of detail. Once happy with your drawing, transfer it onto the block in the usual way. Add a thin layer of acrylic paint.

2 As the sections of this print are small, getting the balance between textured and solid space is important so that the whole print isn't overwhelmed. Here, the pattern of the small cobbles is balanced by keeping the pigeons solid.

3 When starting a new section, it can be useful to carve around the edge of the box, so that you don't accidentally go outside of it when carving the main design.

4 This project is a good way to practise different carving techniques on a small scale, such as these cobbles and bricks.

5 As well as balancing the individual sections, think about the balance of the print as a whole. As three carved sections contain a lot of pattern, I am keeping details to a minimum for the road sign section.

6 Continue carving the rest of the sections, checking the balance between light and dark as you go.

7 If the print looks too dark or too overwhelmed by pattern, carve away some areas to create clear space for the eye to rest.

8 Now your block is ready to ink. As there are fine details here, build ink gradually on the block as adding it too thickly will obscure some of the details.

9 Printing a test onto scrap paper is a good way to check the balance of your print and make any adjustments necessary on the block.

10 You could use this print as the key block to add colour to, perhaps adding a single colour to each section to distinguish them or to change the mood.

1
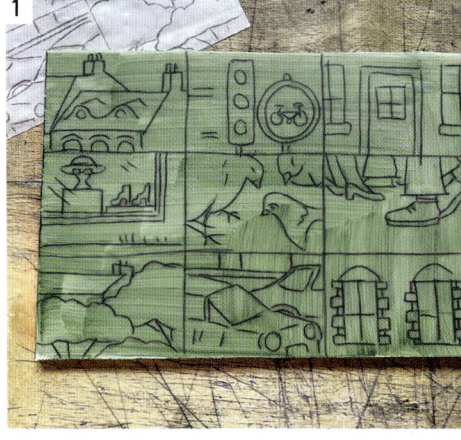

5
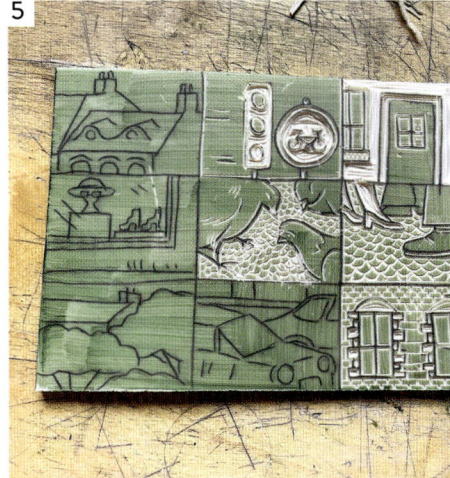

8
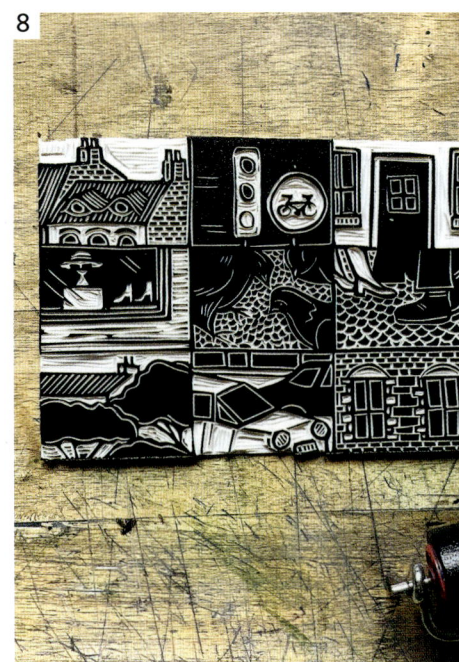

2

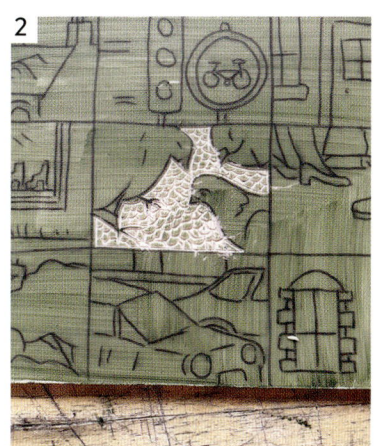

3

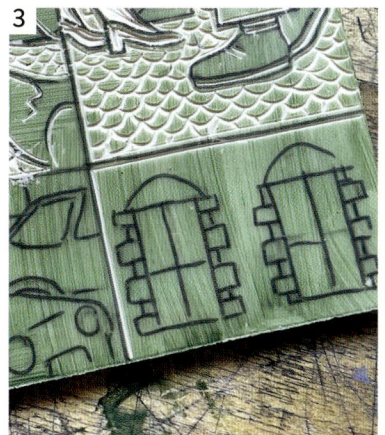

4

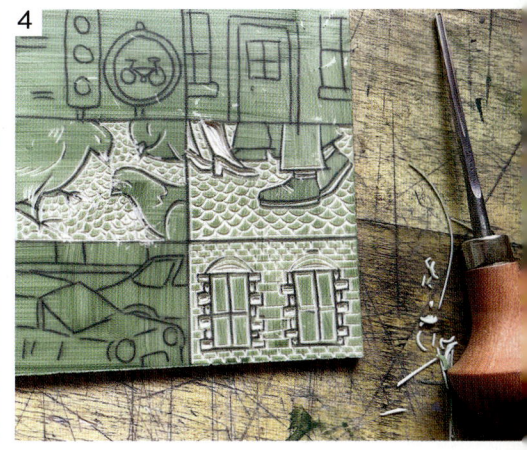

6

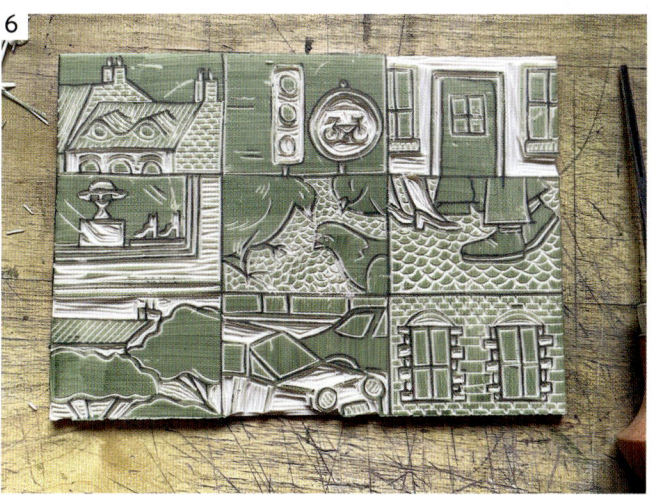

7

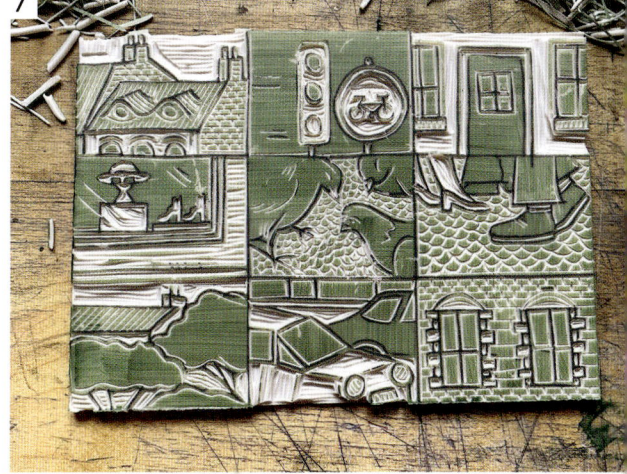

9

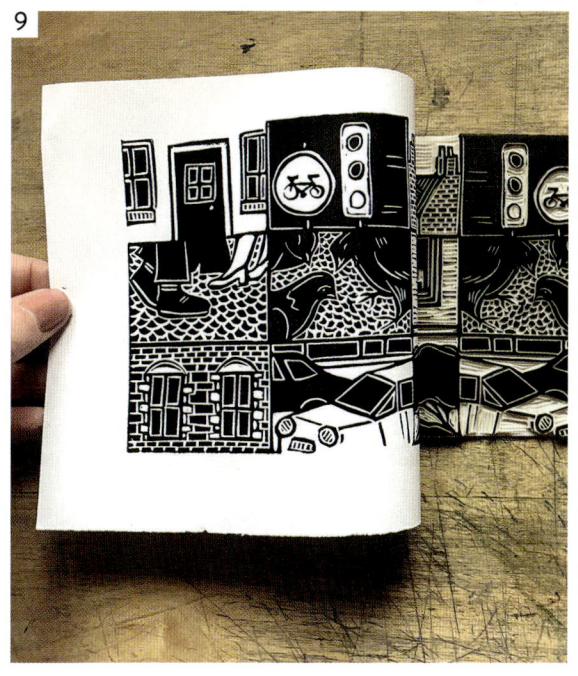

10

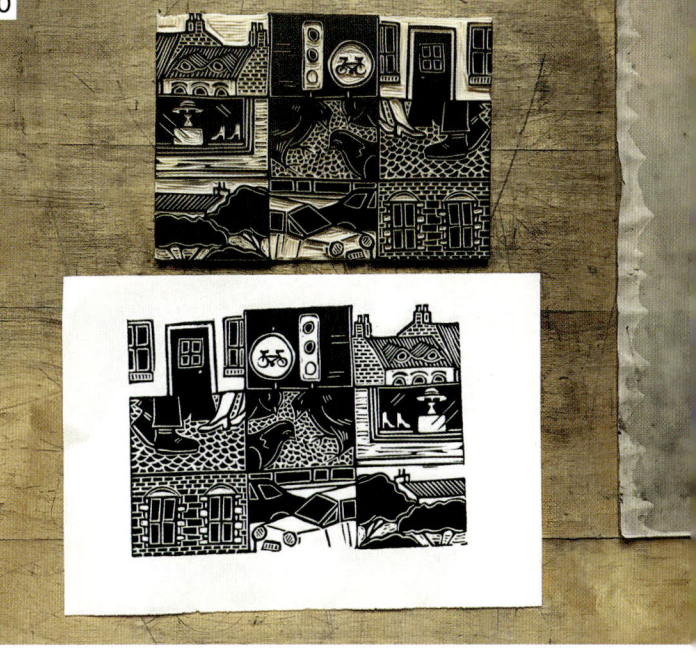

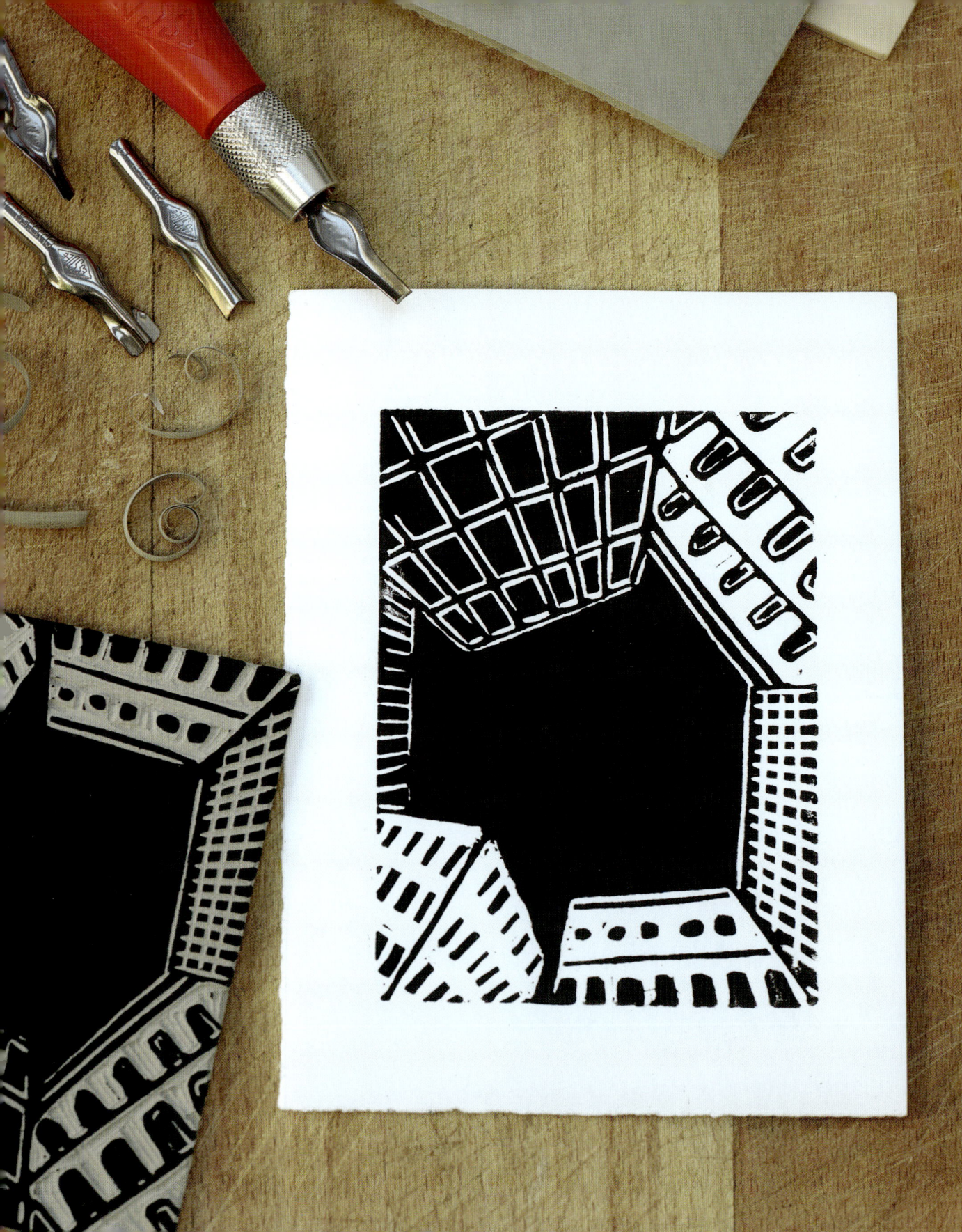

NEGATIVE SPACE

Negative space refers to the space around the objects in your print, and can be used to add extra drama, draw attention to a specific element or, as in this example, to give a sense of scale. In this project, the buildings are used to frame the negative space created by the sky, reflecting the experience of the high-rise urban environment.

SUPPLIES

Tracing paper

Pencil

Pen

Acrylic paint and brush

Narrow cutter

One sheet of lino
7.5 x 10.5cm (3 x 4in)

Ink of your choice

Brayer

Baren

A6 card

Scrap paper for testing

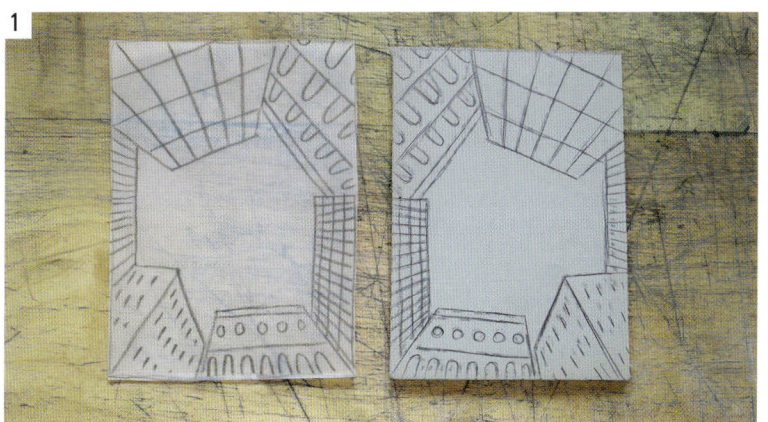

1 Start by sketching your design. Here the empty space of the sky has become the focus of the print. Then transfer your drawing to the lino.

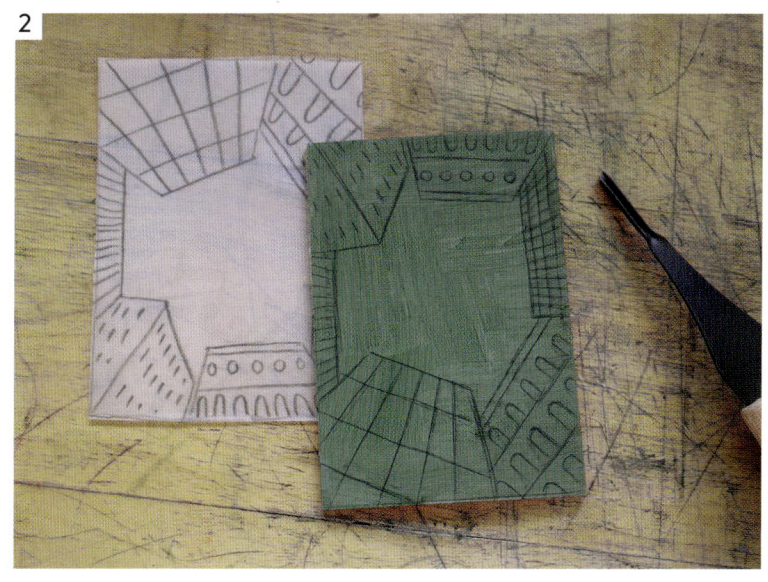

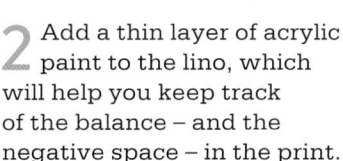 **2** Add a thin layer of acrylic paint to the lino, which will help you keep track of the balance – and the negative space – in the print.

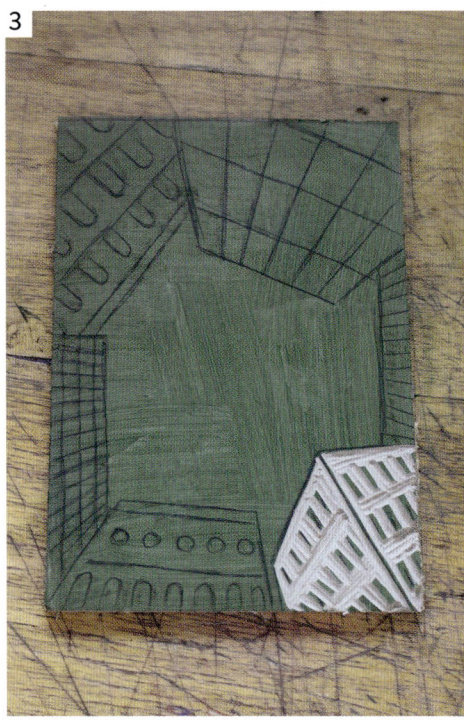

3 Using the same carving technique as introduced in the City Skyline project, add windows to some of the buildings.

4 For buildings with larger windows, define individual panes by carving their outline, leaving thin lines to divide them. A guide for this technique can be found in the Pattern Guide in the Carving Tips section of the first chapter

5 This same technique can be used for curved windows too – here the rest of the building has been carved away to contrast with the ones around it.

6 Varying the size and shape of the windows will add extra visual interest. To create circular windows, hold the cutter still and turn the block as you carve.

7 Carving a grid by overlapping horizontal and vertical lines is also an effective way to create lots of small windows.

8 Your block is now ready to ink. Using a strong colour of ink will really help the negative space stand out.

9 Use test prints to check the balance of light and dark in your print. Here, the solid colour has been kept as the focus, but why not try cutting out the centre and using stamps to create a cloudy sky?

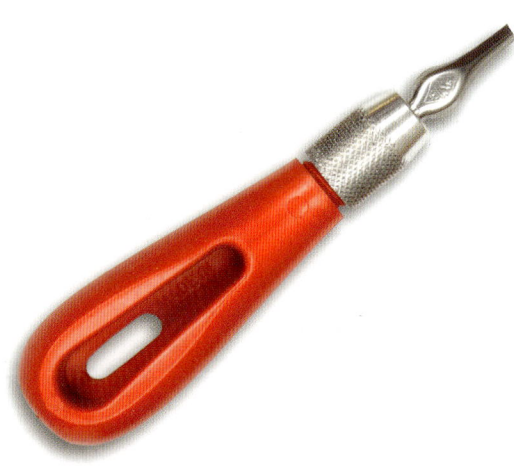

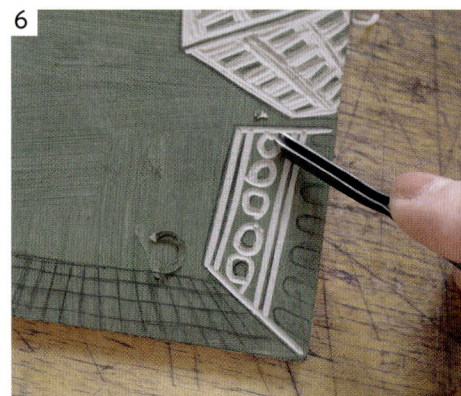

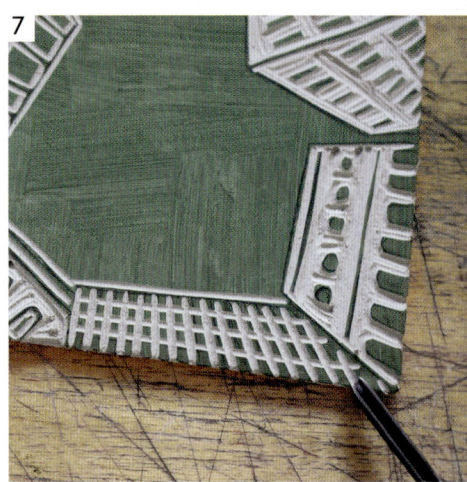

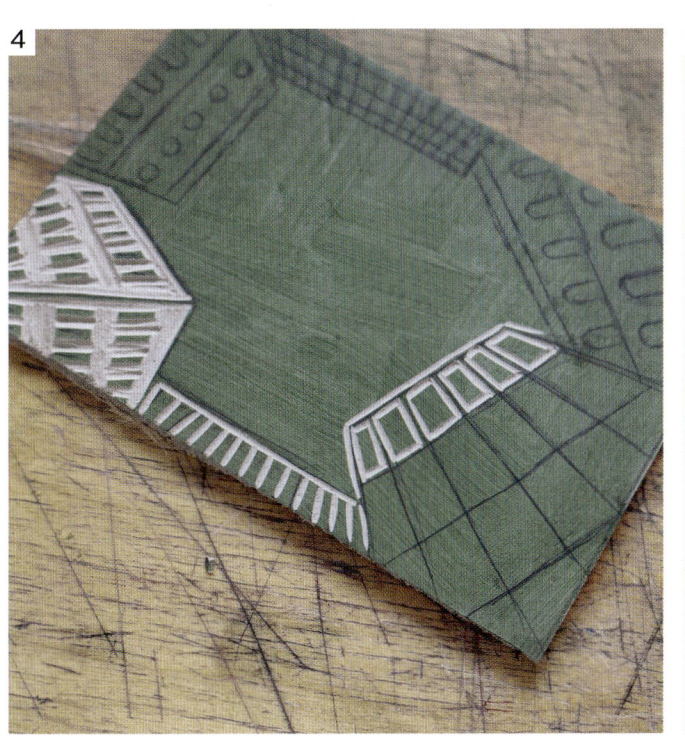

4

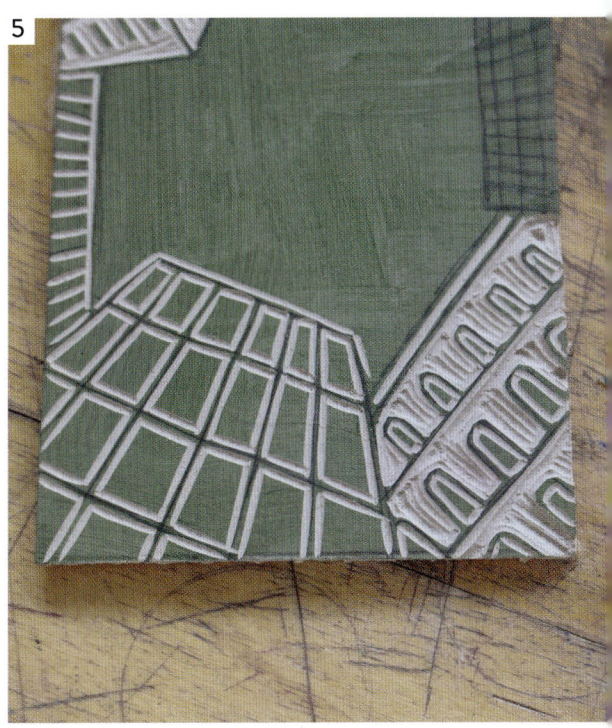

5

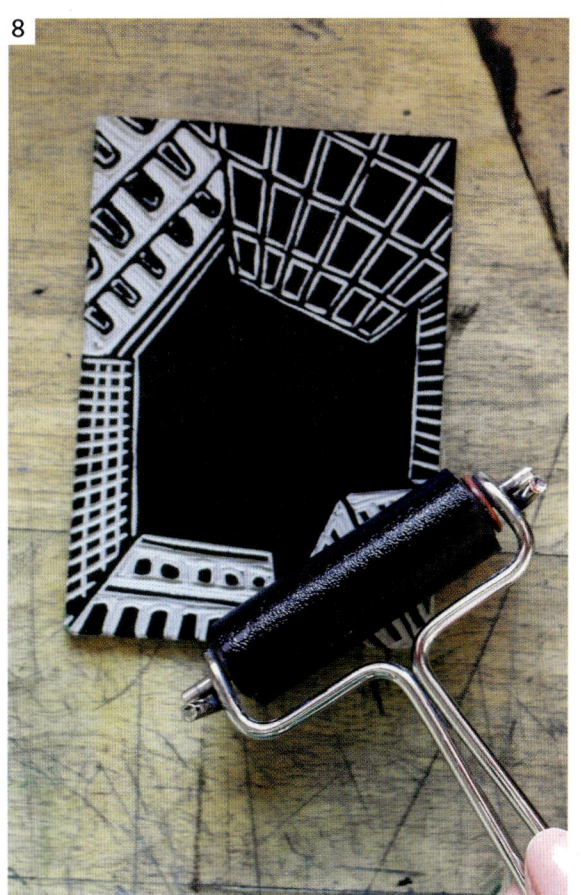

8

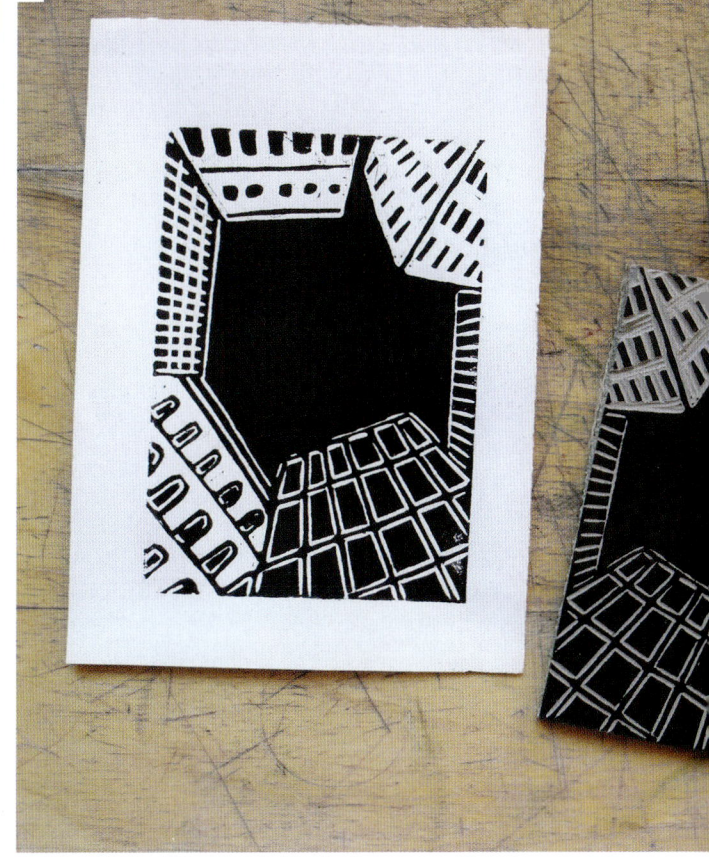

9

SUPPLIES

Tracing paper

Pencil

Pen

Acrylic paint and brush

Narrow cutter

One sheet of lino
7.5 x 10.5cm (3 x 4in)

Ink of your choice

Brayer

Baren

A6 card

Scrap paper for testing

Stiff brush

CLOSE DETAIL

Once you are comfortable with the technique of carving, you can begin introducing more and more intricate detail into your prints. This block is a great way to practise delicate carving by focusing in on one section of an intricate building, such as a clock outside a Victorian railway station.

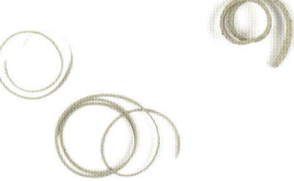

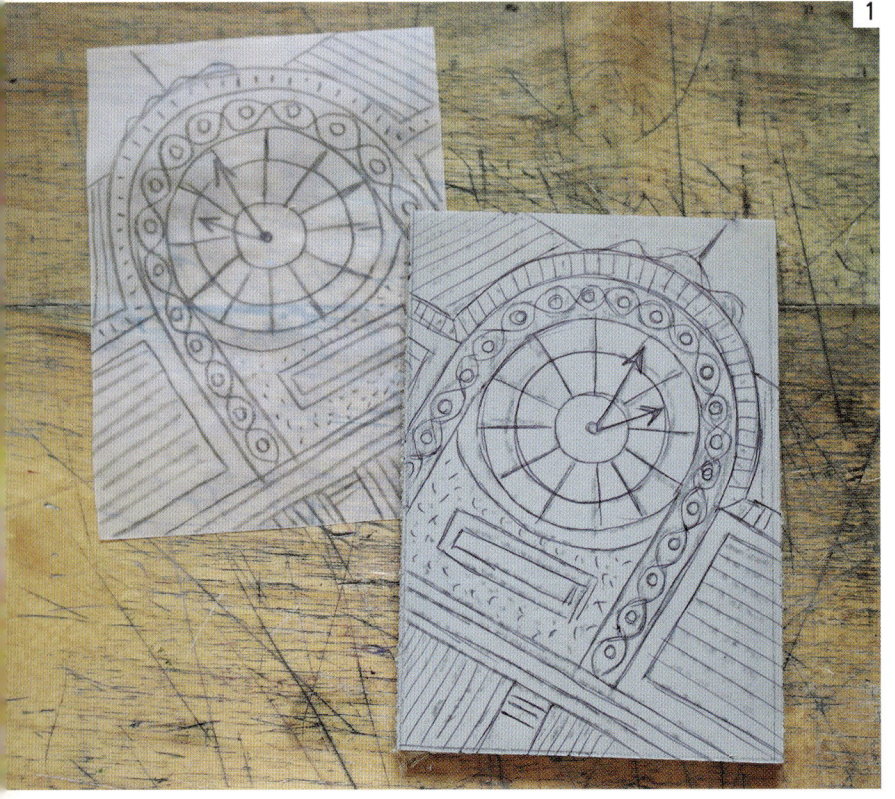

1 Start with your drawing. Think about how to translate the details of the building into print – it might be necessary to simplify some, as very small details may be difficult to carve or (particularly if you are using grey lino) flake away from the block during inking. You can always carve more freestyle details while carving. Then transfer your drawing onto the block in the usual way.

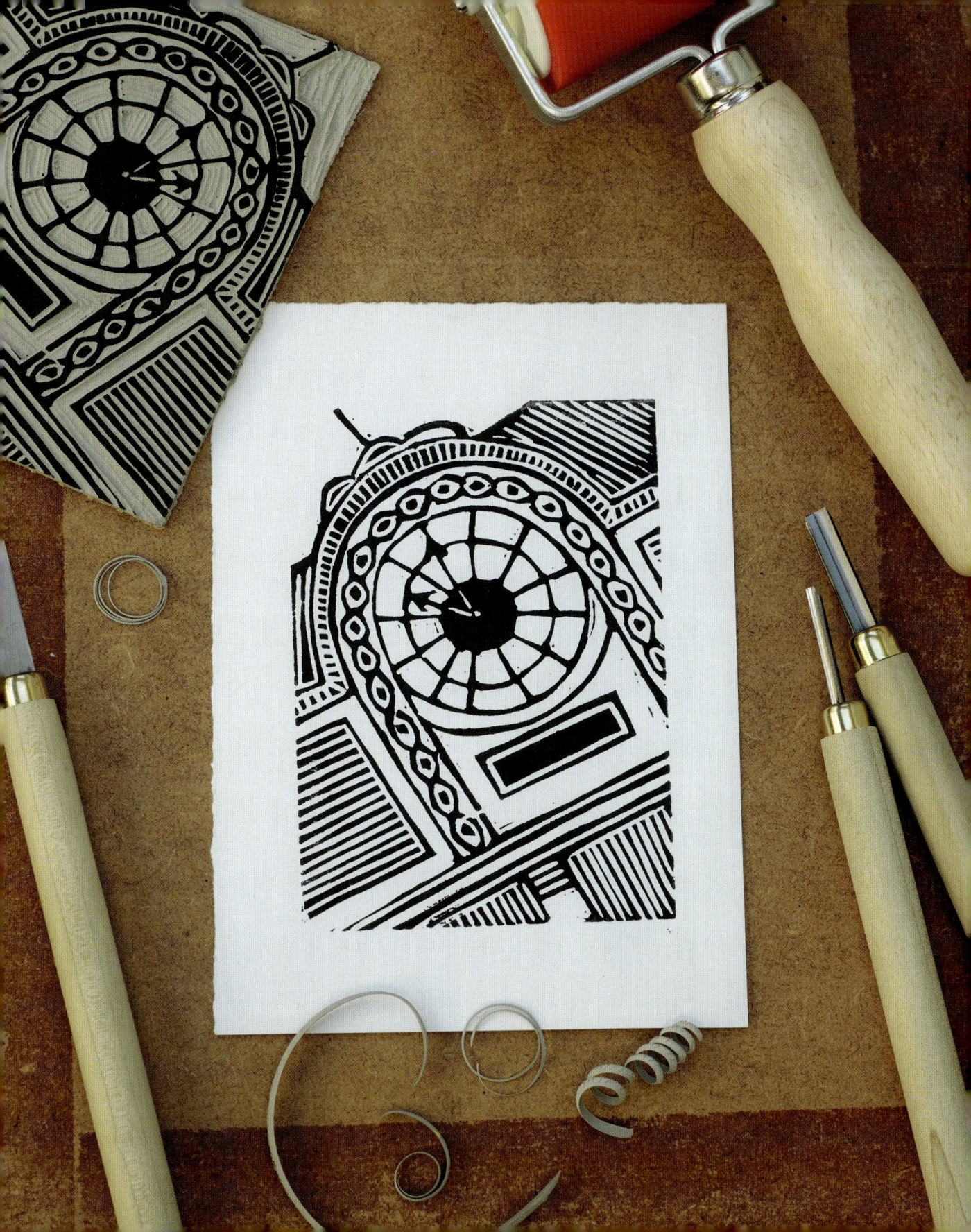

2 When carving, begin with the most intricate detail – that way, if things go wrong, you can make adjustments to the design. These eye-shaped details are a great way to mimic Gothic-style stonework.

3 Close lines can act as shorthand for brickwork or carved stonework, or can add detail to otherwise plain areas of wall.

4 To create the effect of beaded stonework, carve two parallel lines about half a centimetre apart. Then join these with short, vertical lines spaced a little bit apart – this works particularly well as a border design.

5 Continue to add details. Add some areas of blank space to create places for the eye to rest and to prevent the image from becoming too overwhelming.

6 Take a moment to check the balance of the print – too much detail can overwhelm the design, so it may be necessary to remove some areas that you had planned to be pattern.

7 Once carved, use a stiff-bristled brush to clear the block of any small bits of lino that are trapped in the smaller details – this is especially useful when working with grey lino.

8 Carefully ink your block, building up the ink gradually. Inking this block too thickly may cause ink to get trapped in the finer details resulting in a blurry print.

9 You may want to do a test print to make sure that the print is balanced, and to make sure that there are no areas where scraps of lino have become stuck.

10 Once you are happy with your design, it can be printed onto card of your choice.

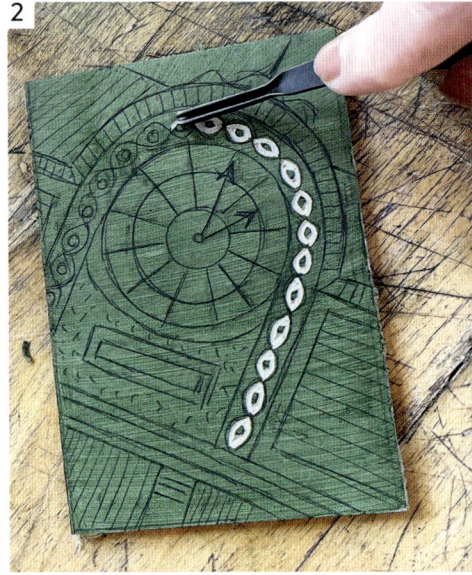

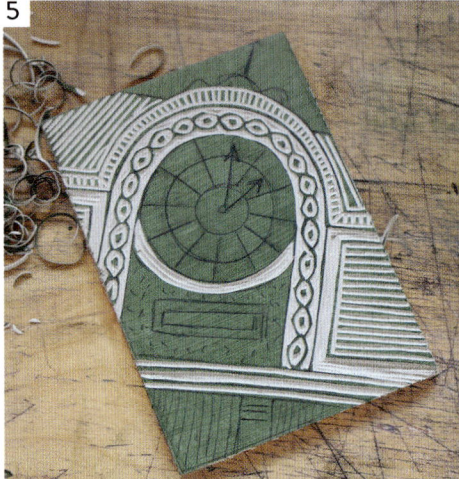

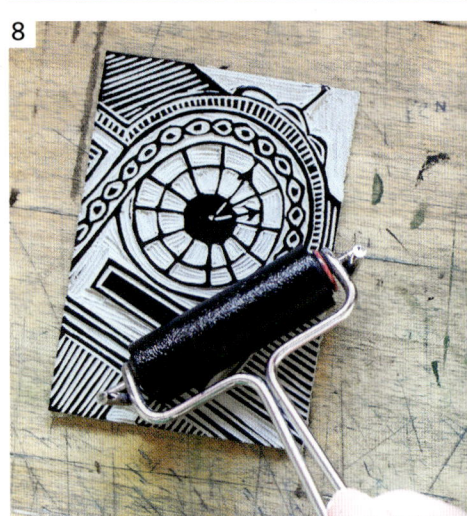

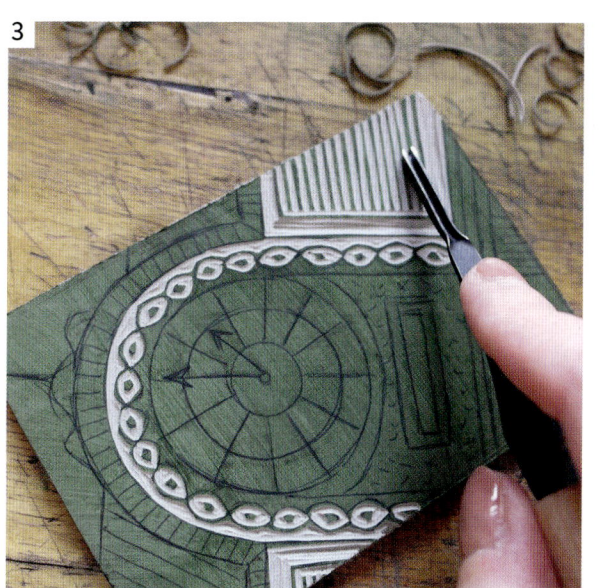

3

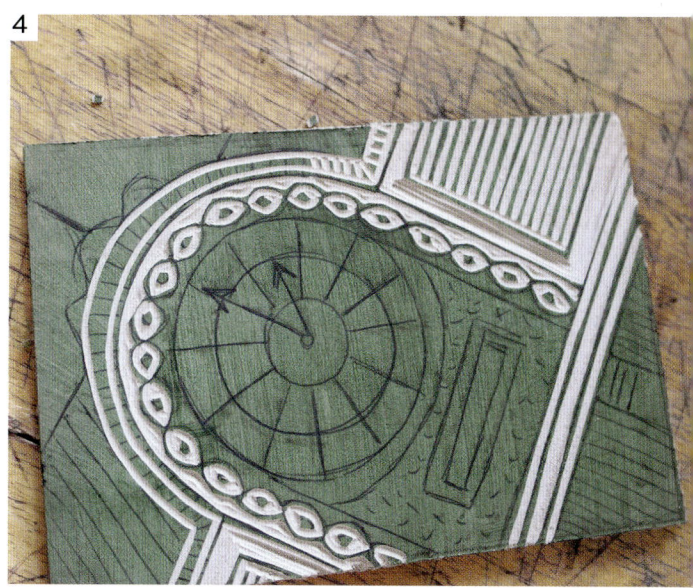

4

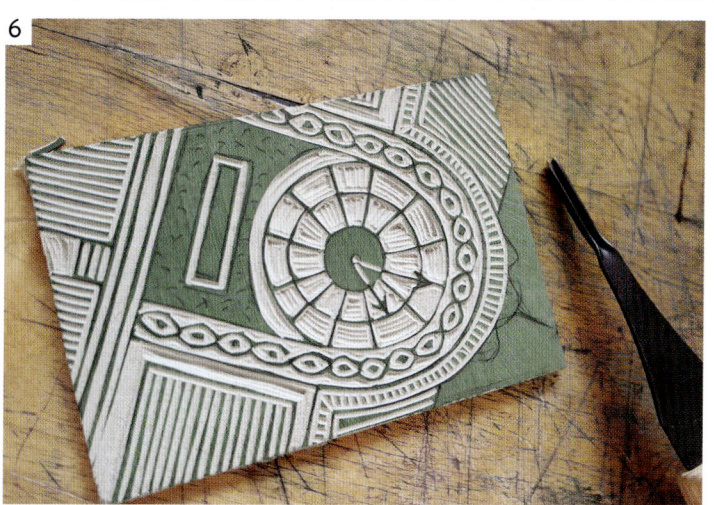

6

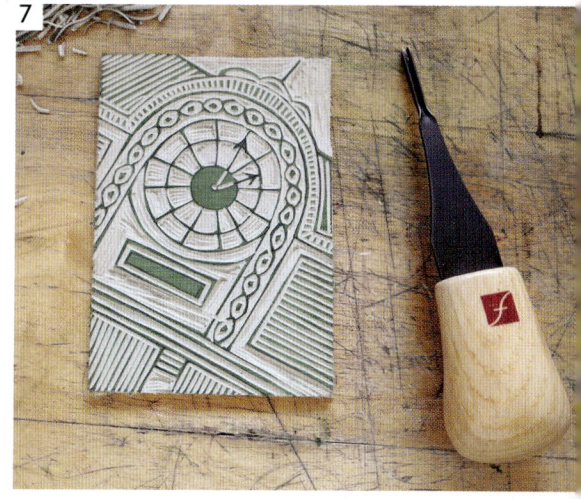

7

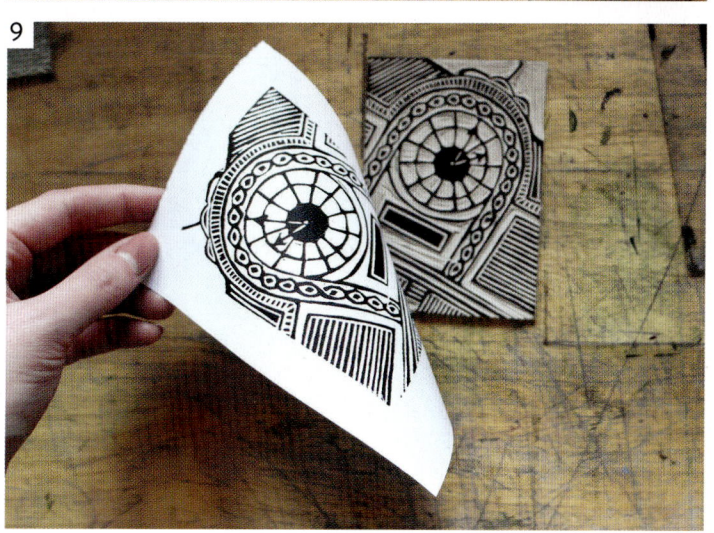

9

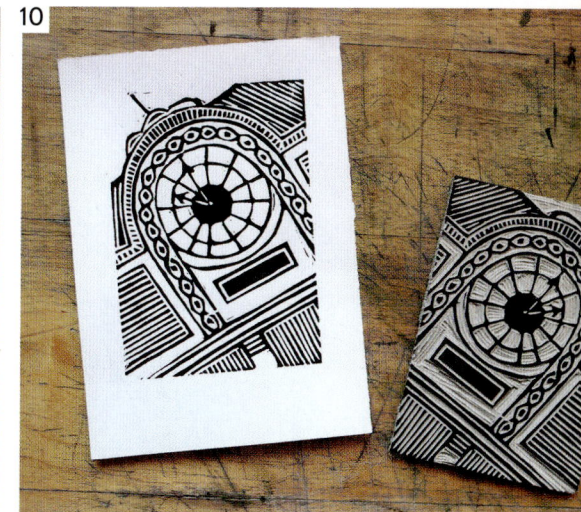

10

SUPPLIES

Tracing paper

Pencil

Pen

Acrylic paint and brush

Narrow cutter

One sheet of lino
7 x 10.5cm (2¾ x 4in)

Ink of your choice

Brayer

Baren

A large sheet of paper or
card, at least ten times
bigger than your block

Ruler

Scrap paper for testing

Fine paintbrush

REPEAT PRINT

Repeat prints are used by printmakers to create designs that slot together and create an endless pattern when printed next to each other – perfect for wallpaper, wrapping paper, or just an interesting design! This block takes inspiration from Art Nouveau windows to create the front of a building when printed together.

1 Begin by drawing your design. Add elements that will connect the print, such as lines that run the entire length or width of the block. Make sure that any of these lines are straight so that they join up.

2 Once you have your design, transfer it onto the block and carve it in the usual way, being especially careful when carving the connecting lines. You can use a ruler as a guide when carving them to make sure that they are straight and will align.

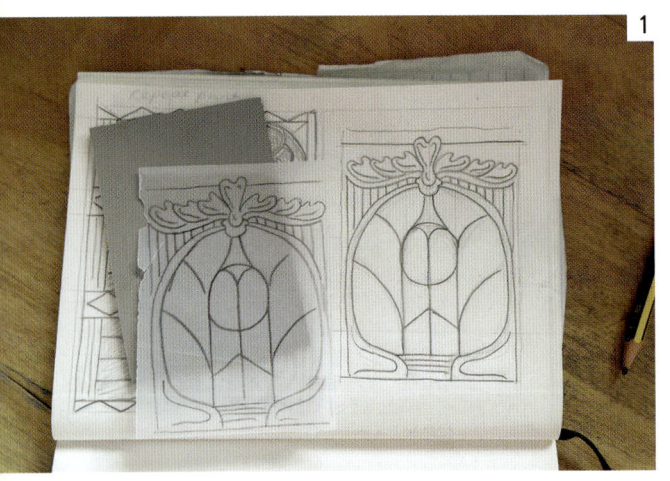

1

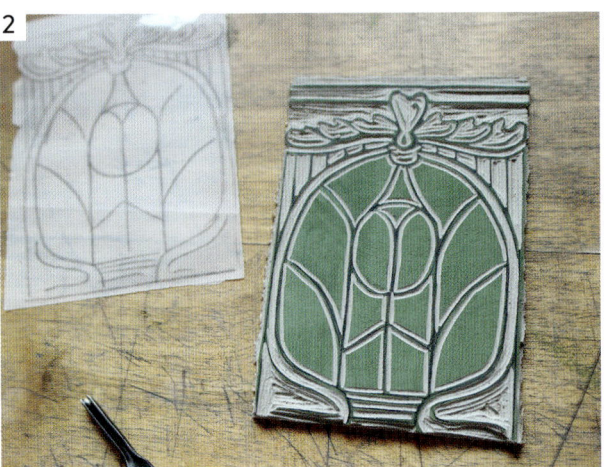

2

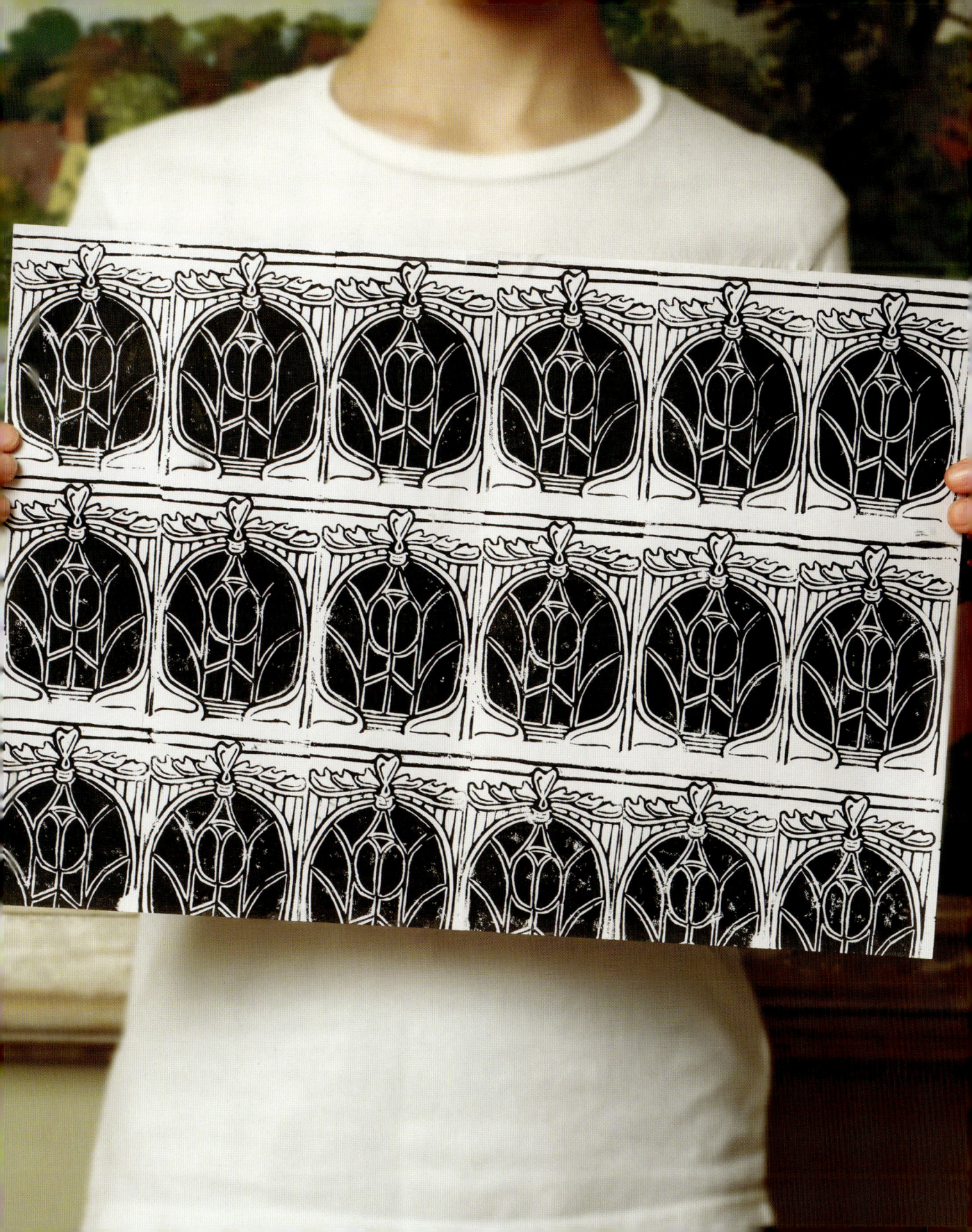

3 Select the ink of your choice and ink your block. You may want to do a quick test print to make sure you are happy with your design.

4 Once inked, place the block face down on your large sheet of paper. It is important to make sure it is carefully aligned at the corner of the paper, as this first print will act as a guide for the rest.

5 Apply pressure to the back of the block. A clean brayer can be used to roll over the back of the block, but be careful not to move it during this process as this will smudge the print. Your first print is now complete. Carefully remove the block from the paper.

6 Re-ink the block. Using the first print and the edge of the paper as a guide, place the block face down and apply pressure again to print the image.

7 You can now see how your blocks connect with one another. Do not worry if the connecting areas do not join completely – this can be fixed later. Repeat this until you have filled the top row.

8 On the row beneath, continue to use the edge of the paper and the other printed designs as guides to line up your block. If you have connecting lines running down you will need to make sure the block is aligned both horizontally and vertically.

9 Continue printing until you have filled the next row. Working one row at a time is best as it prevents misalignment on lower rows.

10 If you reach the edge of the paper and the full block no longer fits on, place a piece of scrap paper beneath your print to stop excess ink from staining your work surface and from dirtying the back of your print.

11 Continue printing across the bottom of the paper until it is full. If you want to join multiple pieces of paper together, make sure to account for any areas of overlap with these incomplete prints along the bottom and sides.

12 Using a fine paintbrush and leftover ink, consolidate the joining lines by filling in any gaps. This can also be used to fix any small registration errors.

13 Your repeat print is now complete. This technique works well for decorative prints or for practical projects and can be used to make wrapping paper or even wallpaper!

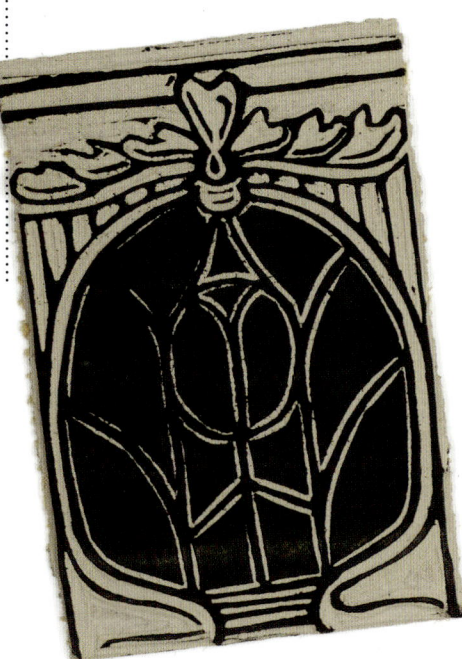

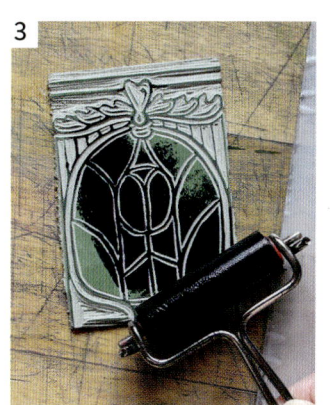

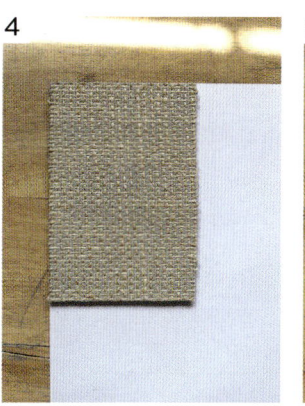

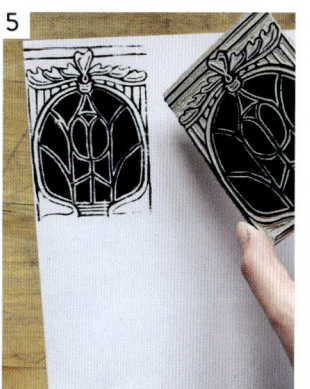

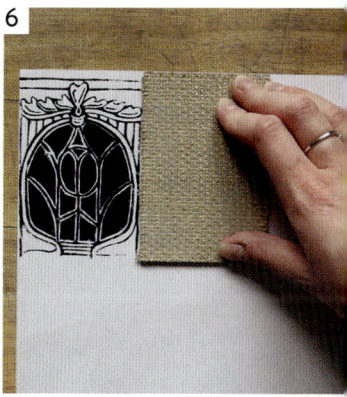

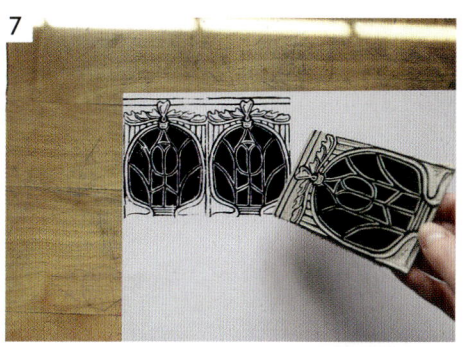

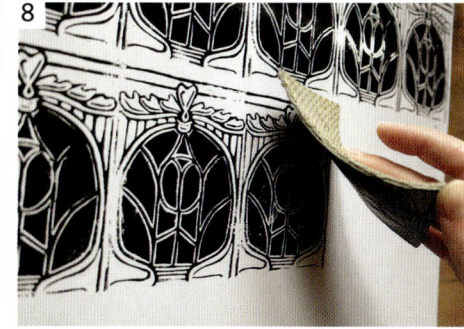

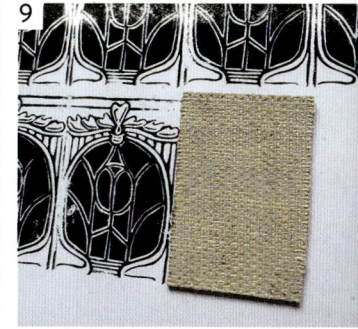

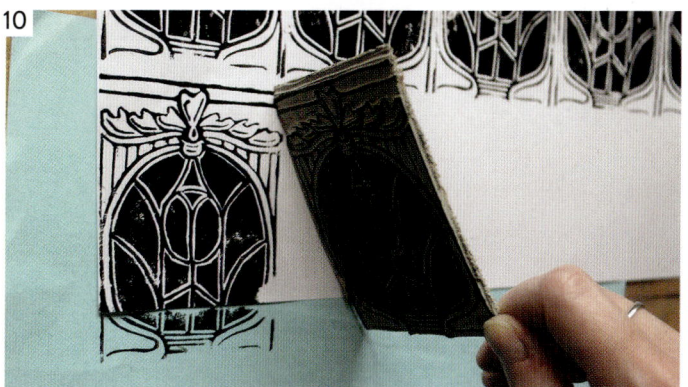

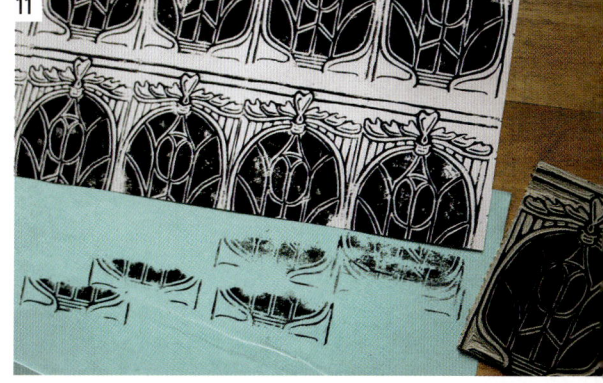

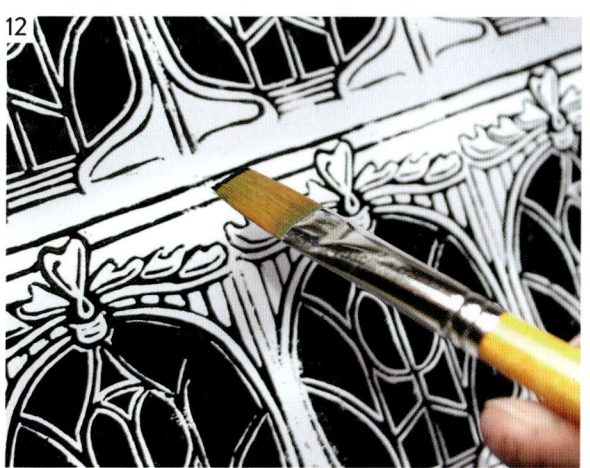

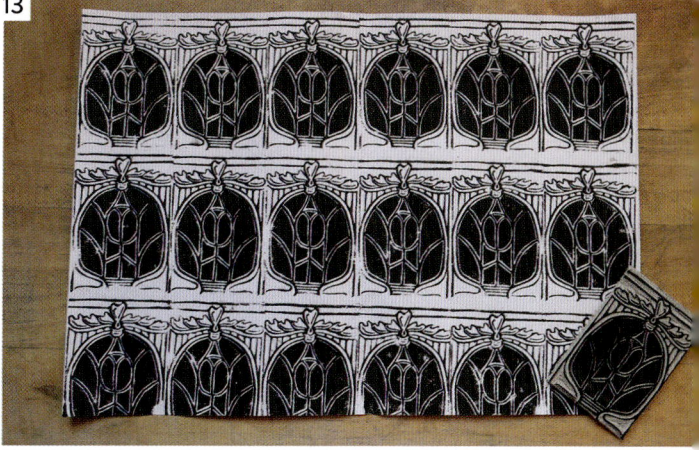

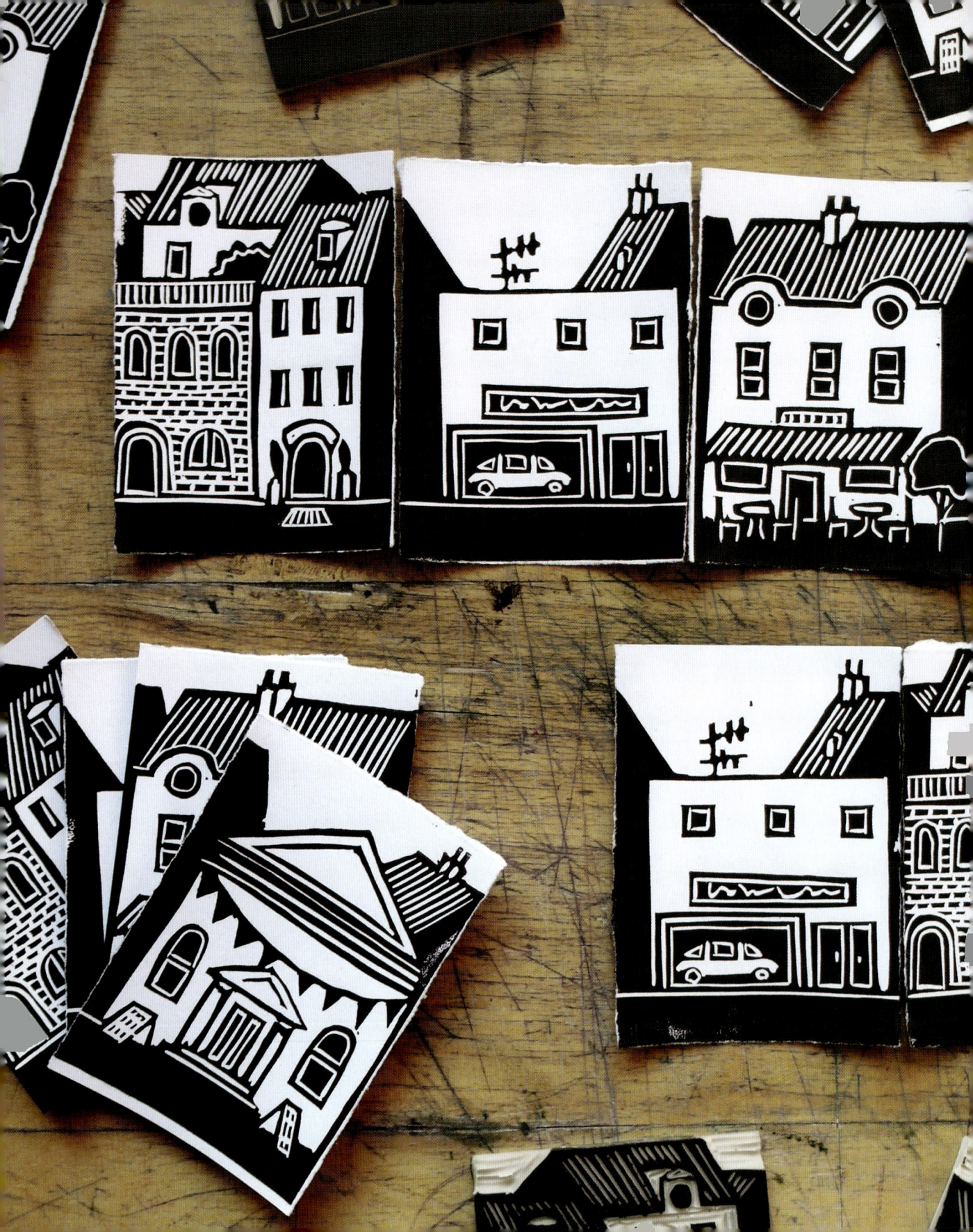

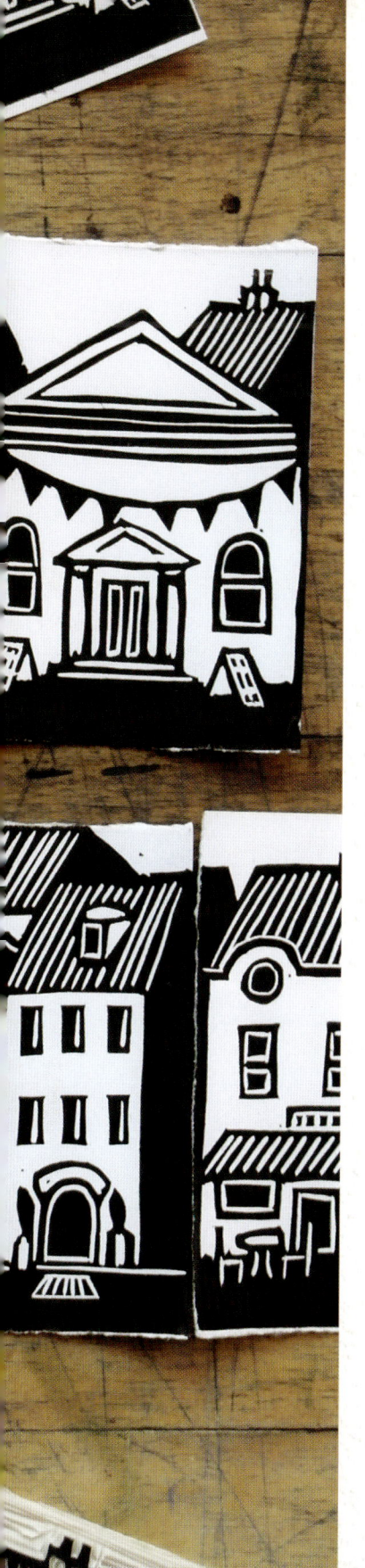

CONTINUOUS LANDSCAPE

Continuous landscape card games originally emerged around the 19th century. Called *myriorama* (a myriad of pictures), these card sets contained images that could be endlessly arranged and rearranged in any order. Create your own *myriorama* with this customisable linocut project of a city street.

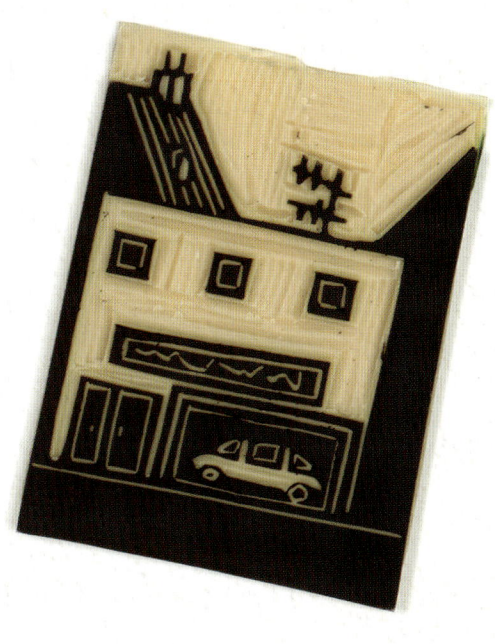

SUPPLIES

Tracing paper

Pencil

Pen

Acrylic paint and brush

Narrow cutter

Four sheets of lino, each 5 x 7.5cm (2 x 3in)

Ink of your choice

Brayer

Baren

Lots of pieces of card, each the same size as the sheets of lino

1 Divide a sheet of tracing paper into four sections the same size as the blocks and draw three horizontal lines – one for the pavement, one for the top of the roofs, and one just below the roofline.

2 Draw a design in each of the four sections. Using the guidelines, make sure that each drawing will connect – for example, the roofline at the edge of all of the drawings aligns with the top line. It may be useful to cut up the tracing paper to check that each drawing matches.

3 Once you have your designs, transfer them onto four individual pieces of lino. Make sure that these blocks are exactly the same size, and that the tracing paper has been lined up in the same place for each design.

4 Add a thin layer of acrylic paint and carve your blocks in the usual way. Keeping the sides of the buildings solid is a good way to ensure that they will fit together. Once all the blocks have been carved, double check that they still align by placing them next to each other in a random order. Fix any areas that don't align.

5 Carefully print these blocks onto pieces of card that are the same size as the blocks, aligning them in the same place each time, using the top corner of the card as a guide.

6 Print multiples of each block – the more cards you have, the more effective your continuous landscape will be.

7 Once dried, the cards are ready to be used – arrange them over and over again for new combinations of your street scene.

8 If you decide to add more to your continuous landscape, use your original drawing as a guide for future additions to make sure that they line up. There's no end to the additions you can make!

9 Alternatively, these blocks can be printed together on the same sheet of paper, using the techniques in the Repeat Print project. Using watercolour paints to add colour to your prints is another way to add detail to your continuous landscape (see the Watercolour project in the Mixing Media chapter).

1
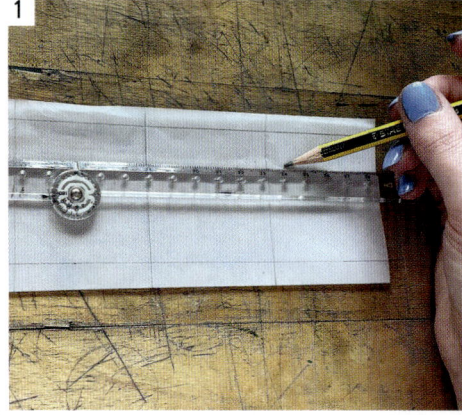

4
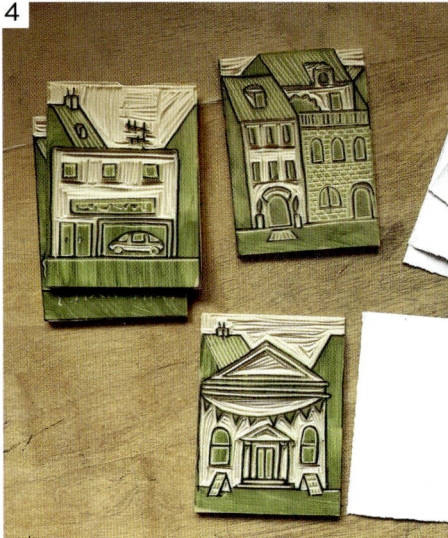

7
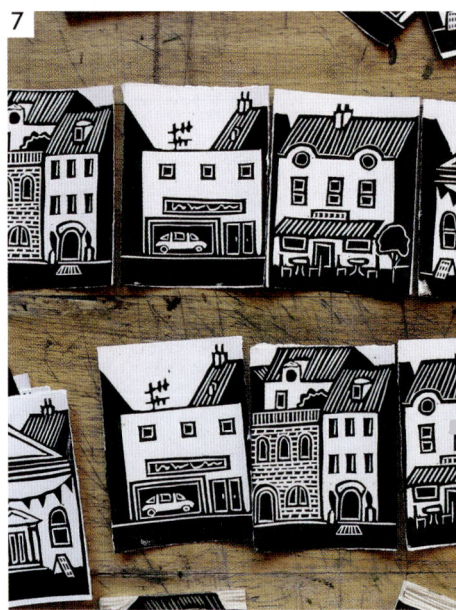

2

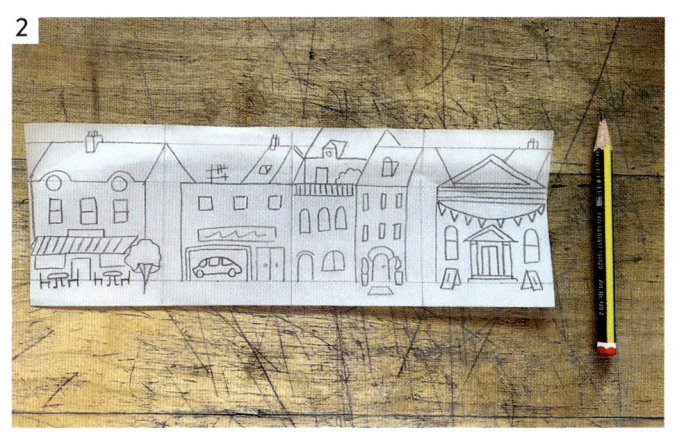

3

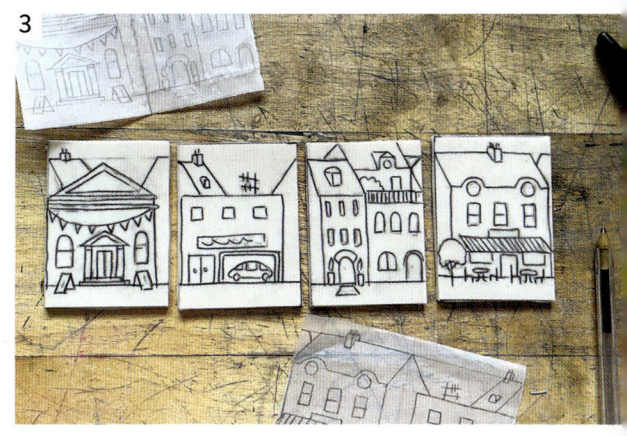

5

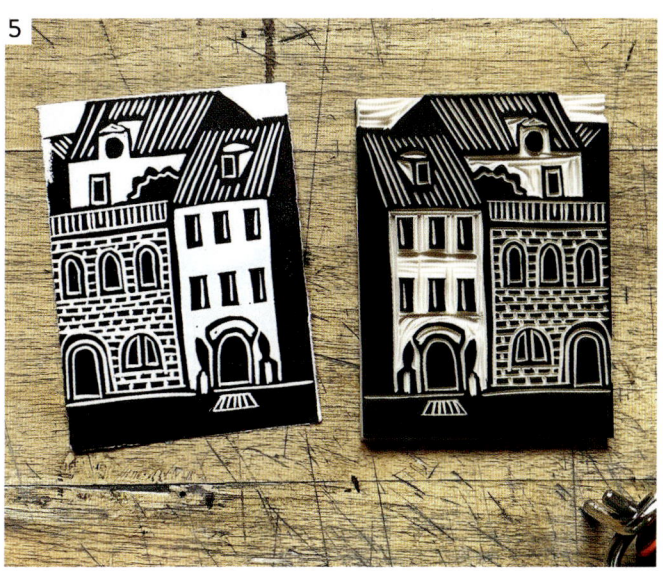

6

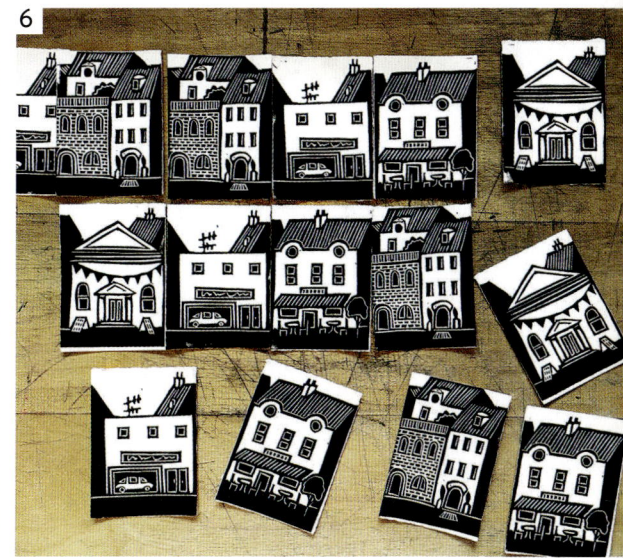

8

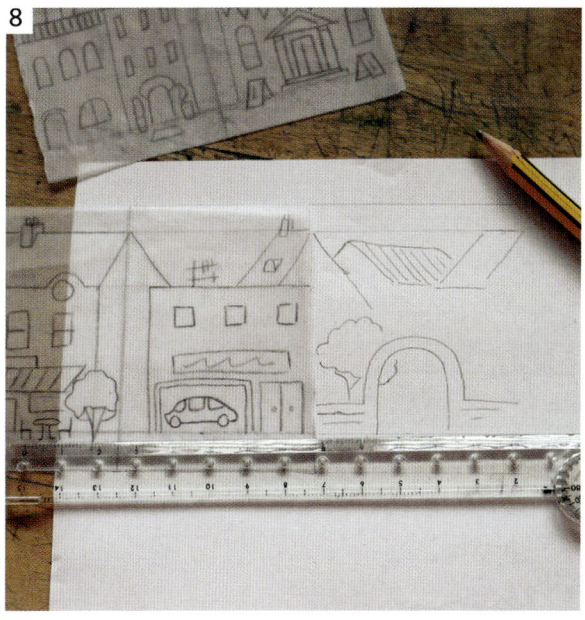

9

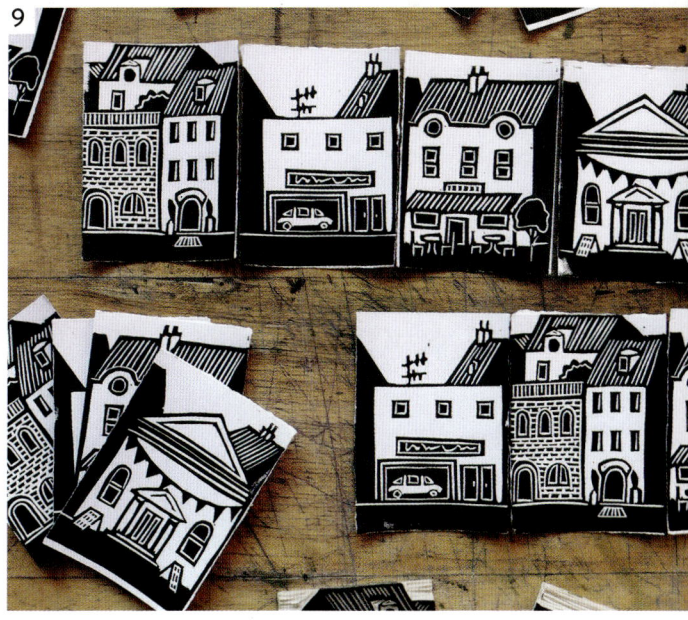

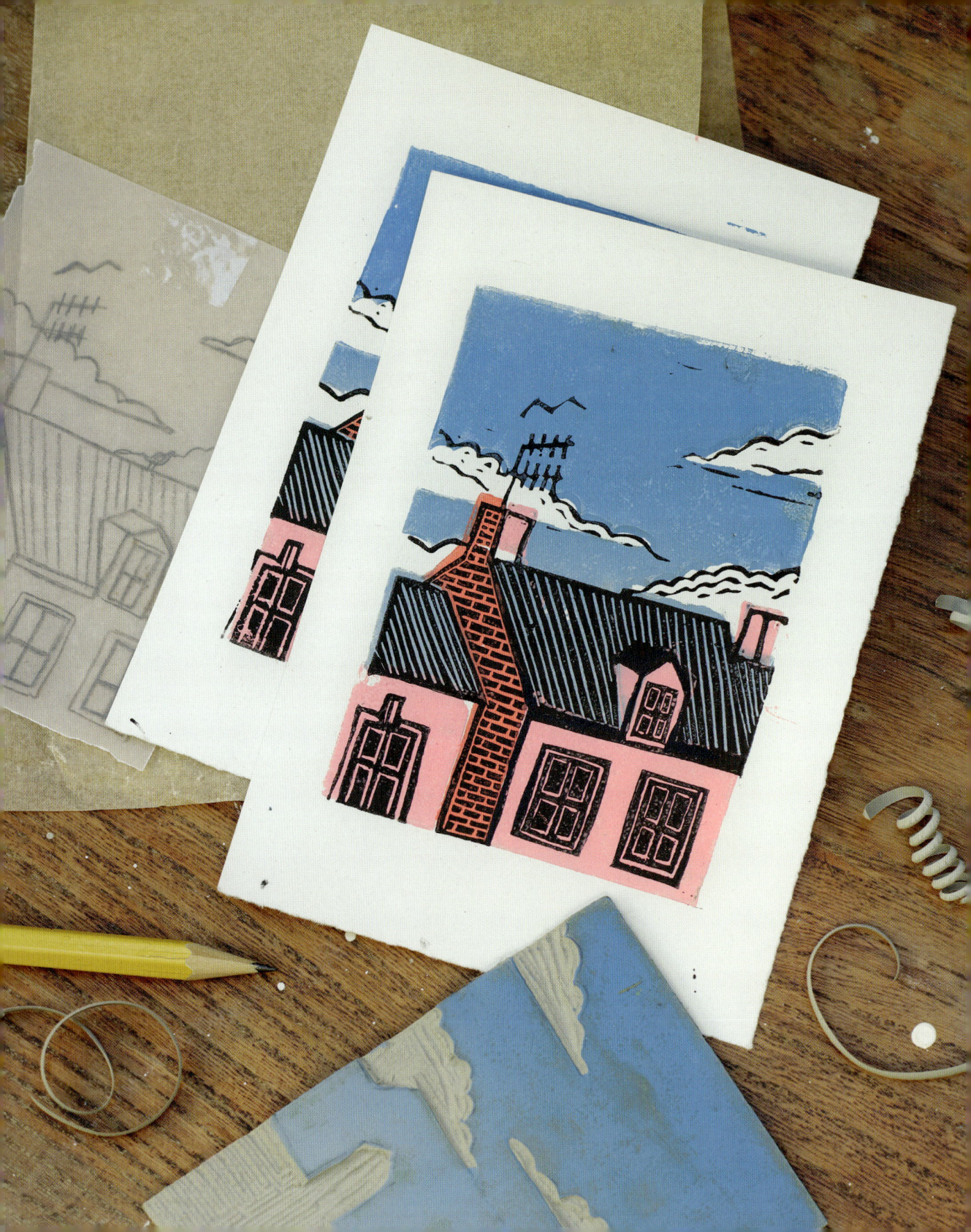

MULTI-BLOCK PRINT

The multi-block technique is an excellent way to introduce colour into your prints using skills you have already developed in the linocut process. Unlike reduction prints which – as the name suggests – involves cutting away a single block to add layers of colour, the multi-block technique allows you to reuse the blocks again and again to try different colour combinations.

SUPPLIES

Tracing paper

Pencil

Pen

Acrylic paint and brush

Wide cutter

Narrow cutter

Registration block

Three lino sheets
7.5 x 10.5cm (3 x 4in)

Ink – red, blue,
black, white

Coloured pencils

Baren

Two brayer

A6 card

Ruler

Craft knife

Palette knife

1 Begin by planning your print. In your initial drawing, plan out the colours you will use, as this will help you calculate how many blocks you will need. The main line drawing will form the key block – the top layer of the print that will bring the design together.

2 Once you are happy with your drawing, consider how best to divide the blocks. For this print, there are four different colours: light pink, dark pink, blue, and black, which are divided across three blocks. The key block must have its own block and be a single colour (in this case black), and the colours are shared across the remaining two. The more colours you want to use, the more blocks you will need. When transferring your print, make sure that all your blocks are the same size and that you line up your tracing paper at the same point each time so that everything aligns.

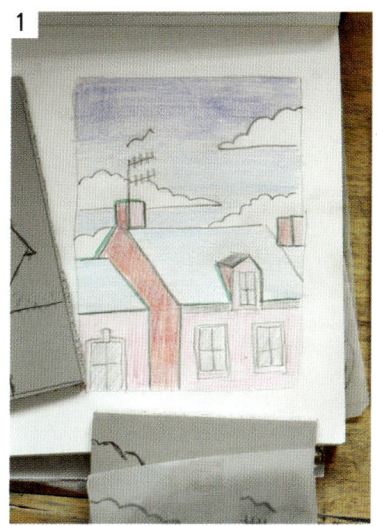

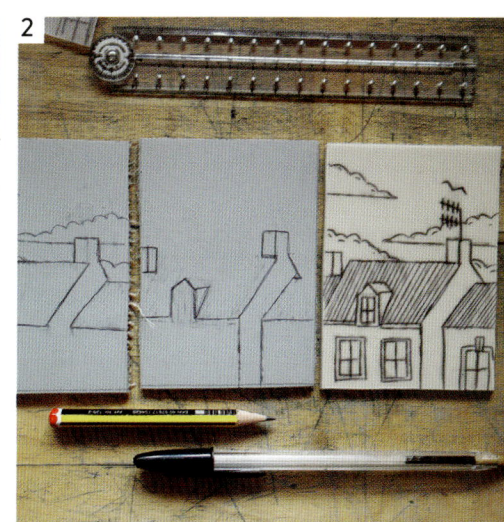

3 Now you can begin carving your three blocks. The key block can be carved like a standard linocut, making sure you leave space for the colour below to show through. The key block will add the main details for the print, and will help define the different areas of colour.

4 For the second and third blocks, carve away everything except the areas where you want the colour to print. If you have a large area that needs removing you can cut this away, which will help reduce unintentional marks on the final print and will give you some scraps of lino for smaller projects.

5 You can also use a craft knife and a ruler to divide the block into smaller pieces where two colours sit directly alongside one another. To ensure these parts fit together snugly, you can use the craft knife to shave off any excess lino across the cut edge.

6 Once your blocks are carved, you can begin printing. When deciding on the order of your blocks, it is best to work from back to front, starting with the colour that will form the background – which for this print is the sky.

7 For the sky block, use a blue gradient to give a more naturalistic feel and add extra visual interest (see Ink in the first chapter). The more white you add to the blue, the lighter the colour becomes.

8 For multi-block prints, it is important to use a registration device to make sure that all the layer align correctly (see Other Tools in the Tools and Techniques chapter). Make sure to ink your block before putting it in the registration device to prevent unwanted ink stains. Print this layer and place to one side to dry.

9 For the second layer, add white ink to the red to mix a light and a dark pink shade for the two sides of the building. Ink the smaller blocks individually, using a different roller for each colour.

10 To assemble the second layer using the smaller blocks, think of them as a jigsaw, fitting the blocks together like jigsaw pieces, ready for printing. A craft knife is useful to push the blocks into place without getting inky fingers.

3
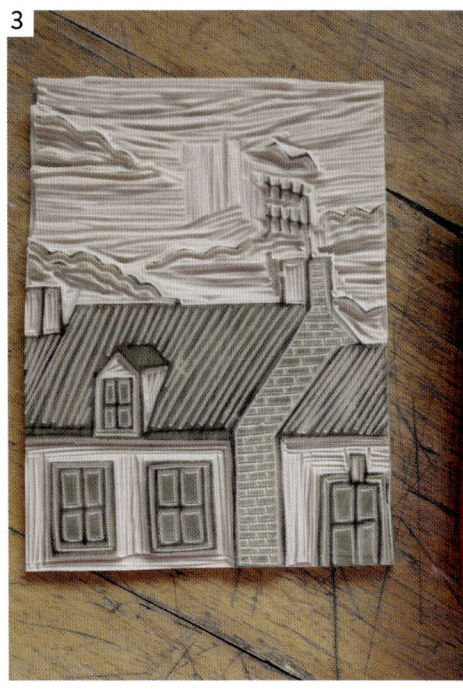

7
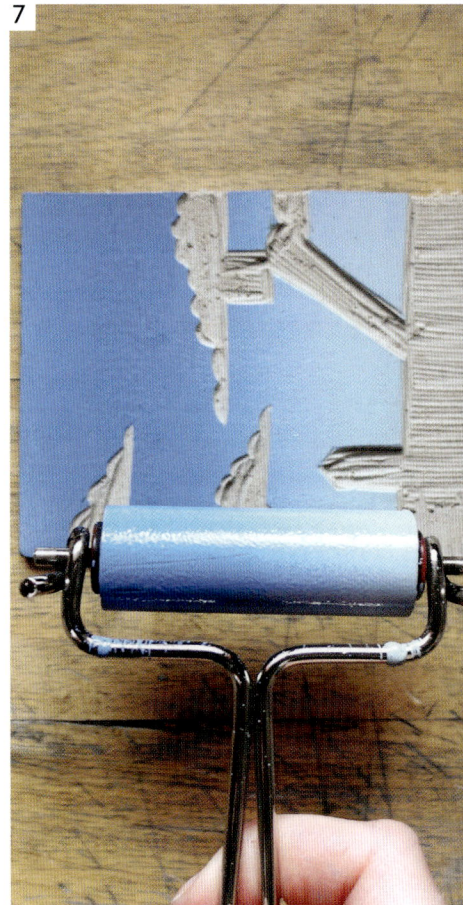

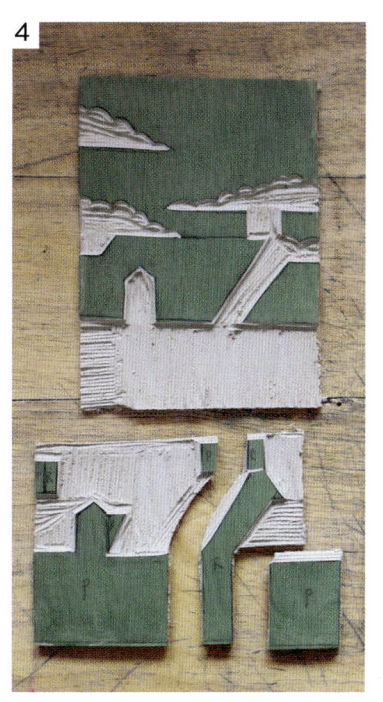

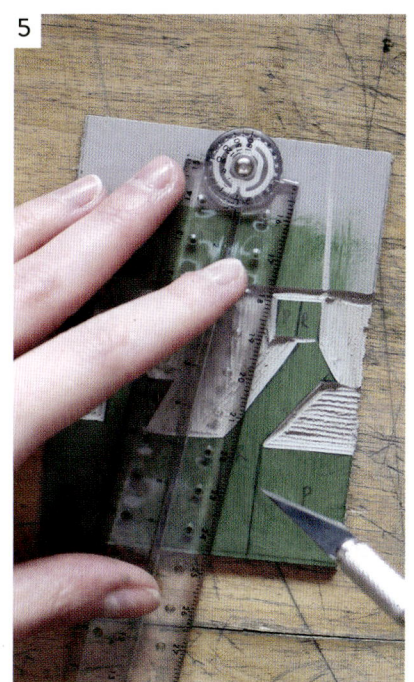

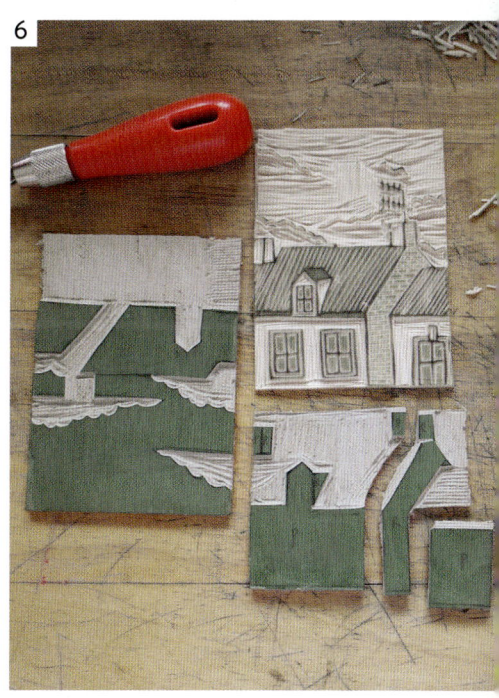

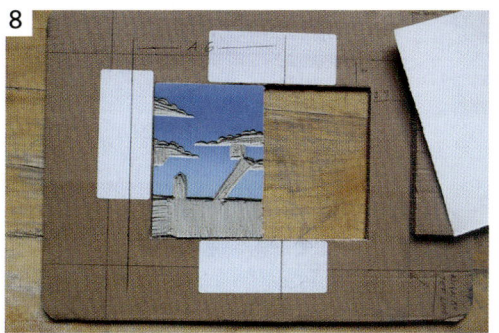

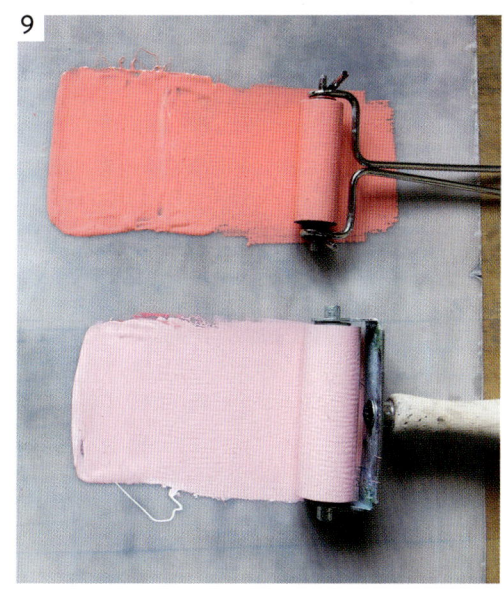

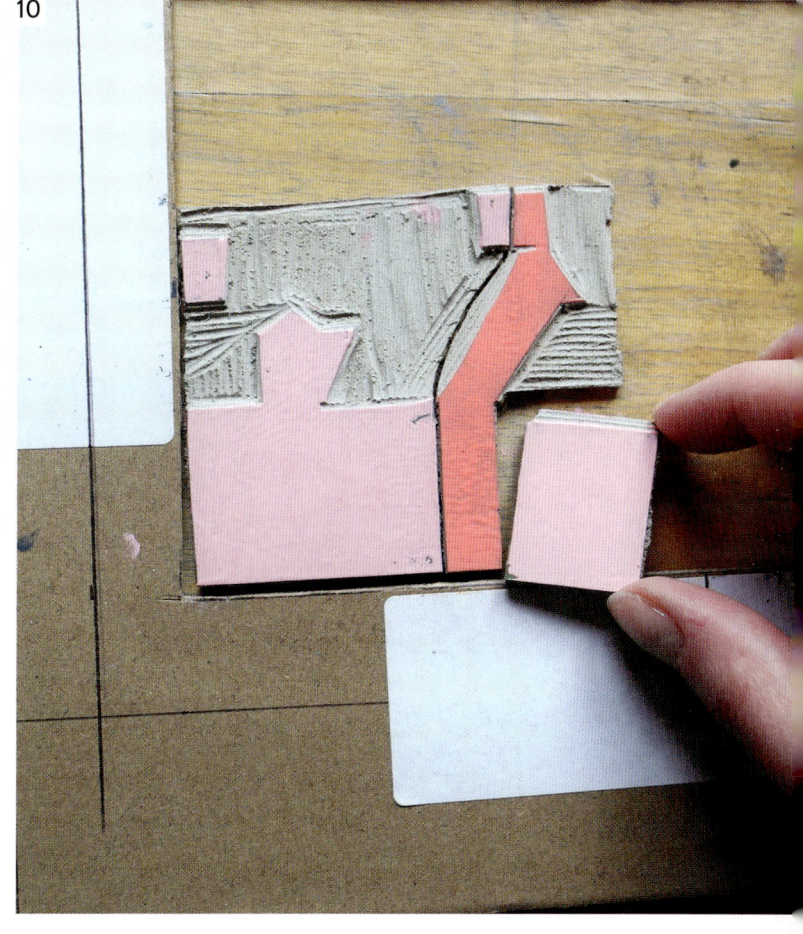

11 When printing the second layer, be careful not to move the blocks when placing the paper on top. You may need to secure these blocks in place by inserting lino or card in the space around them in the registration device. Make sure that you align the paper in the same place as you did for the first layer.

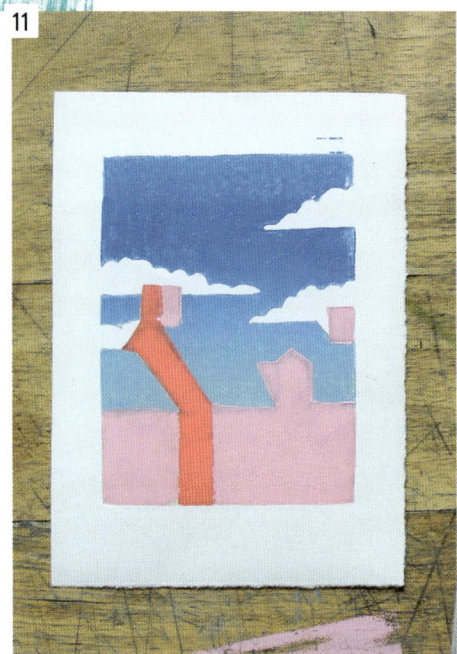

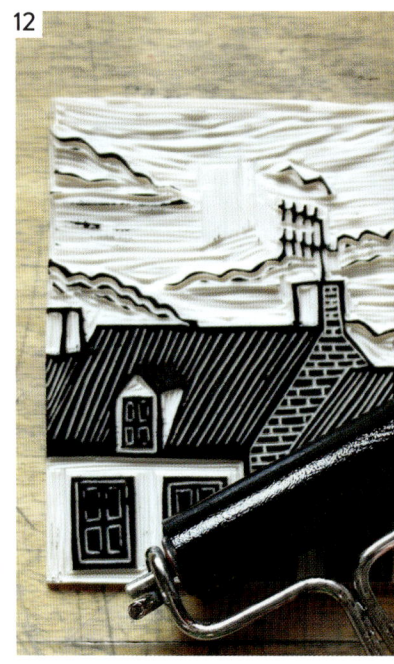

12 Ink the key block with black ink, or any other colour that will stand out from the other layers. You can either print wet-on-wet (printing onto ink that is still wet on the layer below) or wet-on-dry (waiting for the layer below to dry before printing the final layer). Printing wet-on-wet will give a more textured effect, leaving places where the colour below might show through, while wet-on-dry will give a sharper image.

13 When printing the final layer, be extra careful when lining up your paper, as registration mistakes will be more obvious on the key block. This may take a few attempts to get right, so printing lots of copies is always recommended.

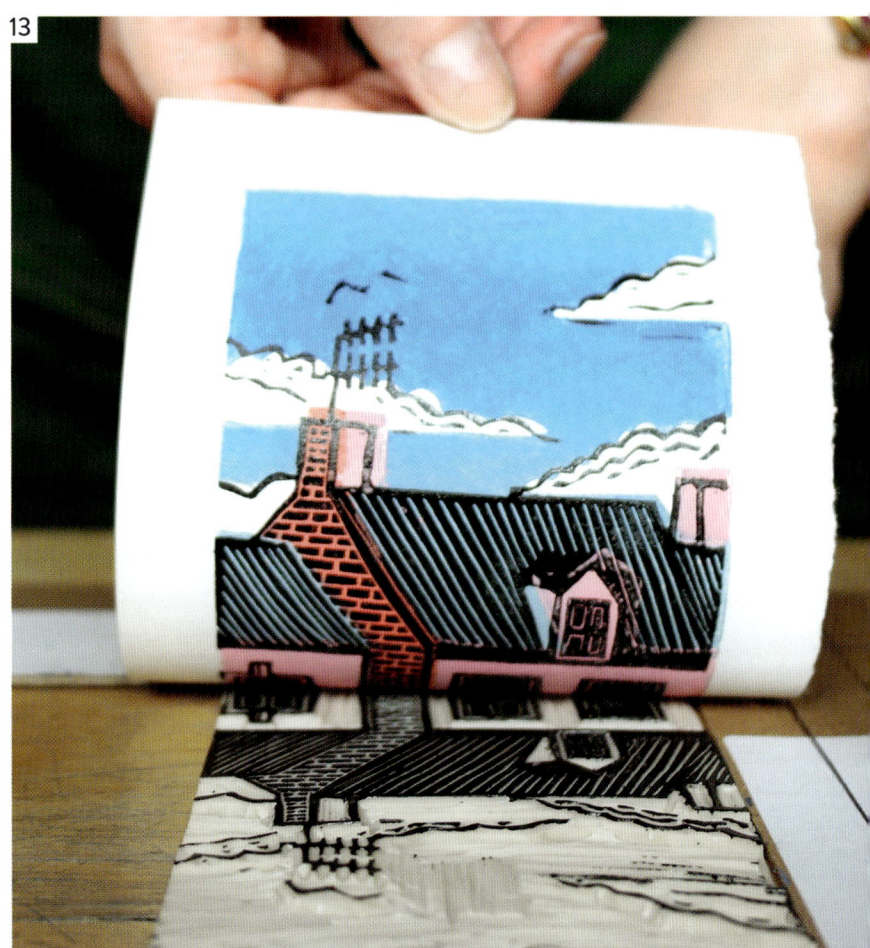

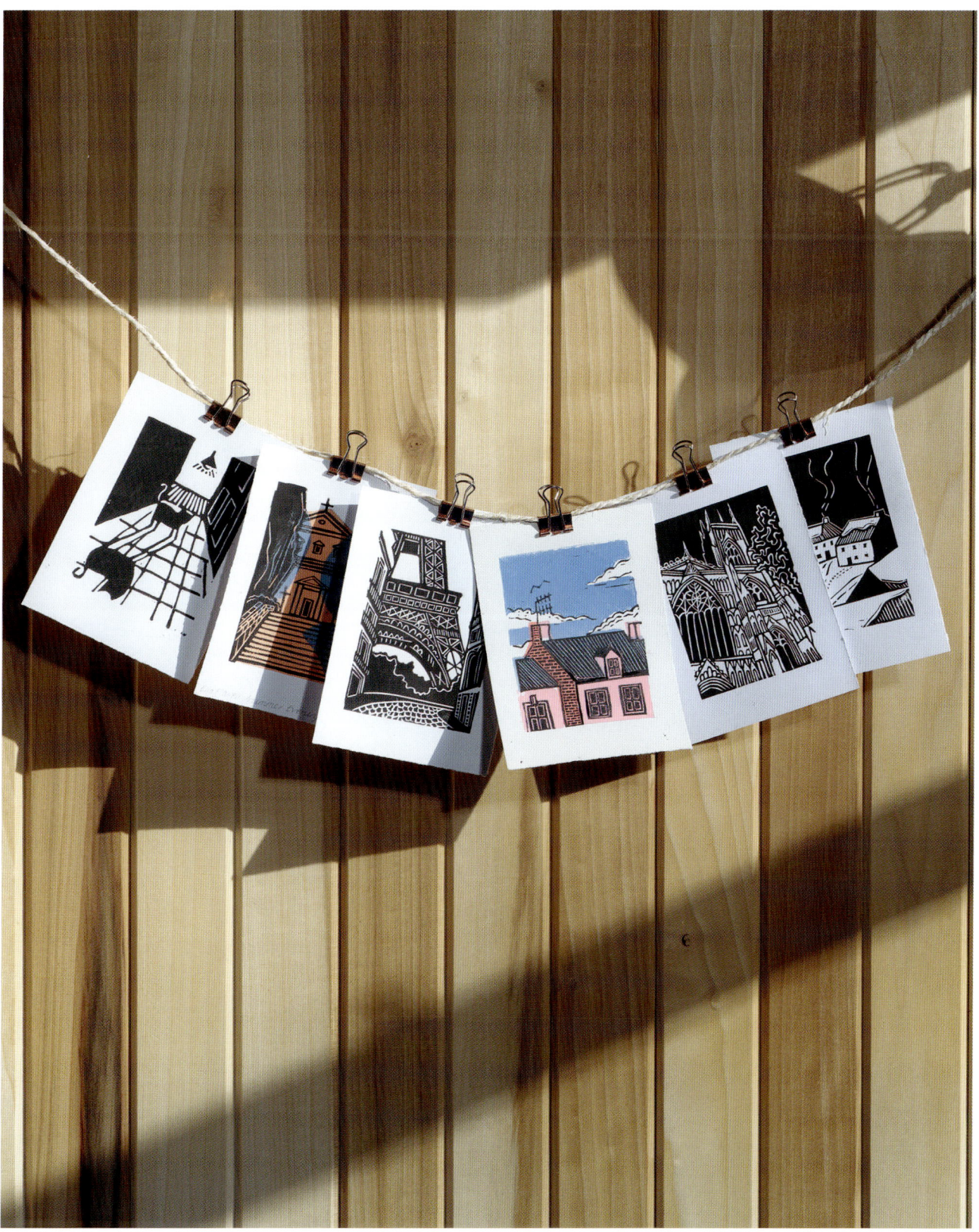

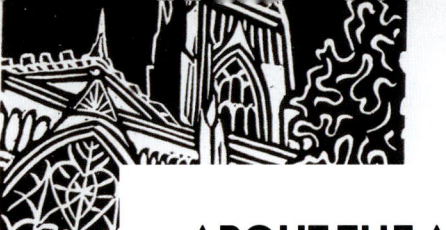
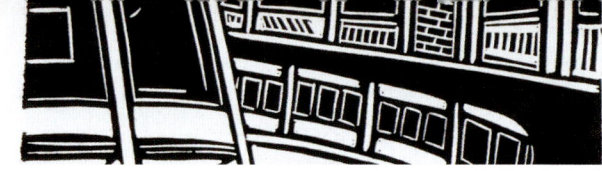

ABOUT THE AUTHOR

Ella Flavell is an art historian and printmaker who has been producing linocuts under the name Burin & Plate since 2016. Her practice focuses on prints of locations of historic and personal significance with an emphasis on unusual architecture, storytelling, and memory. She has completed numerous commercial commissions both in the UK and abroad, designing everything from beer-can labels to Christmas cards. Her work has been featured on the cover of *Birmingham Design Magazine* (2023) and in the book *Carving Blocks: Printmakers and Their Stories* (2024), and she has spoken extensively on her practice in schools and at various design festivals.

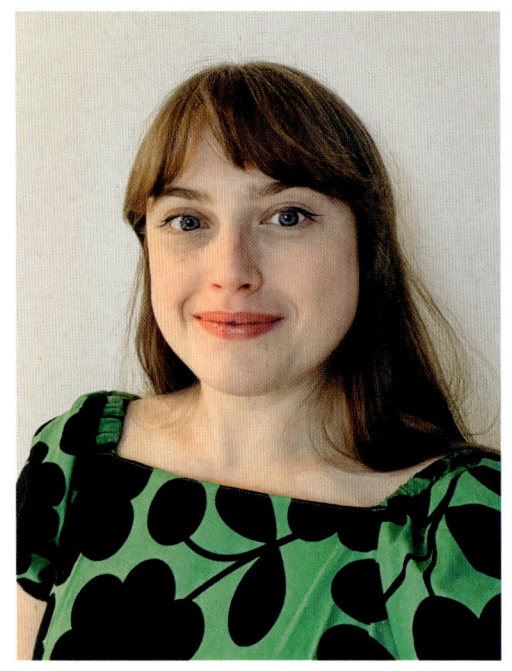

Follow Ella on Instagram at @burinandplate

ACKNOWLEDGEMENTS

I would like to thank my friends, family, and partner for supporting me both through the writing of this book and my other adventures in printmaking. I would also like to extend my thanks to the wonderful team at David & Charles Publishing for all their help, guidance, and support during this process.

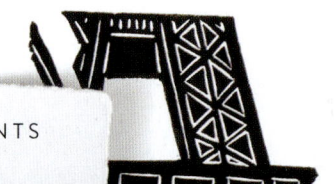
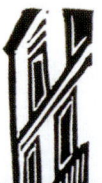
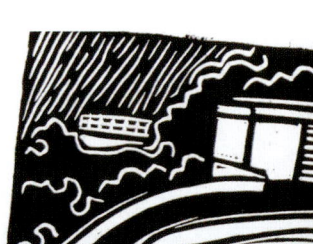

INDEX

This book has been printed on paper
from approved suppliers and made from
pulp from sustainable sources.

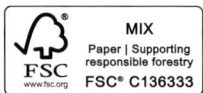

MIX
Paper | Supporting
responsible forestry
FSC® C136333

Printed in China through Asia Pacific Offset for:
David and Charles, Ltd
Suite A, Tourism House, Pynes Hill, Exeter, EX2 5WS

10 9 8 7 6 5 4 3 2 1

PUBLISHING DIRECTOR Ame Verso
SENIOR COMMISSIONING EDITOR Nigel Browning
PUBLISHING MANAGER Jeni Chown
DESK EDITOR Victoria Allen
COPY EDITOR Clare Ashton
LEAD DESIGNER Sam Staddon
DESIGNER Lucy Ridley
DESIGN, LAYOUT AND ART DIRECTION Wayne Blades
PHOTOGRAPHY Neal Grundy
PRE-PRESS DESIGNER Susan Reansbury
PRODUCTION MANAGER Beverley Richardson

David and Charles publishes high-quality
books on a wide range of subjects. For more
information visit www.davidandcharles.com.

Share your makes with us on social media using
#dandcbooks and follow us on Facebook and
Instagram by searching for @dandcbooks.

Layout of the digital edition of this book may vary
depending on reader hardware and display settings.

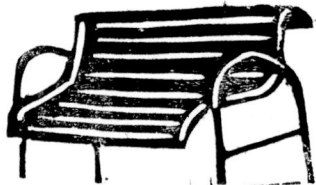